IMPERIAL SIMLA

Isa.—Is not this delicious, Louisa? This fine, pure, bracing mountain air? Dear, dear, darling Simla!

Louisa.—Oh! indeed it is, dear Bella; and it is so delightful to be able to resume all our *active English habits.*

IMPERIAL SIMLA
The Political Culture
of the Raj

PAMELA KANWAR

DELHI
OXFORD UNIVERSITY PRESS
BOMBAY CALCUTTA MADRAS
1990

Oxford University Press, Walton Street, Oxford OX2 6DP
New York Toronto
Delhi Bombay Calcutta Madras Karachi
Petaling Jaya Singapore Hong Kong Tokyo
Nairobi Dar es Salaam
Melbourne Auckland

and associates in
Berlin Ibadan

SBN 0 19 562588 9

Phototypeset by Spantech Publishers Pvt Ltd, New Delhi 110060
Printed at Rekha Printers Pvt Ltd, New Delhi 110020
and published by S. K. Mookerjee, Oxford University Press
YMCA Library Building, Jai Singh Road, New Delhi 110001

Contents

PLATES

Frontispiece
Cartoon, Mems. for Simla

between pages 178 and 179

Captain Charles Pratt Kennedy, Political Agent, 1822–35.

Simla's first house, Kennedy House, built in 1822.

The densest settlement sprawled across the sunny southern slopes.

A *bhishti* fills his *mushak*, as an officer of the Gurkha Battalion looks on.

Annandale—the site of countless fêtes, gymkhanas, dog shows, etc.

The Assembly Rooms and the Jubilee Theatre—the hub of Simla's social life until the 1880s.

The Mall and Scandal Point.

The Ridge—city centre and Piazza.

Viceregal Lodge, built in the Elizabethan style, occupied by Dufferin in 1888.

The new buildings of the 1880s: the Army Headquarters, and the timber-framed 'Tudor' Telegraph Office.

The rickshaw, introduced in the 1880s.

Lower Bazar, a hotchpotch of construction.

Gandhiji and Mahadev Desai escorted by Lala Mela Ram Sood after the Gandhi–Irwin talks, 1930.

'Manorville', Raj Kumari Amrit Kaur's residence in Summer Hill.

The Maidan-i-Gunj in Edwards Gunj, with Vithalbhai Patel addressing a gathering in 1930.

A procession surges across the Mall to bid farewell to Vithalbhai Patel after his resignation as President of the Legislative Assembly, 1930.

For
Surendra
Kartik and Madhurima

Preface

My affair with Simla began when I came to live here in 1972, and I turned to research that culminated in a doctoral dissertation. My fascination for the town, however, grew on, and I spent several years thereafter delving into ideas and material unique to the urban and social experience of the summer capital and its imperial milieu.

The vast amount of material available that reflects British interests and concerns contrasts curiously with offical reticence about its acquisition and choice as summer capital. Unlike for New Delhi, there was no formal Durbar which pronounced the hill station to be summer capital. The Simla tract was exchanged with local rulers in 1830. The document is not enshrined in a Sanad or Treaty, rather it forms an innocuous part of the first Settlement Report of the Simla District compiled by a Deputy Commissioner, some twenty years after the event (see Appendix I).

While innumerable accounts describe British life in Simla, there are no comparable sources that evoke the Indian ethos. Much reliance had to be placed on personal interviews. Old residents were initially selected for their reputation as knowledgeable persons. There was a continuous search for clues about people who might have been political participants, activists, or those who could provide information on an occupation or caste. A wide range of people along the social scale were approached. Although a formal and compact questionnaire was devised, deviations crept in. It proved more expedient to hear the interviewees narrate their experiences, impressions of salient events and catch the nuances of attitude and what they considered meaningful and significant. A follow-up, by counterchecking from other sources (archival, municipal, newspapers), aided in piecing together a coherent account of Simla through Indian eyes.

The restriction of movement of Indians on the Mall exercised so many people, that I have included as Appendix II, the Simla Municipality 'Bye-Law for the Regulation and Prohibition of Traffic'. Finally Appendix III, 'Membership of Simla District Congress' and IV, 'Office-Bearers and Members of the Congress Committee in 1932', offer a factual statement about the mobilization and leadership of Simla Indians.

Local people have always called the town 'Shimla' and hence this spelling was officially adopted in 1983. I have retained the older nomenclature to minimize the confusion that could occur in the scores of references and since it was renowned by that name in the past.

The origin of the name Simla or Shimla is somewhat more difficult to explain. The Simla Kali Bari records link the name to Shyamala Devi and rely on Edward Buck's account that 'Majee' was enshrined in a small temple surrounded by a verandah, that stood in the grounds of Rothney Castle. An Englishman on camp had the wooden idol thrown into a *khud* and made the temple into his kitchen. At night he had a vision of two horsemen attacking him with spears, and awoke shouting for help. When told that the 'Majee' would wreak vengeance unless restored to her house, the idol was installed in a new temple near Christ Church. In 1835, when that was acquired for the Rothney Castle estate, the deity was shifted to Kali Bari.

The Kali Bari records identify the 'Majee' mentioned in Buck, as Shyamala Devi. On the spot where the Kali Bari stands, a tantric Sadhu sat in deep meditation underneath a big deodar tree, before an image of the Goddess Chandi. The Sadhu was held by the people of the neighbouring areas and the Gurkhas in great reverence for his supernatural powers. On his death, in the course of a few years, the image of the goddess and all that remained was taken over by the Bengalis. A wooden *dhajji* structure in the shape of a temple was built and both images, that of Kali and Chandi were installed in it. The image from the Rothney Castle site was installed in the Kali Bari as well.

The Rev. Long's interpretation quoted in the *Simla Guide* of 1870, that Simla derives its name from 'Shyamalay', the house built of slate erected by a fakir on Jakhu, has been described as far-fetched. Simla's origin is not mentioned by early travellers, as for example, Kalka, the gateway to the hills, which is described as a place of worship dedicated to Kali. Both Buck and the official *Gazetteer* are silent on the question. Simla hill folk have usually never heard of Shyamala Devi. The name alters nothing of Simla's past as imperial refuge, although the interest its origin evokes may not be only a matter of semantics but also a pointer to the town's changing identity.

Acknowledgements

I owe many debts of gratitude to the people who made this book possible. My grateful thanks are due to Professor Ravinder Kumar, Director, Nehru Memorial Museum & Library, New Delhi, for intellectual stimulation, advice and encouragement. My thanks are also due to Professor L. P. Pandey, Professor S. R. Mehrotra, and Dr O. P. Gautum of the Himachal Pradesh University for their help and comments.

I extend my thanks to the many people who regaled me with reminiscences of pre-1947 Simla: the late Dr Y. S. Parmar, Lala Mela Ram Sood, Pandit Hari Ram, Mr Dina Nath Andhi, and Mrs Lajja Varma, who spoke of the texture of local politics; Mr Ajit Banta and Lala Ratan Chand Sood, who described trading practices; Mr D. K. Khanna, Mr A. S. Krishnaswami, Dr B. R. Nanda, and Mr Vishva Sood, who conjured up Indian sentiments in the 1930s and 40s; and Mrs Lata Sood, who recalled memories of her father, the late Lala Mohan Lal. I am grateful to Mr Brij Lal Salhotra for details about the Balmikis and to Shrimati Prakaso Devi for the folk songs from her village; Mr Satya Prakash and the late Mr Thakur Das of Thakur Bhrata for information about the Simla Arya Samaj; to maulvi Sanaullah for information about the Kashmiri community of Simla, and Mr M. K. Kaw for translations of the folk songs.

I would like to thank the staff of the following institutions for their help and consideration: the National Archives of India, New Delhi; the Nehru Memorial Museum and Library, New Delhi; the National Library, Calcutta; the Haryana State Archives, Chandigarh; the Punjab State Archives, Patiala; the Simla Municipal Corporation; the Simla Sadar Thana; the State Archives, Himachal Pradesh. My grateful thanks are due to Mian Goverdhan Singh, former Librarian, Himachal Pradesh Secretariat Library, Simla for unstinting assistance.

For permission to reproduce the illustrations contained in this volume, I must thank the Officers Mess, Sabathu, for the portrait of Kennedy; the Himachal Pradesh State Archives for the photograph of the Assembly Rooms; the India Office Library and Records for the photographs of the Mall and Scandal Point, the Ridge with Christ Church, Annandale, and the lady in the rickshaw; Messrs Bindra Studios, Simla, for the photograph of the new buildings of the 1880s; Shri Mela Ram Sood for the photograph of himself with Gandhi; the Nehru Memorial Museum and Library for the photograph of Gandhi at Manorville; and the National Archives of India for the photographs of the procession on the Mall, and of Vithalbhai Patel at the Gunj. The illustrations of the *bhishti* and of Kennedy House have been taken from J. Luard, *Views in India, Saint Helena and Car Nicobar*, London, 1838, and that of the southern slopes of Simla from W. L. L. Scott, *Views in the Himalayas*, 1852. The cartoon reproduced as the frontispiece is taken from Anthony D. King, *Colonial Urban Development*, published by Routledge & Kegan Paul.

I am grateful to Mr Anil Thapa who patiently deciphered and typed the innumerable drafts, as also to Miss Sudha Sharma for assistance. I would like to thank Oxford University Press, especially my editor, who toiled over the text as if it were her own.

Lastly my deepest thanks to my husband, Surendra, who read through its many incarnations with unflagging enthusiasm; and to Kartik and Madhurima who grew, sharing my time and attention, along with my book.

CHAPTER ONE

The Ambience

THE sights and smells of a bygone era are hard to document and difficult to verify. They are images which conjure up an ethos but conceal many answers.

An amorphous mist of nostalgia and romanticism looms over many British pre-1947 accounts of Simla. In the early nineteenth century, its cool climate and steep rugged slopes answered the needs of the East India Company's sick—and homesick—birds of passage, soldiers and civilians, invalids and convalescents. Simla's temperate climate, deodar-wooded hills, and swirling monsoon fog evoked memories of English life, and most found the transformation from scenes of mango and acacia to deodar, pine and fir within a few hours over-whelming. It also afforded an opportunity to build around themselves a world of make-believe.

When Simla was a hill village and had one thatched cottage, a traveller, after he had breathlessly climbed the ascent from Sairi to Boileaugunj for a view of Jakhu hill, recounted that he would remember the journey 'for it reminded me of home, the days of my boyhood, my mother and the happiest of varied recollections.'[1] Later, when by 1837 it had grown into a settle-ment, Emily Eden, sister of Lord Auckland, the Governor-General, pronounced the clear air 'English and exhilarating'. The thick white fog of the monsoons somehow had 'a smell of London, only without the taste of smoked pea soup, which is more germane to a London fog.'[2] As Simla sprawled into a summer capital, the desire to develop its English character became more intense. In 1877, Val Prinsep, returning after a stay in the plains, noticed that 'Everything is so English and unpicturesque that, . . . one would fancy oneself in Margate.'[3] By the 1930s, Malcolm Muggeridge, later editor of Punch, observed that Simla was 'an authentic English production;

designed by Sahibs for Sahibs without reference to any other consideration—not even Maharajahs.'[4]

That Simla was to be English in character was an assumption dyed into the thinking and activities of its residents—structures and appearances that reflected nineteenth-century upper-class values found their way into Simla life. There was a Mall, a Scandal Point (the place of gossip) and scores of cottages with evocative English, Irish, Scottish and Welsh names. It became fashionable (if untenable), to perceive Simla as 'Anglo-Saxon', as a miniscule England, to compare its architectural landmarks with the ones they imitated, to equate the Simla 'season' with that of London.

A standard photograph album of Simla views would represent its English buildings and views, while the bazar would merit one bird's-eye view, panning its slummy squalor from the safe distance of Jakhu Hill. Kipling's description of Lower Bazar as a 'rabbit-warren at an angle of forty-five' found its way into official documents and guide books but scarcely infringed on the consciousness of the English residents. This vast Lower Bazar, which cascaded down the hill in untidy tiers was dismissed, though the monkeys and black-faced langoors with which Simla abounded were sportingly accommodated and even earned immortality in a children's story.

By census counts it required, even in the nineteenth century, a total Indian population of over 85 per cent (29,048 of 33,174 in 1898) to sustain the British illusion. Yet the spell that Simla cast on Indians, though rarely written about, was no less highly-tinted. That Simla was the facsimile of an original British town (which most had never seen) was never doubted. Thus a strange convoluted nostalgia shadows Indian memories: the abiding impression is of a well-planned town, sparkling window-panes, washed roads, even though the majority lived in crouched subservience in the bazar.

Images that the word 'Simla' evoked were the smell of leather and sweat; of *syce* or groom, in an even trot behind the Sahib rider, of breaking into a cold sweat in case the Indian collided with an Englishman; of English ladies with delicate net veils drawn across the face to protect them from the dust of a rickshaw drive; of the turbaned khaki-clad barefoot coolie wheeling a rickshaw; of the overpowering smell of poverty. (It gave rise to the saying, '*Paharis* never bathe'). In spite of these contradictions the impecunious clerk who accompanied the Government of India offices, the petty shopkeepers who set up business in Simla's Lower Bazar, the Harijan who cleaned Simla and its thunder-boxes, the aristocrat and wealthy professional who bought property—all felt privileged to have lived in the *Chhota Vilayat*—little England—of India.

The drawbacks for Indians were many—Simla's prolonged three-and-a-half month long monsoon, its hard-to-digest mineral water, the panting-uphill, and breakneck-down walks, since most Indians could afford neither horse nor rickshaw. Its climate, comfortable in the two summer months of May and June, was cold and wet for the rest of the year. Yet terms purloined from the dominant culture, 'bracing', 'healthy', 'salubrious', became clichés for it used by Indian newspapers, and some thought it could make 'a capital health city'.

Simla, as the summer capital of India, provided an escape not only from the heat, but also from the native culture of the plains. Officials, military and civilian, on postings or on leave, formed the base of Simla's British society in summer; regarding themselves as exiles in India, Simla was for them a spatial creation dedicated to reviving memories of England. If an English official was unable to go on long leave to England he came to Simla, not only to a cooler climate, but also to escape from the relative isolation of district or cantonment where refuge could only be found in clubs. Simla's atmosphere was that of an oversized English club.

The dominant characteristic of British Simla was its contempt for all things Indian. If social interaction between the races was scorned in the plains, it was despised at Simla. In the Government of India, 'the affectation of being English, of knowing nothing at all about India, of eschewing Indian words and customs, spread downwards from the Viceroy's staff and was endemic.'[5] A comment from a local paper of 1894 illustrates this forcefully: 'The use of this khud in an official report strikes us as rather strange. Is there no English word for it? Why must we always be interpolating our speech not only, but our documents as well with these barbarisms? "Down the Valley" would have read just as well and would have had the further recommendation of being English.'[6]

To be English was to be superior. Yet, not every Englishman in India could come to Simla—most non-officials could not afford it. The high cost of living and high rents made it impossible for people of moderate means, earning under 1,500 rupees a month.[7] The presence of the Viceroy, the Commander-in-Chief, the Lieutenant-Governor of the Punjab and their staff made it a very exclusive spot. Hence, in Simla the English tended to be even more self-contained and insulated than in the plains.

Simla aroused mixed emotions in most middle-class Indian residents. Attitudes oscillated between awe at the privilege of staying in Simla and repugnance at the sense of inferiority. This ambivalence is reflected in many Indian accounts. It spawned a host of half-truths and blatant myths.

That 'Indians were not allowed to walk on the Mall' was only partially true. The Mall, a crescent-shaped promenade, was according to a long-time Simla resident, eminent journalist and editor, Durga Das, 'a special European preserve; most of its shops were run by white men. No load-carrying porter was permitted to use it, nor any ill-dressed Indian either. The rule was relaxed only at night, when middle class Indians strolled along the Mall, gazing admiringly at the show-windows of the European shops. . . .'[8]

That vivid description can be corroborated. However, in 1900, despite the European appearance of shops on the Mall, only fifteen were owned by British traders.[9]

It is remarkable how slander sometimes reflects the group psyche and expresses aspects of a town's history. A timeworn myth: Scandal Point on the Mall owes its name to the scandal of a scion of the Patiala family galloping away on his steed, Prithviraj-like, with an English viceroy's daughter or wife. The details vary. Simla people relate the story, being certain they have read it somewhere, promising to let one know where. There is a touch of pity for the inept researcher hunting for documentary evidence (I have not found any) for such a well-established 'fact'.

Investigation did however reveal that the Patiala Vakil Khana (now a primary school) was located in a house in the Middle Bazar, and lay directly below Scandal Point. A Vakil Khana was generally the accredited office of a State and served as a channel of communication between it and the Deputy Commissioner, in his capacity as Superintendent of Hill States, in settling legal disputes and ironing out protocol problems. Doubtless the Vakil carried out sundry other jobs assigned to him by the State Durbar.

What is documented is that a Patiala ruler apparently lost his reputation with middle-class Indians. In 1929, a much-publicized memorial to the Viceroy by ten citizens of Patiala State, levelled charges of abduction, forced labour, illegal arrests, murder and torture. It alleged that the Maharaja's 'moral depravity', 'licentiousnes', and 'profligacy' was the root of misgovernment in Patiala State, and that the honour of no woman who had the misfortune of being young and beautiful was safe in Patiala. It proclaimed: 'At Simla the Maharaja's conduct gave rise to scandals of a grave character', rounding off its twenty-six allegations, listed from A to Z, by the charge that the Maharaja had been emboldened by the government's leniency 'on account of his lavish hospitality towards British officials'.[10]

An inquiry was then conducted by the All-India State People's Conference, and its findings were published in a damning pamphlet entitled *An Indictment of Patiala*. The Maharaja urged that an impartial inquiry take place, and an *in camera* investigation instituted by Willingdon exonerated him of the charges. But people tend to believe rumour more than official reports; rumour satisfies the need for mystery and the belief that truth

is always hidden. The Patiala ruler remained, to popular satisfaction, a notorious figure in Simla.

Was the myth created about him a reaction to British racial
arrogance? Was it a subconscious expression of the sneaking
admiration a daring philanderer was held in by middle-class
Indians who might themselves, at best, have mumbled a defe-
rential greeting to the English lord who passed by on the Mall?
Its significance lies not in its being a fact, but that it arose at all
and that it should linger on.

The Indian response to arrogance was, at the lowest social
level, fear. An easily discernible image of fear is contained in
the gory tale of 'Ram Tel' related by the hill folk of Simla.
According to this, any Indian who wandered about after dark
was caught and hung upside down. His head was shaved and
perforated, and the liquid that oozed out, 'Ram Tel', was an
invaluable balm for seriously-wounded soldiers during the war.
The story is said to have leaked out because a wily villager had
escaped to tell the tale. The ordeal was retailed in huddles in the
villages of the Simla hills—Mian Goverdhan Singh of Jubbal,
who was sent to study in the Municipal High School at Simla
in 1943, was so warned. (In 1975, the basement of the Gaiety
Theatre was pointed out to me as the place where tortures
were perpetrated.)

Did the origin of the story lie in threats made by policemen
patrolling the Simla roads in pairs at night, as they still do,
with instructions to haul loitering servants to the police station?
Was it prefaced by the threat, '*Ulta tang dunga*', 'I'll hang you
upside down?'

Such sentiments of fear and obedience were carefully fostered.
The average Englishman regarded the coolie, at worst, as a
beast of burden, at best as an unkempt, and (horribly) unclean
human being. In the early nineteenth century, Victor Jacquemont, a French naturalist, described the relationship between
European and menial as one between 'hammer and anvil'.[11]
There was no intermediate position between contempt on the
one hand and servile obedience on the other. The European
was advised to administer a thrashing to natives for errant

behaviour—and this could be simply failure to address a Sahib as 'Your Lordship' or 'Your Highness'. Emily Eden expressed her apprehension at being surrounded by about three thousand hill coolies, sitting on the terraces around Annandale. 'I sometimes wonder they do not cut all our heads off, and say nothing more about it.'[12]

But the lesson in respect had been thoroughly instilled. She expressed a sense of relief at the servility with which they bowed to the ground if a European came near.

What did the locals think of English frivolities? In 1858, William Howard Russell, a London *Times* correspondent and critic of the British in India, asked an Indian what he thought of British behaviour. Russell was appalled by the answer:

> Does the Sahib see those monkeys? They are playing very pleasantly. But the Sahib cannot say why they play, nor what they are going to do next. Well, then, our poor people look upon you very much as they would on those monkeys, but that they know you are very fierce and strong, and would be angry if you were laughed at. They are afraid to laugh. But they do regard you as some great powerful creatures sent to plague them, of whose motives and actions they can comprehend nothing whatever.[13]

Simla enters the hill consciousness through many folk songs. The village *hesis* with rustic ingenuity rhymed allusions to Simla in *laman*—couplets sung so as to echo across the valleys. A song from Kulu describes British social mores, as perceived perhaps by an *ayah*, thus:

> *Hoche Shimla Sahib, bare Shimla Missy,*
> *Soone.chandi annu, dongiya, chhati donguie nhaisi.*[14]

> In Chhota Simla lives the Sahib
> In Burra Simla the mem
> Broken jewels can be mended
> Broken hearts are never the same.

The lights of Simla, especially when electricity was tapped, shone across the ranges to Kulu, Narkanda, and Mahasu. The twinkling lights found their way into several verses, and many songs refer to loved ones gone to work at Simla, though not many verses or village tales were woven around the hill people's perception of the life of the English at Simla.

Alice Dracott, who attempted in 1905 to compile the folk tales of Simla, was sometimes asked whether she would like a 'Paharee' man well-versed in folklore to relate a few stories. She was obliged to decline the offer, for many Simla village tales related events that were 'grotesquely unfit' for publication.[15]

European Simla's ritual contact with rural Simla was the annual picnic to Mashobra to participate in the Sipi Fair. Held in the middle of May, it was declared a public holiday and most officials, the Viceroy downwards, visited the fair at least once during their tenure. A typical fair is presided over by the village *devata*, Sipur, a deity in the form of a silver mask, attached to a pyramid-shaped palanquin fixed upon two parallel beams and surmounted by a silver canopy. The fair was, and is, known for its colour, gaiety, and folk dances performed to the accompaniment of the *karnal* (a long trumpet), *dhol* (drums) and the *bugjal* (a pair of circular metallic cymbals). It includes the *thoda*, a ritual dance, in which arrows are aimed at the legs of the dancers, demonstrating their skill in archery. The highlight of the *nati* dance is when the *devata* is made to join the dance. The fair has stalls selling trinkets, bangles, toys, cloth, *laddus* and *jalebis*, swings and roundabouts.

Women sit on the terraced hillside around the small tea-cup shaped valley to rest and view the fair, which was regarded as a marriage mart, with prospective brides being put on show for sale to 'prosperous *jampanis*'. In the early nineteenth century, this was perhaps taken as evidence of *rit* (a system of matrimony involving bride price, described in the *Gazetteer* of 1888–9 as a temporary marriage without any formal ceremony. It is dissolved by the woman when taking a new husband, who pays the first husband the money originally paid to the girls' parents, ordinarily seventy rupees). In 1882, a newspaper commented that the newcomer is promptly told that 'the real business of the day is purchase of wives, and a part of the hillside is pointed out to him where the youth and beauty of the surrounding county is closely packed together, decorated with nose-rings and bright chudders, and showing willingness to respond to critical inspection with smiles of the most winning frankness.'[16] The typical Pahari woman was 'as a rule, extremely good-looking, and a born flirt; she has a pleasant, gay manner, and can always see a joke; people who wish to chaff her discover an adept at repartee.'[17]

Curiously, Indians from the plains tended to type hill women as 'simple, shy and innocent'. (Women in the hills, it may be mentioned, are the economic mainstay of a family—they cultivate the fields; fetch water, fuel wood and fodder and tend cattle, in addition to doing the household chores. Considered an economic asset, hill women enjoy relatively greater independence than those of the plains.)

The 'unique' features of Sipi fair appear to have been whispered to successive visitors and find mention in several accounts such as those by Buck in 1905, and Randhawa in 1952.[18]

The fair was likened in 1882 to the Derby—in that it attracted rich and poor, old and young. As in the Derby it was not the race alone that counted. 'The native matrimonial Seepee has gone down in importance, the European tiffin-eating Seepee has been magnified into an important ceremonial. Standing back a little you had the luxurious shamianas with their luncheon tables and groups of scarlet waisted khitmutgars waiting about in the left foreground; then in the middle foreground the European guests, ladies in riding habits or bright dresses, and the men in all imaginable varieties of riding costumes. . . .'[19]

The social life of the rulers in the summer capital had many faithful chroniclers. British writers were generally more interested in portraying their own lives and the Simla which they loved, or occasionally hated, than writing about the natives. A recurring theme in contemporary British accounts and newspaper articles is of the 'red-tape tempered with picnics and adultery' variety, an exposé or defence of British society in Simla. The nostalgic reminiscences of a retired civilian, published in 1946, give a vivid, if idealized, picture of social activities:

> A very pleasant place was Simla—pleasant the frolic and the fun, the good friendships made, the manifold interests that work and society provided.... Do the Black Hearts still delight society with their lavish dances? Does the theatre still scintillate with amateur talent? Are the boxes still auctioned to those who are anxious worthily to accommodate youth and beauty at the play? Do those charming and intimate little dinners still take place at the Chalet? Do crowds, on horseback or in rickshaws still wend their way to sumptuous parties and return in the small hours when moonlight kisses distant hill and deep valley and wakens dreams of romance in youthful bosoms? Do gallant calvacades ride forth to Mashobra or Wildflower Hall along ways overshadowed by deodars. . . .?[20]

The presence of English women in the hills in large numbers enhanced the holiday and social image of Simla. They, more than their men, tended to withdraw into their own closed, artificial circle. For them, Simla was an endless session of balls and archery, fetes, fun-fairs, picnics and amateur dramatics, and their diaries, letters, and novelettes covering the span of almost a century, from the vicereine to the official's wife, hardly venture beyond an account of the social rounds. There is a remarkable similarity in the content of the Simla letters and diaries of Emily Eden in 1837–8, Lady Dufferin from 1884 to 1888, and even of a plebeian officer in the Women's Auxiliary Service during World War II.[21]

Their view was further perpetuated by fiction. Simla had its Rudyard Kipling, who masterfully peopled the summer capital by larger-than-life images in his novels.[22] Serving as a correspondent of the *Civil and Military Gazette* and the *Pioneer* between 1882 and 1889, he learnt much about social life at Simla from his frequent visits there, and from his sister, Mrs Fleming, who portrays Simla's social scene in her novel, *A Pinchbeck Goddess*. So vivid was Kipling's evocation that the array of dowagers, policemen, officers, administrators and antique dealers, portrayed in several stories, soon became 'real' characters, whom

British visitors hoped to encounter even a quarter of a century
later.

Many of Kipling's literary creations have become Simla's
'historical' legacy. For instance, a letter writer in 1913 recommended Kipling for an insight into the 'real life' of Simla.

> By docket, billet-doux and file,
>   By mountain, cliff and fir,
> By fan and sword and office-box,
>   By corset, plume and spur,
> By riot, revel, waltz and war,
>   By women, work and bills,
> By all the life that fizzes in
>   The everlasting hills.

'The above, Sir', he concludes 'is life in Simla in a nutshell—
strenuous work and strenuous play.'[23]

Edward Buck's historical account of Simla, *Simla Past and
Present*, written at Curzon's behest, also relies largely on British
sources. Buck, a Reuter's correspondent and Chairman of the
Associated Hotels of India, was a Simla resident of long
standing, who meticulously brought together almost every
published reference to the town from articles, letters, diaries
and books. He describes with feeling the world of viceroys,
lieutenant-governors, commanders-in-chief and their aides;
important residences, buildings, clubs and amateur theatre.
Predictably, the underlying thread of his chapters is illustration
of a facet of the life and attitudes of the official, white section
of its society.

Sometimes the mystique of a town is taken to represent its
reality. Simla has been overburdened with images of British
life. Such images both help and hinder our understanding of
the urban and social reality of Simla. These perceptions pre-
suppose a set of assumptions and prejudices. Much is known
about the Gothic and quasi-Gothic structures scattered across
Simla, less about its morphology and the parameters of its urban
plans. Much is known about individual houses and their owners,
less about the pressures against which successive administrations

strained to prevent a change in the pattern of that ownership. Much is known about the people who gave Simla its English façade, less about those who lived on its underside. It was customary to dismiss Simla's Indian population as migratory and functional. What then were the issues that local politicians raised in the small, cramped and crowded Gunj Maidan in the Lower Bazar?

Simla was a microcosm of the vast mosaic of forces that were shaping modern India, it was unique, and yet part of a larger pattern. Much is known about picnics, excursions and shikar along the newly-built roads along the crests of mountain ranges. Less, that the creation of hill-stations and dak bungalows created linking roads that altered the nexus of development in the hills. Trade that had once been channelled along routes and towns situated in the river valleys diminished in importance, whereas hill-stations like Simla were imperceptibly converted into entrepôts.

CHAPTER TWO

The Beginnings

THE first mention of 'Semla, a middling-sized village' comes in 1817 from the diary of two Scottish officers, Lieutenants Patrick and Alexander Gerard, as they surveyed and mapped the newly-subjugated hill states.[1] They climbed the summit of Jakhu Hill, the highest point on the ridge, for a bird's-eye view of the surrounding area and took the bearing and altitudes of the peaks visible there. They noticed that the area was well cultivated on the banks of the rivulets but not near the road. The Sutlej valley provided a broad natural highway linking the Punjab with the plateau of western Tibet. Tibet was known as a rich source of precious metals, and for its soft and highly-valued *pashm* or shawl wool, of which the East India Company hoped to acquire the monopoly. The more frequented trade route through Ladakh and Kashmir lay through the hostile territory of the Sikh ruler, Ranjit Singh. There now seemed a possibility of an alternative route through Bushahr, the largest and northernmost hill state.[2]

In 1814, Colonel Ochterlony, in charge of the army in this sector, had pondered over the information that an elephant given in dowry had been sent from Nahan to Bushahr.[3] The revelation had opened up glimpses of a wide road leading to Bushahr, which had acquired importance as a half-way stage on the route from Tibet and Ladakh. It was at Rampur, its capital, that traders from the plains met sellers with sheep-loads of merchandise from Tibet, Ladakh and Yarkhand. Simla lay on this trade route, traversable for six months in the year, between Rampur in Bushahr and Sirsa in the plains.

The hill states of Kumaon and Garhwal had been conquered by the Gurkhas towards the close of the eighteenth century. Armed with three-pound guns, which they dismantled and carried as headloads over hill paths, and clad in red uniforms in

imitation ot the East India Company's Bengal army, the
Gurkhas had terrorized the warring hill state rulers into sub-
mission. The Gurkha conquest paved the way to control of the
key Himalayan passes to Tibet and all the trade that passed
through them. But Gurkha policy excluded all foreign traders,
denying the British merchants' access to Tibetan marts.

Ochterlony's first task was to wrest the hill forts between
the Ganga and the Sutlej from the Gurkhas. In a series of well-
planned manoeuvres in 1814–15, the Gurkhas were defeated
and forced to sign the Treaty of Sagauli.[4]

The immediate sequel to the Gurkha wars was the parcelling
out of territories. The Company assumed the role of provi-
dential arbiter of boundaries: the hill rulers were reinstated
with respect to each other as nearly as possible in the position
they had occupied before the Gurkha conquest. It was surmised
that the 'natural effect of our exertions for the restoration of
these Chiefs and of the political influence and ascendency
which our success will bring with it, will be to make them
look to us for advice and assistance in their difficulties which
we shall be at liberty to afford.'[5] The eighteenth-century Bara
Thakurais (Twelve Lordships) and their off-shoots and feuda-
tories, the Athara Thakurais (Eighteen Lordships) were formed
into the twenty Simla Hill States under the Assistant Political
Agent posted at Sabathu.

The hill rulers, as anticipated, looked to British advice and
assistance when there were disputes. A delicate balance of
hostility, it was calculated, would be useful for British interests
and ensure the 'preservation of tranquillity' for British commercial objectives. Some of the larger states were cut to size.
Keonthal (from which much of Simla was later carved) was
deprived of half its territory for demurring on paying its share
of the expenses of the Gurkha war; Baghat (the area near Solan)
forfeited three-fourths of its territory for being 'unfriendly'.[6]
On the other hand, for its assistance with troops and supplies,
Patiala was given the confiscated portions of Keonthal and
Baghat, yielding an annual revenue of 35,000 rupees. The
Company then seized the opportunity to replenish its coffers.

Patiała was required to pay a *nazrana* of 2,80,000 rupees for the privilege of acquiring hill territory.[7]

The hill states were in return obliged to construct twelve-foot-wide roads through their territories, to provide armed retainers in time of war, and to keep the Company supplied with a specified number of begarees throughout the year. The Company retained the strategic forts of Sabathu, Kotgarh, Raingarh and Sandoch. A newly-formed Nasiri Battalion, welded together from fragments of the defeated Gurkha forces, was posted at these forts.[8] Simla itself went unnoticed during the course of the Gurkha war.

The distinction of founding the future summer capital of India rests with Captain Charles Pratt Kennedy, posted as Garrison Officer until 1821, and thereafter as Political Agent and Commanding Officer of the Nasiri Battalion stationed at Sabathu.

The thickly-wooded Simla ridge was clearly visible from the cantonment at Sabathu. Its forests, full of hyena, bear, leopard, barking deer and jackal, became a hunting ground for officers posted there. So popular and prolonged were these summer trips that in 1819, Lieutenant Ross, the Assistant Political Agent, built a thatched cottage in Simla. In 1822, his successor, Kennedy, built the first permanent house—a pretty gabled cottage called Kennedy House.

As Political Agent, Kennedy was assigned the task of supervising the hill states, and ensuring that they complied with the provisions of the treaties they had signed. The difficulty of governing remote and isolated hill tracts had led General Ochterlony in 1817 to recommend that local officers exercise 'a power analogous to that of the magistrates of cities and zillas', both in the hill districts retained by the Company as well as in the 'independent' states.[9] Kennedy consequently was vested with wide magisterial powers and the task of revenue collection.

There is a touch of irony in Jacquemont's description of Kennedy's awesome duties: 'He discharges the functions of collector. With an independence equal to that of the Grand Turk he acts as Judge over his own subjects and, what is more, those of the neighbouring rajahs, Hindus, Tartar and Tibetan, sending them to prison, fining them and even hanging them when he thinks fit.' Kennedy apparently adapted easily to the authority he wielded. A middle-aged bachelor, he was reputed 'the most rigorous of dandies and the greatest of sticklers for form and of having the most stinking pride of any of the princes of the earth.'[10] For fourteen years, till he retired in 1835, Kennedy made Simla virtually his 'royal estate', and was associated with and responsible for much of the town's growth.

Simla's *First Settlement Report* recounts that from 1824 onwards, 'European gentlemen, chiefly invalids from the plains,' built many of the earliest houses. Land for house construction was leased 'free of rent' from the rulers of Keonthal or Patiala, depending on the site chosen.[11] *Begarees*, building material and wood were also secured from them, and the transactions recorded in Kennedy's office.[12]

Simla was chosen in 1827 by Amherst, the Governor-General, for a summer trip. He came with his entourage and 1,700 coolies in attendance.[13] Amherst spent an uneventful summer at Kennedy House, leaving Simla after two months—apprehending that it would be unhealthy after the middle of June, once the monsoon set in. The visit created a precedent.

It also left six large houses that had been built for his entourage. The smallest of them could accommodate four bachelors or two married families. The officers requested these for accommodation for invalids, 'a boon very gratefully received by all classes and particularly those whose means or distance from the Presidency render a voyage to sea . . . impracticable or greatly inconvenient.'[14] The request refers to the practice of sending invalid soldiers to the Cape of Good Hope or to England to convalesce.

The hill settlements built in India occupy a special place in the history and consolidation of the British Empire. In the early nineteenth century, when a series of conquests extended British sway all over India, many of the hill towns were strategically placed to serve as military outposts or sanatoriums for convalescing soldiers. Camps such as Simla obviated the necessity of sending convalescents out of the country.

The earliest houses at Simla were built on flat pieces of land, preferably near springs. Sometimes a tent pitched at a spot for a few seasons became the site for a house. There was a shortage of accommodation—Captain Mundy, aide-de-camp to the Commander in Chief Lord Combermere, considered himself lucky to occupy an attic below a wooden roof, where he could stand upright only in the centre. 'I enjoyed . . . a splendid view . . . and the luxury of privacy, except at night, when the rats sustained an eternal carnival, keeping me in much the same state as Whittington during his first week in London. I soon grew tired of bumping my head against the roof in pursuit of these four-footed Pindarees, and at length became callous to their nocturnal orgies and kept a cat.'[15] He writes that in 1828 hundreds of mountain labourers and coolies were employed for cutting timber, laying blocks of stone and erecting buildings. The leisure hours of many officers were spent supervising the construction of their houses and afterwards in enlarging and beautifying them.

There were instances of what in current urban usage would be termed 'squatting'. A Major Spiller pitched his tents on a plot for two seasons, from April 1929 to September 1930, and then claimed the right to construct a house on the site. Kennedy averred that he had selected the site for the office and establishment of the military department. Spiller retorted: 'a fact known to every person in Simlah, [is] that the ground in question has been occupied by my tents and my servants ever since I have been on this location.'[16] His claim was granted but later he was accused of encroaching upon additional land. Spiller then went on to construct his house but had problems obtaining timber, which the Rana of Keonthal had refused him. 'If I give all my trees how will my subjects be able to live in my country?'[17] Spiller and another officer thereafter made a deal with a local zamindar, Bisumber, who agreed to supply 150 trees for fifteen rupees. The trees were felled, but the Rana's retainers prevented Spiller's servants from removing the wood, and a scuffle ensued. Thereupon the officers struck a bargain with the Rana's *vakil* to lift the timber on payment of an additional twelve rupees. The Rana protested to Kennedy,[18] who reported the matter to the Governor-General. In spite of his protests, Spiller was reprimanded by the authorities for unjustifiable usurpation of land and for his efforts to procure timber illicitly.

Spiller's determination to construct a house must be viewed in the context of the prevailing housing shortage. House rents were high and investment in property yielded lucrative returns, as one-third of the cost of a house was usually charged as rent for a six-month season. A Simla house was, therefore, an excellent investment, especially for a resident who could have it properly attended to.[19]

By 1830, a township of thirty British-owned houses scattered over the Simla tract had come up. It was then acquired by the East India Company. Patiala was asked to part with four villages (Kainthu, Paghog, Cheog and Aindari) which came within Simla. They spread from Bharari, across Kainthu to Prospect Hill, including the plague post on the Cart Road, upto Jutogh railway station. The Maharaja was compensated with seven villages in Bharauli. The Rana of Keonthal was given the area near Ravin, minus the fortress of Raingarh, in exchange for the twelve villages of Panjar, Sirian, Dharma, Phagli, Dillen, Kiar, Bamnoi, Pagawag, Dhar, Kanlog, Kilian and Khalini—villages that lay between Tara Devi across Simla upto Kasumpti. Simla town now comprised an area of about six square miles.[20] It was surrounded by princely states. Patiala lay on the north and west; Keonthal on the south and east; and Koti, which included the suburbs of Sanjauli, Mashobra, Kufri and Naldehra, on the north-east. A chain of hill states lay along the route from Kalka via Simla to Bushahr, and on towards Tibet.

Once Simla had passed under the direct jurisdiction of the Government, the first civic rules were formulated. The earliest houses, paths, and water reservoirs built by individuals were now brought within the general scheme of 'improvement' of the town. Bentinck, the Governor-General, suggested that two hundred square yards be the utmost allowed an individual for construction of a house. As a first step, the boundaries of houses and the land attached to them were demarcated. A graduated ground tax, ranging from twenty to forty rupees, depending on the built-up area, was fixed.[21] The proceeds from the *chowkidari* tax were meant to defray the cost of policing the town.[22]

In 1832 Bentinck appointed a three-man committee to suggest measures for improvement of the town. The main problems which confronted the three members, Captain Kennedy, Colonel C. B. Stevenson, the Quarter-Master General of Subathu, and MacSween, a house-owner, were how to improve the water supply and roads in Simla. Since springs were the only source of supply, water was a perennial problem and a few reservoirs had been built in 1828 and 1830. One of the first instructions to the committee was that 'every spring that can be turned to account for the purpose, with the roads and pathways leading to it, must of course be considered public property.'[23] Narrow, but clearly-marked tracks linked the various houses. The first 'fine, broad, level road around Mount Jakhu, about three miles in length', was built in 1828 under the supervision of Combermere, the Commander-in-Chief.

Right from the beginning, Simla established a reputation for gaiety. Visited by the affluent, fashionable section of the East India Company's civil and military servants, its popularity grew as wives and families returned to the plains with rosy complexions. Mundy mentions there were sixteen women in 1828, while Jacquemont encountered 'the most friendly and lively of the rich idlers and imaginary invalids'. Annandale, the name given to a flat semi-circular amphitheatre, about a quarter of a mile in circumference and surrounded by tall majestic deodars, was a readymade play and recreation ground. The first funfair was held in Annandale in September 1833 to raise funds for a girls' school at Sabathu. Subsequently it became the site for countless balls, dinners, picnics, fêtes, flower shows, dog shows, archery competitions, hack races and even rickshaw races. By the late nineteenth century, the ground had been enlarged and it was possible to hold gymkhanas, polo, cricket

and football matches there. Annandale's legacy to Indian sport
was the annual Durand Football Tournament, inaugurated by
Mortimer Durand in 1888.

Annandale in all likelihood owes its name to a small valley in
Dumfriesshire in Scotland, the home of several families well
known in the Indian services. It is referred to as Annandale in
an article published in 1834 in the *East Indian United Service
Journal*. However, a guide to Simla published after 1881 called
the grounds Annadale, according to a romantic legend about
Kennedy being so struck by the beauty of the place that he
named it after Anna, a youthful love of his in England.[24]

The sustaining core of the new hill-station, the bazar, on the
Ridge, formed a 'neat little village, snugly situated under the
shoulder of Jako, which protects it from the north-east wind.'[25]
The market was dominated by three *shroffs*, four cloth-sellers
and four grain-dealers. Rughbur Dass, a commission agent
and banker, monopolized the trade, loaning money at 24–7
per cent interest per annum, both to the retail shopkeepers and
to spendthrift British officers.[26] A *kotwali* (police post) was
located adjacent to the bazar. Kennedy's earliest instructions
issued to the *kotwal* pertained to security against theft by
servants, coolies and vagrants, and prohibition of gambling
and drinking in the bazar. By night, the scores of labourers and
coolies slept in huddles in the open or in improvised sheds.
Kennedy's paternalistic instincts directed that 'Shops of every
description to be shut at 9 p.m. Lights extinguished, and no
natching or other noise allowed after that in the Bazar.'[27] All
servants found strolling about after 10 o'clock except servants
who waited at table, were also picked up by the police. In 1832,
Kennedy sited a new bazar at the eastern end of Simla. It came
to be known as the Chhota (small) Simla bazar.

To provision Simla with essential foodgrains, the construction of several new routes and the diversion of others was
required. Simla did not lie on an established trade route; traders
from the *mandis* (wholesale markets) of Hoshiarpur and Jagadhri
had to travel there. The creation of *chowkis* by hill rulers charging
transit duties posed a problem here. Along the Pinjore-Sabathu-

Simla route, the Patiala ruler farmed out *chowkis* at Barh and Haripur to the highest bidder. The ruler of Bilaspur levied a tax on traders travelling from Kangra to Simla. In 1824, all duties levied by hill rulers were abolished.[28] The trace of an alternative mule road to link Simla via Sabathu across Nahan, with the markets at Jagadhri, was made. In 1832, octroi and other transit duties imposed at Simla were abolished and traders were free to trade without 'search, detention or question'.[29] Traditional items of trade between Bushahr and the plains passed through the Simla market, the principal imports from the plains being grain, cloth, cotton, silk, copper and brass, while the exports included hill produce—opium, cumin seed, borax, shawl-wool, ginger, walnuts and honey.

By 1827, Kennedy claimed to have achieved the object of the subjugation of hill territory—a twelve-foot-wide road between Pinjore and Bushahr, a distance of two hundred miles, all at the cost of the work of a company of Pioneers for a few years. Kennedy did not add the contribution of the hill coolies. There were complaints of non-payment of wages from two local zamindars: Perunah and Jolah petitioned that they had supplied forty coolies for ten months to complete the road from Simla to Sabathu. The Political Agent refuted the charge as untenable as the hill rulers were under treaty obligations to keep the roads in repair.[30] Kennedy denied another accusation of keeping six coolies for six years without pay.[31]

This road was not permanent because it takes several years before paths cut into hillsides can stabilize into roads. The monsoons often wash segments down into khuds while landslides carry stones and rocks down on to the roads. Despite a laudatory note from the Governor-General's Secretary, commending his zeal and meritorious services in road construction, Kennedy was refused a request for a special allowance.[32]

Kennedy's less-known contribution, in which lay the seeds of an agricultural revolution, was in distributing potatoes for planting to villages along the new route between Fagu and Theog. The potato flourished and became a cash-circulating medium for impoverished hill villagers. Because of the cool climate, disease-free potatoes were produced and these were soon accepted as the best seed potato in the country.

Kennedy's Christian sensibilities were alarmed at the lax religious feelings of the hill people. He recommended that a mission of the Unitas Fratum or Moravians be set up in the area as he felt that they would be the most suited for 'the moral and political upliftment' of the local people. The mission was set up in Kotgarh.[33]

Captain Kennedy's imperious manner and the authority he wielded as Political Agent were resented by his compatriots. The records are full of complaints against him and of cases sent up for redress to the Governor-General and his Council.[34] A Captain Elliot accused Kennedy of deliberately routing a public path through his garden. He protested that Kennedy had not been 'so scrupulous with regard to the benefit of the public when his own interest was concerned; he having turned the high road from Subathoo to this place (Kennedy House) to his own advantage certainly but not to that of the public.'[35] Kennedy in his reply pointed out that the road was made up to the office of the Political Agent, which was housed in his home. A Major Stacy protested about a path to a water tank being made through his lawn, thus injuring the value of his property.[36] A Colonel Torrens through whose backyard the newly conceived Chhota Simla bazar road was routed, fulminated: 'There are a hundred spots available at that side of Simla, more convenient, which will injure no one, without fixing on mine. Should a bazar be raised on the spot suggested, it will not be on the Public road, but this Road looking backwards all over my premises [Torrentium] and which unquestionably I would not have purchased at any price, had there been reason to suppose that such a nuisance was likely to be erected in their vicinity.'[37]

Kennedy's failure to curb the extortionate demands of middlemen and check prices led fourteen officers to loan money to retail shopkeepers to buy merchandise directly from the plains, and thus evade the 27 per cent interest charged by local commission agents.[38] They felt obliged to pass a resolution that 'no want of courtesy' existed towards Captain Kennedy. Kennedy decreed that their decision was illegal and intimated to Simla's Indian merchants the 'necessity of the greatest circumspection in their dealings with military officers'.[39] Various allegations prompted Kennedy's Commissioner to demand action against persons using 'disrespectful language' against the local officer and to enforce obedience to his orders.[40]

Kennedy, however, ingratiated himself with the men who mattered. Mundy said of him, 'a merrier man I never spent an hour's talk withal'. Jacquemont described Kennedy's work routine as occupying 'one hour after breakfast. . . . [He] passes the rest of his time in loading me with kindness.' Kennedy maintained a well-stocked cellar and a meticulously run household. 'Is it not curious to dine in silk stockings at such a place, and to drink a bottle of hock and another of champagne every evening—delicious Mocha coffee—and to receive the Calcutta journals every morning?' Kennedy's other important guests were Lord Amherst in 1827, and in 1828 Combermere, the Commander-in-Chief, who stayed at Kennedy House for seven months.

A new house, Bentinck Castle (Grand Hotel now stands on this site) was constructed for Bentinck, the next Governor-General to visit. Bentinck, who was unpopular with British officers because he had reduced their travelling and daily allowances, had a hill, said to resemble his profile, named 'Bentinck's nose', and there was some consternation when Lady William Bentinck converted a Simla billiard hall into a church. But Bentinck's visit in 1831 made Simla the 'establishment' hill-station. Thereafter, until it was formally established as summer capital, every successive Governor-General visited the town at least once during his stay in India.

During his fourteen years' tenure, Kennedy rose from the rank of lieutenant to major. On the eve of his retirement from the Political Department in 1835, he made a futile bid to obtain a raise of salary. His military pay and allowances were 663.10 rupees, while his civilian pay, based on the revenue collection of 50,777 rupees from the North-West (later Simla) Hill States, raised his salary to 1450 rupees a month,[41]—more than the

revenue of many hill states. The Governor-General did not
'perceive any sufficient reason' for granting him an increase
in salary.[42]

However, it was Kennedy's dominating, aristocratic manner
which set precedents. It was he who sited the houses, bazars
and roads in the rugged and wooded hills of Simla and transformed it into a summer resort. By the middle of the nineteenth
century, Simla had grown into a town of a hundred houses
with a British population of three hundred and twenty during
the summer.

The densest settlement emerged on the sunny southern slopes
in the heart of Simla. This was linked by the Cart Road, the
only vehicular artery in the town, to the Simla–Kalka road.
The bazar on the Ridge spread southwards down the slope.
Some of the European estates were located below and adjacent
to the bazar. The hub of British social life until the middle of
the nineteenth century—the Jubilee Theatre and the Assembly
Rooms (now the Meat Market)—were at the eastern end of
the bazar.

Some of the earliest houses were constructed near springs
and their courses near the Combermere ravine on Jakhu.
Townsend, Abergeldie House and Cottage which belonged to
Colonel Tytler (referred to as Titla Hotel still) was a hotel in
the 1860s. Bonnie Moon was a boarding house in the 1840s. A
spring near the United Service Club served the club and
Richmond Villa, as did the Chalet and Swiss Cottage. Further
downhill were built Ravenswood and Central Hotel. A cluster
of houses, Rooksley and Rooks Nest, and below the Mall,
Glenarm Hotel (now Marina Hotel), were probably constructed
around the spring there. Lakkar Bazar and numerous houses
near Blessington mushroomed into a colony around the several
springs in that area.[43]

Simla's growing importance and size was reflected by the
administrative changes made in 1841. Both Captain Kennedy
and his successor, Colonel Tapp, had held dual charge as both
Commanding Officer of the Nasiri Battalion stationed at

Sabathu, and Political Agent to the Simla Hill States. The two offices were now separated: The Political Agent was redesignated Deputy Commissioner of Simla and Superintendent of the Simla Hill States, subordinate to the Resident of Delhi (and after 1911, Ambala).

Despite the opening up of the sanatoriums, the popularity of Simla as a 'salubrious abode of Hygeia', and the visits of succeeding Governors-General, access to Simla remained difficult. The forty-one mile winding, precipitous hill path from Kalka via Kasauli and Sabathu to Simla was only 'passable by foot passengers, horses, mules, ponies or cattle'. The men usually rode, while invalids and women were jolted along in a *jampan* (a curtained sedan chair carried by four coolies) for the twenty hours the journey took. The hills were sparsely populated and there was often difficulty rounding up local peasants to serve as coolies. A journey to Simla could be an ordeal for both passenger and coolie.

The political and military vicissitudes in the Punjab gave a major impetus to the development of Simla. The deployment of British troops in the Punjab during the Sikh wars had two consequences: first, it necessitated the creation of sanatoriums and convalescent homes for wounded and sick British soldiers, for which the Simla hills, overlooking the Cis-Sutlej states and trans-Jamuna north-west provinces, provided a favourable location. Secondly, these hills formed valuable strategic and tactical bases for it was possible to rush troops down to the plains at short notice from these posts.[44]

Ranjit Singh's death in 1839 and the ensuing chaos opened up possibilities of the occupation of the Punjab; within a decade, Dalhousie had accomplished annexation. In preparation for the conquest of the Punjab, the Government established several sanatoriums and cantonments in the Simla hills. In addition to Sabathu, acquired after the Gurkha war, Kasauli was made into a military station. Its barracks contained accommodation for over five hundred European troops. Kalka was requisitioned in 1842. As the gateway to the hills, Kalka was considered

necessary 'for the formation of camps, for the erection of
magazines, for the reception of military stores for the use of
regiments serving in the hills'. In 1843, Jutogh, three-and-a-
half miles from Simla, was a cantonment for a detachment of
British infantry. Similarly, in 1847, Dagshai, sixteen miles
south of Simla, was formed into another cantonment. The same
year, the Lawrence Military Asylum was founded in Sanawar
near Kasauli for the education of the orphans of British soldiers
who had served in India. Finally in 1861, Solan, thirty-one
miles south of Simla, was acquired as a rifle practice ground
for troops stationed in Kasauli, and later, had a 'strong detachment' of British infantry stationed there during the summer
months. These military posts provided a ready-made ring of
protective cantonments around the future summer capital of
India.[45]

British plans for conquest of the Punjab led successive
Governors-General to tour the northern provinces so as to be
near the arena of military activity. They invariably came up to
Simla to escape the summer heat of the plains, and often spent
seven months, from April to November in Simla. Every such
trip added to the mystique of Simla—a mystique not associated
with the other hill stations of India. The trips were not yet an
annual feature and officially, neither the Council nor the Secretariat staff moved from Calcutta. In 1837, when the centre of
political interest shifted to the Afghan question, Lord Auckland
spent two years in the region, when Auckland House was
constructed for him. Auckland's visit to Simla was not merely
a holiday trip, for his advisers, secretaries and staff had travelled
up with him. Auckland's successors, Ellenborough and
Hardinge, visited Simla in 1842 and 1846 respectively.

When Ellenborough visited Simla, he sanctioned funds for a
safe, level road to be constructed from the cantonment of Jutogh
to Simla. A Captain Pengree who was convalescing, was placed
at the disposal of the local authorities for supervising road construction in and about Simla.[46] A broad road connecting the
entry to Simla to the eastern part of the settlement, which by
then was referred to as Chhota Simla, was built.[47]

Another stretch of road was made linking Jutogh to the approach to Simla, which in turn facilitated the entry of loaded cattle to the Gunj or market there.[48] The locality was named Boileaugunj, after the eccentric brothers, Colonel John Theophilus Boileau and Alexander Henry Edmonstone Boileau, both engineers in the North-West Provinces. Buck relates that they once received the Commander-in-Chief at a dinner party, each brother standing on his head by one of the main pillars of the central porch. The older Boileau was a keen astronomer and in 1840–57 was in charge of the Simla Magnetic Observatory (later, Observatory House was occupied by the private secretary of the Viceroy). Above all he was a talented architect, and designed Christ Church at Simla and St Georges at Agra.

During the annexation of the Punjab, Dalhousie spent three consecutive summers in 1849–51, at Simla. Assuming that Simla had been the headquarters of government for twenty-five years, he chafed at the criticism voiced by Calcutta's British commercial interests in the newspapers. 'When the Governor-General remains at Calcutta, the up-country journals abuse him for wallowing listless and inactive in "The Ditch". When he goes up to the North-West Provinces, the Calcutta papers abuse him for amusing himself wandering about the country, and enjoying cool leisure in his "mountain retreat". Hit high, hit low—stay up or go down—there is no pleasing them.'[49] He himself found Simla overrated, both for the climate and everything else, though he thought nothing of the distance and the five-day journey from Calcutta to Simla. He writes of a 'terrible fortnight' filled with festivities, balls, funfairs, plays and concerts. But he found Simla a suitable 'eyrie from which to watch the newly-annexed plains that stretch below.'

Dalhousie's 'eyrie' during the monsoons was about one hundred and fifty miles from Simla in the interior, at Chini (Kinnaur) in the protected hill state of Bushahr. His answer to critics who pointed out its inaccessibility and remoteness was: 'The mail will be only 46 hours from Simla, and can get there in four days, so that I am ready if wanted.'

Dalhousie's visits to Bushahr led him to re-examine the

possibility of a trade route to Tibet envisioned during the Gurkha wars. The outcome was construction of the 'Grand Hindustan and Thibet Road' commencing from Kalka. The first lap of the road, constructed in 1850–1, was rerouted to pass through Dharampur, Solan, Kandaghat and Tara Devi to Simla. 'I returned to Simla by the new road, which I commenced one year ago,' he wrote in 1851, 'and which when it shall be finished will not be surpassed, I flatter myself, by any mountain road in the world.' The Hindustan–Tibet road upto Simla came to be used for wheeled traffic by the 1860s. Dalhousie, however, could not convince the Board of Control at London about the comparatively low cost of construction despite the use of forced labour. After the Punjab conquest there also was concern at the utility of the road and the high cost of maintenance. The road beyond Simla, therefore, remained a 'small cut bridle path'.[50] It was never more than seven or eight feet wide, zig-zagging from Simla to Theog, Narkanda, Kotgarh, along the right bank of the Sutlej river to Rampur, across the river at Wangtu bridge, to follow the left bank of the Sutlej to Chini.

The popularity of excursions along the Hindustan–Tibet Road, and the increasing number of holiday visitors to Simla and the surrounding cantonments required the use of *jampans* as a mode of transport. This meant rounding up from fifteen to twenty thousand villagers to serve as porters and coolies.

The clause on the supply of labour in the 1816 treaty affected the Simla Hill State villagers the most; those living in villages along the roads were compelled to serve as coolies to carry luggage in accordance with the custom of *begar* prevalent in the hills. It also entailed *kar* or *atwara*, free service given by the various *pargana*s of the state in rotation, and *rast* or *rasad*, the right to free provisions for officials of the State on tour. When the East India Company became the suzerain power, Company officials availed themselves of the existing system of *begar* and *kar*. Under this, the hill rulers were to supply a specified number of porters for transporting the baggage of government establishments, army regiments, and for officers on tour. The Rana of Keonthal in 1816 was cautioned not to disregard Government orders requisitioning *begarees* from his territory in time of need. The difficulty of providing labour experienced by several hill ranas led to the commutation of labour requirements at the rate of three rupees per porter per month. A sum of 13,788 rupees per annum was collected by the Company, which was used to pay the labour employed by officials.[51]

Hunting and sight-seeing trips to the Simla hills, especially along the Hindustan–Tibet Road, were some of the attractions of the Simla season, and the treaty obligations were easily stretched to cover private outings since the system provided inexpensive labour. It became customary for individuals to apply to the Political Agent for a *purwannah* or permit which would enable them to obtain porters at the various stages at government-approved rates on their excursions and hunting trips. The burden fell heavily on villagers living along the more frequented routes. In 1921 it was one of the issues on which it became possible to mobilize the otherwise docile hill population.

While most British visitors had no compunction in utilizing a system sanctioned by treaties, some officials such as William Edwards were repelled by it. Edwards, Simla's Deputy Commissioner and Superintendent of Hill States from 1847 till 1852 viewed *begar* as 'nothing short of an insupportable and fearful system of serfdom'. Anxious to promote education in the Simla hills, Edwards passed an order that those parents who sent their children to Government schools would be exempt from *begar*. The privilege was so highly appreciated that the Simla school attendance rose to a hundred.[52] Edwards also tried to limit the use of *begar* to the terms of the treaty, and had the following notice displayed in 1851 at Dak Bungalows outside Simla:

> Coolies or Porters are not to be supplied to any private parties whatever, either in the Station of Simla or travelling through the District, by the Government officers European or Native. All such private parties are to make their own arrangements, but they are particularly warned from endeavouring to supply

themselves by forcibly impressing the people of the country
either themselves or through their servants or otherwise than by
mutual agreement with the people.[53]

A complaint against Edwards' order described the impossibility
of complying with it, since 'Gentlemen and their Hindustani
Servants' could not search for labour in villages. Privately
procured coolies charged 7 annas per day as against the 4 annas
(quarter rupee) per day paid to those requisitioned by government. British travellers complained that they had to pay 'double
hire' to procure coolies and this spoiled the pleasure of their
trip. 'The English have inherited this system', a traveller
reasoned, 'and instead of honestly recognizing it as being a
necessity, and working it on the Oriental lines but with British
fairness, they have mixed up with it Western ideas of the "freedom and liberty" of the subject.'[54]

The demand for coolies was so great that Edwards' scheme
was abandoned by his successor, William Hay. The Government decided that 'complete free trade' was not possible for
'its tendency is to encourage and engender a spirit of incivility,
if not of insolence and extortion, on their [the coolies'] part
towards Europeans.' The solution was found in making
available a moderate number of coolies through the formal
appointment of an influential man of the neighbouring areas, a
chaudhri. With withdrawal of the concession, the Simla school
benches were also almost emptied of hill children.

The efforts to abrogate a system which caused 'extreme mis-
ery and hardship' to the hill villagers were one among several
novel features initiated by William Edwards. A Haileybury
graduate, he had joined the Civil Service in 1837 and was
allocated to the Bengal Service. Poor health and the need for
convalescence led him to be posted as Deputy Commissioner of
Simla.[55] Young, enthusiastic and full of ideas, Edwards was
sensitive to the problems that beset the Simla hill people. What
was rare was the solutions he sought to implement. They were
largely reversed by his more aristocratic and authoritarian
successor, Lord William Hay.

Edwards introduced Western schools in the hills partly to meet the British Government's need for script writers and accountants as well as that of the hill state rulers, and partly because, to his Victorian perceptions, the people were 'totally ignorant and barbarous'. He collected the '*nuzzurs*' he received when he toured the hill states (usually regarded as a perquisite of officials attached to the Agency) into a fund for a central school at Simla, and other schools in the district at Jubbal, Kotkhai, Bharauli and Baghat. Elementary school books were prepared by the Irish Education Society and published at Simla.

Edwards' zeal was also directed towards an experiment to exclude the middlemen and commission agents of Simla's Lower Bazar and fix the prices of essential commodities such as foodgrains,[56] which were expensive in Simla. An earlier attempt by army officers had been declared illegal by Kennedy. Edwards felt that the Ahrties received a commission of one and a half per cent on all transactions which constituted nothing more than a 'customs or transit duty'. By a proclamation of 7 April 1848, he abolished the institution of commission agent.

In 1848, Edwards planned a market, called the Gunj (later named Edwards Gunj) where traders from the surrounding hills and from the plains could sell their grain to retailers at their own risk. The Gunj was below the Lower Bazar, in a shaded spot, and a spring supplied water. Free accommodation was built for itinerant traders. A *chaudhri* and weighers, paid by the Government, were to replace the commission agents and middlemen.

Prices were worked out on the basis of one month's average, and traders were authorized to sell at one seer for the rupee over and above the rate prevailing in the Gunj. Several circumvented the prohibition and met traders on the way into Simla, making bargains with them. When Edwards found that traders did not sell at the Gunj he fined the *kotwal* 50 rupees and ordered that nothing was to be bought or sold except at the Gunj.

The result was that grain was cheap and the buyers content. But traders from the *mandis* complained that their grain was

often left unsold because some commission agents also functioned as shopkeepers and drove petty traders out of business
by leaving them no margin of profit. After Edwards left Simla,
requests and petitions came in from grain dealers and shopkeepers criticising his system, and suggesting that traders would
not supply the Simla market. Consequently directions from
Fort William advised the gradual removal of restrictions to
free trade.

Edwards' system was abandoned, after a trial of four years,
by his successor, William Hay. The middlemen, commission
agents and money-lenders were thereafter firmly entrenched
at Edwards Gunj, gradually expanding their business to supply
commodities to bazars in the Simla Hill States. Simla did not
develop into a significant market for goods from Tibet and
beyond. The wool trade was re-channelled through Kashmir.
Finished products were sold at Amritsar which, owing to
Ranjit Singh's policies in the early nineteenth century, had
emerged as the mart for trade with Central Asia. There was
'literally no traffic on this side of Rampur', except in November
and December when the Lavi and Dhal Melas of Rampur were
held. But Simla became a natural entrepôt for goods to and
from the surrounding hill states.

The injunction to all the Simla Hill States to construct twelve-
foot-wide roads throughout their territories converted several
pathways into mule tracks. Simla became the focal point where
no less than sixty-three routes, directly or indirectly connected
by intervening routes, converged. By the 1870s, travellers
invariably started out from Simla for expeditions to Tibet, the
Upper Indus Valley and Central Asia. Small bazars, such as
Kufri, Theog, Matiana, sprang up near the dak bungalows,
located at stages of ten to twelve miles along the newly-built
roads. Trade had been the primary reason for the Gurkha wars
and the assertion of paramountcy over the western Himalaya.
It receded into the background once it was discovered that the
siting and development of sanatoriums and cantonments were

a more tangible gain. While in 1814, Ochterlony had wondered how an elephant could be transported through the hills, half a century later, the Simla hills were ready to receive another elephant, a large white one—the Government of India offices and its staff.

CHAPTER THREE
Government Moves

WHY should the Government of India have found it expedient to travel over 1,200 miles from Calcutta, across the length of the Indo-Gangetic plain, to govern from Simla? Both its inaccessibility, and its siting on a rugged crest of ridges, made the development of Simla as a plausible summer capital an unlikely possibility. In the 1860s, the Government of India's annual transfer of official, clerk and peon, with files and dispatch boxes, from Calcutta to Simla, amounted to a veritable expedition. The government official travelled from Calcutta to Ambala by train. At Ambala, he hired a Dak Gharry run by the government or from a private agency known as Jeethu and Son. The journey to Kalka was continued in stages of five miles; the Ghaggar river was crossed in bullock carts, and some took the opportunity to visit Pinjore *en route*. The British official stayed overnight in Kalka at Lumley's Hotel or Lawrie's Hotel; the next day, with a break for lunch at Solan, he arrived at Simla. The clerk complained that for days he had to 'dance attendance' at the post office at Ambala for conveyance. Each government employee claimed a tour allowance for the period of absence from Calcutta, and a month's camp allowance on every occasion for trips to and back from Simla. The Governor-General sanctioned the staff gratuities at the end of the tour.

Yet, John Lawrence, as Viceroy, decided that Simla was the most suitable hill station to be the summer headquarters of the Government of India. He deployed every argument to get this accepted by the India Council at London. Lawrence's career had been shaped in the Punjab; in 1849, he was appointed Administrator of the Punjab, and from 1853 to 1859, he was Chief Commissioner of the province. His association with Simla dated to visits during the Punjab campaigns. On account of ill-health, he had accepted the Viceroyalty on condition that he be allowed to spend summer in the hills. In a letter to Charles Wood, Secretary of State, he summed up Simla's strategic advantages:

> This place, of all Hill Stations seems to me the best for the Supreme Government. Here you are with one foot, I may say, in the Punjab, and another in the North-West Provinces. Here you are among a docile population, and yet near enough to influence Oude. Around you, in a word, are all the warlike races of India, all those on whose character and power our hold in India, exclusive of our own countrymen, depends. No doubt there is the danger of being cut off from the seat of Government. Still, on the other hand, railways will lessen that danger.[1]

This was the most forceful argument there could be for converting an inaccessible hill station into a summer capital. The decision has to be viewed against the backdrop of the changes taking place.

Concurrent with British annexation of vast tracts of territory in the nineteenth century, a well-organized administrative framework was being created to govern the country. Careers in the army and the civil services in India were actively encouraged. This led to the influx of a large number of Britons into India, for whom an extended stay in an alien, hot and humid land several thousand miles away from England was a severe ordeal which the establishment of hill stations helped to mitigate.

There were parallel developments among other European colonists. By 1808, the Dutch in Indonesia had decreed that the highland town of Buitenzorg be developed for its proconsuls and their permanent staff. In the Philippines, Spanish colonists established a sanatorium at La Trinidad.[2] In India over eighty hill stations were created by the British in various regions, both as sanatoriums and holiday resorts. The largest number were in the foothills of the Himalaya.

In the 1850s, another pattern was set. District and provincial administrations moved their headquarters to the nearest hill station in the summer: the Madras Government spent six months at Ootacamund, the Bombay Government was four months at Mahableshwar and four at Poona each year, the

Bengal Government went to Darjeeling for three months, and
the Government of the North-Western Provinces and Oudh
was in Naini Tal for five and-a-half months.

Lawrence's choice of Simla as summer capital stemmed from
the current preoccupation with Punjab and domination of the
north-west frontier. Britain's own expansionist interests in
India and West Asia made her apprehensive of Russian ambitions. Punjab provided the key to the security of the newly
established empire against the bugbear of a Russian advance,
either from the Mediterranean or from Central Asia. Throughout the nineteenth century, Britain feared a Russian attack on
India through Afghanistan and north-west India, and viewed
with alarm her expanding control in Central Asia; Britain
wishing both to safeguard her northern frontiers as well as to
develop Indo-Tibetan trade, and exploit Tibet's rich mineral
resources. Simla and the ring of cantonments around it provided
a ready force of British soldiers and commanded access to
potential trouble-spots in northwest India, as well as to
Central Asia.

The 1857 Uprising demonstrated Simla's other advantages—a
docile population, and submissive hill rulers. The hill ranas
demonstrated their loyalty during the Uprising in 1857 when
the Gurkhas of the Nasiri Battalion at Sabathu 'mutinied and
marched off with a sum of Government money to join their
comrades at Jutogh.' The fear of mutinous Gurkhas from
Jutogh, and alarm at the 'turbulence of the Mohemmadan and
the Poorbeas' of the Simla bazar, led panic-stricken British
inhabitants to flee from the town. They found refuge with the
local ranas.[3]

The hill rulers furnished armed retainers for the protection
of Simla. A contingent of soldiers sent from Sirmour guarded
the bazar, while another from Bilaspur occupied Boileaugunj,
the approach to Simla. In 1858, William Hay, Simla's Deputy
Commissioner, reported that 'Simla was the safest place in
India during the mutinies of 1857.'[4] The Simla hill population
was described as 'simpleminded, orderly people, truthful in

character and submissive to authority so that they scarcely required "to be ruled".'[5]

From Simla, troops could be rushed to Delhi and deployed in the plains, even during the rainy season, as the events of 1857 had demonstrated. Keeping in view the security of the British empire, and the Uprising of 1857, Simla appeared the logical choice as a summer capital.

Lawrence opted for Simla for administrative reasons as well. It was customary for Governors-General to make extended tours throughout the country for several months each year, and Charles Wood, Secretary of State, had readily agreed that Lawrence should visit the various hill stations of India in the summer. Lawrence countered that file work made such an arrangement unfeasible, since the work had become 'probably treble, possibly quadruple, what it was twenty years ago, and it is, for the most part, of a very difficult nature.'[6] Secondly, in 1861, the various departments of Government (Home, Legislative, Revenue, Military, Finance and Public Works), had been divided between members of the Executive Council. All important questions were discussed by the whole Council which met once a week. Before the constitutional change, decisions were taken by the Governor-General-in-Council through files perambulating to members of the Council, beginning with the Governor-General. Lawrence, therefore, formally assembled the Executive Council at Simla in 1864. While the larger Legislative Council did not move, a number of Government secretaries and their clerical subordinates also came to Simla.

In 1864, 484 persons, including the secretariat staff, clerks and servants, were transported from Calcutta to Simla for six months.[7] Apprehending objections to the cost of the move, the Government of India drew up accounts to show that, of the 4,00,000 rupees spent during those months, a trifling 64,000 could be attributed to assembling the Council and 'of having the entire Government of India at Simla'. It was assured that the cost in subsequent years would be less, since the secretarial staff had been provided with offices, furniture, duplicate copies of proceedings and reference works. The extra expenses, Lawrence wrote, were offset by the fact that 'I believe that we will do more work in one day here than in five down in Calcutta.'

Wood communicated to Lawrence that the question of moving Government annually was too serious to be decided 'off hand'. He was sure the Council would disapprove. He continued, however: 'It is only by some *management* that I have prevented their [the Council's] objections to going to Simla year after year. They could not I am sure agree to its being cast down as the *rule* formally: but I may in each year prevent an objection till it becomes the practice. But you must not try them too hard: They will get out of their unfashionable notions in *time*.'[8] The question of the Simla move was also linked with the location of a new capital—one which would suit Europeans climatically and avoid the need for a double capital.

The need for a more centrally-located capital than Calcutta had been voiced once the trauma of the 1857 Uprising had subsided. Calcutta was also regarded by Europeans as a vast pestilential vapour bath for six months in a year. A more central location would enable the Government to take swift action against an uprising in any part of the country. Calcutta was also the most distant point in India from the Punjab and the north-west frontier where Russian intrusions were seen as threats to the Empire itself.

Canning had suggested that the new capital be placed in Central India. Jabalpur, Allahabad, Agra or Delhi were other possibilities. Since there had been much criticism by Calcutta's commercial interests of the proposal to shift the capital permanently out of Calcutta, Wood recommended Darjeeling, a hill station only one day's journey away from Calcutta by rail, where the Government could hardly be cut off in the event of another rebellion. Lawrence rejected Darjeeling because he felt the accommodation available was inadequate, and dismissed Allahabad, Agra, Delhi, Central India as out of the question.

As a second best choice, he advised the transfer of Government to Poona. Poona was connected by rail to Bombay and was well placed for communications with England. But it was in the western part of India, and the Vindhyas blocked access to the north. 'In the event of commotions the communication with upper India would be cut off.' Lawrence suggested that the winter capital be at Agra or Delhi with the summer capital at Simla. Wood had reacted sharply against the proposal to eliminate Calcutta altogether. When arguments failed to convince, Lawrence provided a solution by suggesting the retention of 'Calcutta as the capital and allowing the Government to come to Simla.'

Uncertainty dogged Lawrence's choice of Simla as summer capital, for Wood had not been 'prepared to say . . . that such an arrangement shall be stereotyped for all time to come.' It took a dozen years before the hill station was formally accepted as summer capital, and then, as foreseen by Wood, as a *fait accompli*. The Viceroy and Government continued to spend the summer at Simla each year and the town continued to grow.

There were apprehensions about the reliance on natural springs as a source for the increasing need for water. Lawrence's successor, Mayo, recommended Ranikhet which had more water and level land available for construction as the more suitable site. Accordingly, surveys were conducted, but none of the sites was acceptable. Lytton then tried to end the controversy over Simla being the summer seat of the Government of India.

Once communications improved, Government's move became more acceptable. The construction of the railway-line from Calcutta to Delhi and thence to Ambala in 1869 was one such step. The construction of a cart road from Kalka to Simla through Dharampur and Solan was another. By 1874, a bullock-cart service for goods and a tonga service for mail and passengers came into general use. In 1874, a traveller calculated that the Viceroy with his staff, the members of his Council, and secretaries to Government could be at Ambala in about twelve hours after leaving Simla. Fifty hours by rail would get them to

Calcutta and sixty to Bombay. The Government was in close
proximity to the Punjab, for the railway-line connected Ambala
to Lahore, Multan, Delhi, Agra, and most towns in the northern
region.[9] With the current pace of Government business and
activity such 'speed' was considered adequate.

It was over a quarter century before a narrow-gauge railway
was built upto Simla. The Ambala–Kalka link was extended in
1891; twelve years later the first passenger train arrived at Simla
on 9 November 1903. Designed by H. S. Harington, the Chief
Engineer of the Kalka–Simla railway, the construction was a
sixty-mile engineering feat. From Kalka at 2,100 feet above
sea level to Simla at 7,000 feet, it climbs the steep ascent by a
series of loops and in a succession of tight curves. Its 103 tunnels
take up five miles while two miles of it are arched viaducts
balanced across precipitous chasms.

The contract for construction of the Kalka–Simla line was
given to the Delhi Umbala Company in 1898. Estimated to
cost 86,78,500 rupees, the cost mounted to twice the original
estimate. Funds were raised partly by advances by the Secretary
of State and partly by privately-raised capital. Initiated as a
commercial venture, it ran into a loss and was taken over by
the Government.

Three major establishments were a presage of Simla's emerging characteristic as a bureaucratic town *par excellence*. The
offices stationed in the town throughout the year formed the
backbone, and held Simla active through the five winter months.
The decision to maintain Army Headquarters permanently in
Simla was taken in 1864, in view of Simla's strategic location
regarding Punjab and the north-west. Soon the offices attached
to the Army Headquarters, the Director-General and Examiner
of Military Accounts, the Directors General of Ordinances,
the Army Removal Department, the Imperial Service Troops
and the Indian Medical Service, were also located permanently
in Simla. These constituted about a third of the Government
establishments in Simla and imparted a sense of continuity to
the town and to its social life.

The Punjab Government came up from Lahore for five months, in 1871–3, and then continuously from 1876,[10] after Lytton had felt it necessary to summon the Lieutenant-Governor of the Punjab for consultations in regard to the north-western region. However, only the officials and a skeleton staff of clerks and peons came up. The bulk of the Secretariat functioned from Lahore although a duplicate set of printed records was maintained in Simla. A daily *dak* brought in all the urgent files.

The Government of India's annual move was more like a mass migration. The major part of the Departments of Home, Finance, Education, Foreign and Political, and Legislative had to be transported. The movement of routine records and files was also cumbrous. 'The records and waste paper, which are better left in some dusty recess, are brought up here at an enormous cost for no earthly reason for no sooner have they arrived than they are relegated to the lumber rooms,' expostulated the *Tribune*.[11] With the increasing complexity of government's work there was a steady rise in the files and number of people transported to Simla annually.

The secretaries of departments together decided suitable dates for the move each year. The Viceroy and his Council usually left Calcutta at the end of March or the beginning of April. They stayed at Simla until the end of October and after a winter tour in the plains returned to Calcutta by the middle of December. A query from the India Office about the uncertain dates in 1889 elicited the reply that discretion must necessarily be given to the Viceroy-in-Council to determine the dates on which the movements between the two capitals were made. For 'it is not desirable, owing to climatic reasons, to lay down a hard and fast rule and the main consideration must be the state of public business.'[12]

The Government stay at Simla stretched out to seven months and more.[13] While the plains were punishingly hot from April to July, it was muggy and oppresively warm from August to October. On the other hand, Simla had clear weather from April to June. The Simla season commenced in April once the officials came in from Calcutta (after 1911, Delhi), and Lahore.

It took about a month to be fully launched, after the officials, convalescents and holiday-makers settled in by the end of May. This coincided with the week-long celebrations for the Emperor's birthday. By the end of June the monsoons set in and until mid-September the climate was 'as perfectly English as England is, nearly three parts of the year.'[14] It confined people to indoor entertainments and to offices. When the shikar season commenced, it kept sportsmen out on the surrounding hills. The forests of the hill state of Dhami were reserved as shooting grounds for the Viceroy and his entourage. Mashobra, six miles away along the Hindustan–Tibet Road was the 'country-side'. Country houses dotted the landscape, where the élite of Simla drove out to spend weekends. Normally the stay came to a close by the end of October, although 'public business' often kept many officials busy for a few days in November as well.

Criticism of the Government move to Simla turned into a daunting annual event, first by the non-official British community of Calcutta and later by the nationalists. Calcutta society, its European house-owners and commercial interests never took kindly to these moves. Calcutta's mercantile community complained that the transfer would necessarily mean the isolation of the Imperial Government from commercial opinion. Further, that Simla was the cradle of more political insanity than any other place within the limits of India. Auckland's disastrous Afghan policy was traced as being secretly hatched in the seclusion of Simla; its atmosphere produced adventurous decisions and was fatal to a sense of purpose and responsibility.

Historians have projected hill stations as being European cultural enclaves. Anthony D. King summarizes their development in Asia as exhibiting three crucial variables. These highland settlements accounted for a particular set of environmental preferences, demonstrated the distinctive residential models available for the colonial community, and explained the ethno-medical theories supporting the view that hill stations were healthier than residence in the plains.[15] As a holiday resort and sanatorium,

Simla's British society had become notorious for its uninhibited conviviality and merry-making, described by Russell as 'Mohawkery' (mohawks were a class of aristocratic ruffians who infested the streets of London in the eighteenth century). He had been shocked at 'the lax notions of discipline and decency'.[16] The impression endured over the century and found an echo in the Indian nationalist press:

> These summer sojourns,. . . are fraught with evils in a variety of ways. Of the greatest among them is the laxity of morals that is generally found to prevail. . . . Their example . . . often contaminates our young men.[17]

Once it became established as an official town, the holiday atmosphere receded to the background, although Simla continued to have a wide range of social activities. It was also an image that two generations of civil servants tried to erase. They pointed to Simla's distinguished society, highlighted the quantum of work possible and argued that the social life in Simla was over publicized, since bureaucratic routine could merit little press coverage.

The 'exodus question', as the Government transfer to Simla was nicknamed, was to exercise nationalist opinion for over half a century. In the 1880s a broadside of petitions, letters, and editorials in the Indian press led to an enquiry by the India Office on the duration and costs of the annual move. Criticism of the 'gigantic picnic' rested on several counts: the remoteness and isolation of the bureaucratic machine from the realities of the plains below for more than half the year; the cost that it entailed; the time involved in the annual migration; the periodical dislocation of public business and the loss of touch with public opinion.

'And is it wise, is it moral, is it politic, to allow this waste of so large an amount of public money, year after year, for the luxury of a Governmental trip?' asked the *Tribune* in 1883.[18] Time and again Government was forced to disclose the costs, calculated at six lakhs in 1883. The nationalist criticism was principally that Simla isolated the Government from public

criticism and popular opinion. It readily conceded the Viceroy's
need to stay at a hill station during the summer months but
reacted to the entire Government moving. *The Bengalee* wrote:
'While the people are groaning under a load of taxation, to
which additions are from time to time still being made, Civil
and Military servants, who have long been acclimatized to the
country, take advantage of the culpable weakness of the
Government to indulge at the public expense in a luxury to
which the head of Government alone is entitled.'[19] If the cost
appeared high, Government stressed the fact that 'work was
more efficient.' Nevertheless, approval and endorsement were
not a universal British official verdict. Guy Fleetwood-Wilson,
an unpopular Finance Member, found it outrageous that

> sedition, unrest, and even murder may have been going on
> elsewhere. . . . Up at Simla the news of an outrage is received
> with languid and transient interest. The burning questions are
> polo finals or racing, with the all-absorbing tennis tournaments
> to fill up voids in the daily life.[20]

He maintained that consistent and sustained policy was apt to
disappear at Simla. The Indian feedback to Government's
policy, which was an important feature in Calcutta, Lahore or
in other provincial capitals, was absent in Simla.

The Indian press voiced the opinion that efficiency was
impaired. As there were no representative institutions, it was
especially necessary for the Government to watch every
expression of public opinion. 'The great objection to Simla as
the capital of the Empire is that it deprives the Government of
touch with the people. . . . The natural order of things is inverted.
Foreign problems assume an undue importance, while questions
of domestic reform are relegated to the background.'[21] Some
officers on the other hand, argued that residence at any Presidency town gave a provincial tilt inconsistent with impartial
and balanced rule.

Such sustained criticism impelled British officialdom to
devise a whole vocabulary of rationalization to justify the move
to Simla. British officials in fact found it more comfortable to
spend the summer but made it out that the Simla stay was

essential to the Empire itself. Nineteenth-century Victorians often viewed themselves as a tough island race which had won its way to democracy in an environment invigorated by cold northern blasts. The history of India on the other hand, was of a country swept by successive invasions from the north, of invaders gradually enervated by a tropical climate. The lessons from Indian history were clearly drawn. Charles Dilke, member of Parliament, confirmed this view when he elaborated: 'The climate of Simla is no mere matter of curiosity. It is a question of serious interest in connection with the retention of our Indian Empire.... Simla gives vigour to the Government, and a hearty English tone to the State papers issued in the hot months.'[22] If essentially British qualities were to be reinforced, the annual stay in a cool, bracing, invigorating climate such as Simla's, was an obvious necessity.

The Simla Gazetteer of 1889 described the annual transfer almost as an organic development. 'Year after year, occasionally at first, but before long with perfect regularity, the seat of Government was transferred for a few weeks in every summer to the Himalayas.'[23] Rudyard Kipling summed up the compelling irrationality of the rationalizations and the more telling reasons of confidence born of commercial prosperity:

> Though the argosies of Asia at her doors,
> Heap their stores,
> Though her enterprise and energy secure
> Income sure,
> Though 'Out-station' orders punctually obeyed
> Swell her trade,
> Still, for rule, administration, and the rest,
> Simla's best;[24]

In fact, the move reflected a sure and optimistic phase of the British Empire. A Government hand-out to the press in 1884 explained the seven-month sojourn of the Government of India as a 'source of vigour and energy to the men who expend and exhaust their strength in administering the affairs of the Indian Empire.'[25] By the 1880s, the choice of Simla as summer capital was a settled fact.

CHAPTER FOUR

Imperial Summer Capital

WHEN Lytton made his first Viceregal tour to Simla in April 1876, the place struck him as being a 'mere bivouac'.[1] He was dismayed at the makeshift temporary arrangements, but what particularly irked him was the lack of a viceregal residence. He thought Peterhoff,[2] a rented house occupied by the Viceroy since 1863, was a 'sort of pigstye'. Till the fate of Simla as summer capital had been decided, the India Office was unwilling to sanction funds for residences, office buildings, water supply and essential services.

Lytton, at first, regarded the town as a mere appendage to the Government—something like 'a large public office, with its accompanying bazars'.[3] But as the buildings took shape, they began to mirror emerging imperial self-assurance: the restructuring of Simla would reflect Britain's unbounded confidence in its imperial destiny.

The morphology of the summer capital had nevertheless to be set into the frame of a half-century's erratic urban growth; a holiday resort and sanatorium adapted to Government needs. The holiday resort had grown after 1864 to meet the annual needs of Government departments for office and residential accommodation. The initiative had come from private builders, British and Indian, who ran up structures to meet the demand for houses and offices.

All Government houses and offices were rented, including the residence of the Governor-General, unless he built one as Bentinck and Auckland had done. For instance, in 1875, the Home Office was in St Mark's, Finance in The Yarrows, Public Works in Herbert House, the Foreign Office in Valentines, Military in Dalziel Cottage, and Revenue and Agriculture in Argyll House, all in central and western Simla. The Adjutant-General carried on his work in Strawberry Hill (outside the municipal limits), and the Quarter-Master General in Portmore, in east Simla. They were thus scattered across the length of Simla. In 1882, the Government of India rented eighteen private houses to accommodate their offices; the establishment included 103 officers and 1,082 clerks.[4]

The number of houses increased from 290 in 1866 to 1,400 in 1881. They were tenanted by Government offices, civil servants, the army and holiday-makers. No housing plan was followed, although the municipal by-laws broadly regulated structures, and individual owners built houses to their own specifications. These were entered in a register maintained by the municipality for the purpose of assessing ground rent and house tax; the first town settlement showing maps of house boundaries was only made in 1905.

No master-plan was drafted for the imperial capital, nor was any agency or individual delegated the task. Thus, no parallel can be drawn with the New Delhi designed by Lutyens thirty-five years later, nor with the decisiveness with which the United States Government, in 1903, selected city planner Daniel H. Burnham to prepare an urban design for the hill station of Baguio, the American summer refuge in the Phillipines. Part of Simla's growth was dictated by the exigency of the time; the rest was the result of Viceregal direction. The new buildings were dispersed on the sites and estates available in those years. From 1875 to 1881, sites for Government buildings were chosen (and changed), and plans for the water supply, sanitation, and roads made on the basis of reports drawn up by Government committees. A Simla Imperial Circle of the Public Works Department was set up in 1877, with the task of translating official ingenuity into drawing-board sketches and earth-bound construction.

The plan, as it developed, placed the viceregal establishment in the relatively sparsely-occupied western half of Simla. In 1879, a project had placed the secretariat offices adjacent to Viceregal Lodge; two years later in 1881, a committee of officials shifted them to central Simla. General Frederick Roberts' house, Snowdon, in central Simla was acquired as the permanent resi-

dence of the Commander-in-Chief. It seemed fitting to assign
the eastern part of the town called Chhota Simla to the Chhota
Lat Sahib, the Punjab Governor, for his residence and offices,
as distinct from the Viceroy, the Mulk-e-Lat Sahib.

For municipal and functional purposes the town was divided
into two wards, Station Ward and Bazar Ward. The division
not only signified the residential and commercial areas respectively, but also, broadly, the European and Indian enclaves.
The division can be conveniently used to describe the social
gulf between those who lived in the two areas.

Bazar Ward meant all the five bazars—Boileaugunj, Kainthu,
Lakkar, Chhota, and the largest, Bara or Lower Simla Bazar—
in the different localities of Simla. The Indian bazars, regarded
as the necessary 'excrescences' to an otherwise essentially British
town, were meant to house and support the Indian population
necessitated by Government residence. Lower Bazar, the largest,
served as the residential area for one-fifth of Simla's population,
while the other bazars were pockets of Indian shops and residences strewn over the town. Lakkar (wood) Bazar, atop a
number of wooden depots containing stacked timber brought
from the interior, is near the Ridge. A few grain shops supplied
the needs of the locality. Its distinctive feature was a colony of
Sikh carpenters from Jullundur district who had set up shops
selling wooden toys, kitchenware and walking sticks, for
which it was famous. The bazar in Boileaugunj near Summer
Hill, the Chhota Simla Bazar in the east, and Kaithu Bazar on
the way to Annandale, were clusters of Indian shops and traders
in these areas.

Station Ward consisted of most of municipal Simla and,
dotted with upwards of 400 privately-owned cottages, villas,
and castles, each built on an acre or more of land, had a distinctively English character. The planners had consciously trans-
planted as much as they could of nineteenth-century Victorian
England to Simla.

In a note entitled *European Architecture for India*, Captain
Cole, architect and engineer of the Simla Imperial Circle, outlined the principle that buildings should bear a distinct classical

or Gothic impress.[5] Since the Mughals had left exemplars of Muslim architecture, the British as successor imperialists should create structures that bore the stamp of ideal European architectural forms. It was customary for architects and engineers on leave in England to study architectural trends in the design of houses and public buildings there. The Victorians liked imposing buildings and revelled in ransacking old styles.[6] A diversity and blending of styles was the hallmark of English architecture in the nineteenth century, and these trends featured in the Simla buildings. A wide range of styles were utilized and moulded to suit the edifice, the available material, and official tastes, while the lack of skilled labour and certain materials led to an even greater medley. The end result was some startling architectural compromises, with each building differing wildly from the next, although it was possible to trace its English origin.

Government structures of the 1880s were designed and built under another constraint: a stream of reprimands for overspending from the India Office. The Public Works Department tried to allay these fears by assurances and estimates showing that the cost of construction would more or less equal the capitalized rents of houses hired as offices, or by the sale of government properties and that no appreciable financial outlay would be required.[7] Yet building plans until construction began were little more than rough sketches.

There was also the constant nagging doubt whether Simla would remain the summer capital. Allocations for a new viceregal house were held in abeyance lest this forced the India Office's hand in accepting Simla as summer headquarters. In addition, the decision of whether or not to construct a new viceregal residence was altered by three successive Viceroys themselves—Lytton, Ripon and Dufferin.[8]

Lytton, an imperialist and aristocrat, found Peterhoff unsuitable, uncomfortable and cramped. Most Viceroys had found Peterhoff inconvenient, since it did not have enough room even for a small durbar of hill chiefs. It was a building which was owned by General Innes until 1869, and thereafter by the Raja of Nahan. Lytton, architect of the policy of welding the Indian princes into pillars of the imperial organization, believed that though their political power was circumscribed, 'their cordial and willing allegiance' was essential to the maintenance of the Empire. The loss of political power was compensated by, among other features, introducing an elaborate hierarchy of status and position. He believed that small favours and marks of honour such as an additional gun to his salute, the right to a return courtesy call from the Viceroy, or a more honourable place in durbar, were quite as highly prized and appreciated as the more concrete benefits of augmented zamindaris conferred in earlier times by the Mughal emperors. The grand Delhi Durbar of 1877 had been Lytton's brainchild. It thus seemed inconceivable to him that a summer capital should be without a durbar hall.

Durbars at Simla were held in a *shamiana*, a marquee, pitched on the lawns of Peterhoff. Lady Dufferin who witnessed a durbar from the vantage point of her window at Peterhoff described it enthusiastically: 'The tent was lined with pale blue and white; there was a scarlet carpet on the floor; the Viceroy's Throne was on the far end of the tent; the Chiefs and their families were ranged all down one side of it, while European officials sat on the other side.' But Simla's torrents of rain could sometimes seep through the canvas top, dampening the solemnity of the occasion. An irate Lytton communicated to the Secretary of State that if the Governors of Madras and Bombay were having suitable summer residences built it was indispensable that the unbecoming arrangements at Simla should cease.[9]

In 1877, Lytton selected a site on the summit of Observatory Hill in the western part of Simla. The assumption was that a Government House raised on an eminence would impress the imagination and convey an aura of dignified authority. A thickly-wooded 330-acre estate covered the whole of the Observatory, Bentinck, and Prospect Hills.

Captain Cole was deputed to prepare the designs for it during his stay in England. He drew a fairytale palace, and exhibited an etching of it at a Fine Arts show at Simla in 1878. His good taste and study of English architecture was not, however, matched by any experience as a builder. Cole was disinclined to supervise mundane details and left them to his assistant, Girling, who thought it no crime to take a fixed percentage from all contractors. It was discovered that a newly-built road to the top of Observatory Hill had given way; a foundation wall was narrower at the bottom than the top. Besides, a thousand deodar trees, purchased from the surrounding forests had to be measured, sawn, stacked and seasoned for the new Viceregal Lodge.[10] Cole seemed incapable of overseeing the construction, item by item.

In 1880, Cole was replaced by Henry Irwin as Superintendent Engineer and Architect of the Public Works Department. Irwin was a resourceful and influential architect, who designed most of the large buildings in the 1880s, many of which were to become landmarks.

Irwin drew up the plans of a somewhat more modest residence than Cole had done, costing five to ten thousand pounds less. These had to be shelved soon after since India Office postponed the question of providing a residence for the Viceroy to a future date. In December 1885, when the scheme was revived again, Irwin wrote that the plans had been worked out only in 'suggestive form' and not in detail.

Ripon, Lytton's successor, was a serious man, known for his moral earnestness. He felt that while Viceregal pomp and state might be justified in Calcutta, it was absurd at Simla. He was anxious to cut down the 'swagger' as much as he could and revert to simpler precedents—a preference in congruence with financial constraints. So Peterhoff continued as the Viceregal residence.

Irwin had suggested another storey be added to the house to make it a more spacious 21,478 square feet. A new residence would have cost 8,00,000 rupees while Peterhoff could be overhauled for 3,00,000. Ripon favoured the redrawn Peterhoff, with its additional and more comfortable dressing rooms and bathrooms, observing however that though on a grander scale than in the Observatory scheme they were not always quite 'what I should call convenient in detail.'[11]

Ripon's frugality met with a barbed response in the Anglo-

Indian press. *The Pioneer* expostulated: 'Self denial of this kind
is quite characteristic of the Viceroy, but it is a little hard on his
successor—if half the stories told about the shaky state of the
present Viceregal residence be true.'[12] The plans and work
remained suspended until the close of Ripon's tenure in India,
although a dispatch in November 1884 gave preference to Peterhoff. Ripon left the final decision to his successor—Dufferin.

Dufferin had a choice of three plans: the Cole and Irwin
designs for a new Viceregal house, and Irwin's drawings for a
restructured Peterhoff. His first reaction soon after his arrival
at Calcutta, but before a visit to Simla, was to concur with
Ripon's decision. 'The Viceroy does not want a palace at a hill
station but a healthy and convenient house.'[13] Work was therefore begun by Irwin and his executive engineer, Hebbert, on
Peterhoff in February 1885.

The decision was revoked soon after Dufferin's arrival in
Simla in April. Dufferin was a diplomat, cultured, charming,
who enjoyed durbars, receptions and fancy-dress balls. His
otherwise colourless viceroyalty was filled with entertainments. It was not suprising that Lady Dufferin thought Peterhoff
a cottage, 'very unfit for a Viceregal establishment'.[14] Meanwhile, Irwin and Hebbert had had problems restructuring the
old house according to plan because of the instability of the
foundations in the north-east, and being tied to an arrangement
in which it was impossible to install sanitary fittings, water
and gas. Irwin, sensing Dufferin's wavering commitment to
the old house, suggested abandoning the old building in favour
of a new one on its lawns and added that 'the cost would
probably be not much more.'[15]

Dufferin revived the plans made for the Observatory Hill
site in the summer of 1885. Lord Randolph Churchill, the new
Secretary of State, was more amenable about sanctioning funds
for the new residence. Dufferin was enchanted with the prospect
of overseeing the new construction. He had fancied building a
mansion on his estate in County Downs in Ireland, and later an
official residence at Quebec when he was Governor-General
of Canada. Neither had materialized for lack of funds. His

dreams were now realized with the construction of the Viceregal Lodge at Simla. He examined and approved the general plan and suggested modifications as construction progressed. For two Simla seasons his hobby was to visit the site almost every morning and evening, to the dismay of the Public Works Department officials.[16] The Dufferins moved into the Viceregal Lodge on 23 July 1888, only a few months before their departure from India.

The mounting costs and necessity for hurried completion so that it could be occupied by Dufferin before his term ended, led to changes in the original plans. The upper walls of the main gallery, around which the main rooms were arranged, which was meant to be twelve feet wider, had to be narrowed in width to cut down on costs. Later, Curzon perceived an exterior tower to be out of proportion to the rest of the building. It was raised in height to correct the defects of the structure.

The Viceregal Lodge, designed by Henry Irwin for Dufferin, was by far the most impressive structure in Simla; yet it had its critics. Lady Curzon found its appearance a trifle ludicrous— one in which a 'Minneapolis millionaire would delight.' Many years later Montague, Secretary of State for India, thought it resembled 'a Scottish hydro'. But a part of its appeal lay in its location on a watershed, from which, on the one side the rivers flow into the Sutlej and so into the Arabian sea, and on the other into the Jumuna on its way to the Bay of Bengal. Buck found it a suitable site for the residence of the Lord of the Indian Empire; and indeed, from a distance with its grey silhouette, it looks somewhat like a castle in Scotland.

The location of Viceregal Lodge determined the sites chosen for the Viceregal establishments and the offices of the Government of India. In 1877, when it was decided to locate Viceregal Lodge on Observatory Hill, Peterhoff and the estates and houses on the adjacent hill were selected as Government of India offices. Accordingly, several houses on this hill, Beatsonia, Boorj, Mount Pleasant, Annandale Lodge, were acquired by the Government. The proposal for locating offices in these houses was, however, abandoned because by then Ripon had chosen to keep Peterhoff as the Viceregal residence.[17]

In 1881, a committee of secretaries headed by the Member of Public Works in the Executive Council considered it 'undesirable' to locate offices near the Viceregal residence. They recommended alternative sites in central Simla which would be equidistant for its office-going population, Indian as well as English. A cluster of sites adjacent to and above the western corner of Lower Bazar were selected for Army Headquarters, the Civil Secretariat, the office of the Deputy Commissioner, the Treasury and Court of the District Judge, the Ripon Hospital and a Roman Catholic church. Private properties were accordingly chosen, acquired and rebuilt for offices. The committee chose Dahlia Lodge for the Secretariat and Littlewood, adjoining it, for Army Headquarters.[18]

Henry Irwin designed two sturdy iron and concrete buildings for the two offices, as recommended by the committee. They were completed in 1885 at a cost of over 1,700,000 rupees. *The Pioneer* described the functional structure of the new buildings:

> No style of architecture has been followed. . . . The designer happily made the most and best possible use of existing ways and means, in the most practical and possible amalgamation of iron and concrete; the walling is of concrete, the framework of cast and wrought iron. In fact from foundations to chimney-stacks, staircases, and even chimney tops, there is no other material used but concrete where iron was not necessary. Excepting in verandah floors and ceilings of upper rooms, which are of local deodar, the joinery is of teak.[19]

Modelled on the Peabody buildings in London, they were one of the sturdiest landmarks of Simla, and reminded some of the 'huge warehouses that are to be seen in the business parts of London and Liverpool.'[20] Simla's nineteenth-century English society never quite forgave the ugly buildings for which Ripon's Government was mainly responsible, and which seemed to them to deface the landscape.[21]

In 1904, the Civil Secretariat was shifted to a new office at

Gorton Castle and the vacated block was handed over to Army Headquarters. Gorton Castle has the appearance of a forbidding, eerie castle, with grey stone walls surmounted by a high-pitched roof with pointed towers, presenting an uneven broken skyline. The preliminary drawings were made by Sir Swinton Jacob, but modified and redrawn by Major H. F. Chesney as construction progressed.

On the terrace above Army Headquarters was Simla's magisterial and law-enforcement bulwark, the Kutchery, the court and offices of the Deputy Commissioner of Simla. This edifice, in contrast to the iron and concrete of the adjacent buildings, was a massive stone structure in Norman Baronial style.

Between Army Headquarters and the courts was the Roman Catholic church, which had been designed by Henry Irwin in French Gothic style in grey stone. The church was consecrated in 1886 and the steeple added in 1900. To the east of Army Headquarters Ripon Hospital was constructed, also a timber-framed building with Gothic details, designed by Irwin and built by Campion and Learmouth. It had a distinctive open staircase surmounted by a corrugated iron roof.

Two houses, Conny Cot and Conny Lodge, lying across the newly widened Mall, were pulled down. A Tudor brick-and-timber structure for the Post Office and a Telegraph Office were also designed by Irwin. The Public Works Department office was situated near Gorton Castle and constructed on the site of two old residences, Herbert House and Lowville. The building burnt down in 1896 and was reconstructed two years later. A site between Chaura Maidan and Viceregal Lodge was selected for the Foreign Office and a picturesque Swiss chalet constructed for it in 1887. (It now houses the All-India Radio, in a new concrete structure, the old building having burnt down).

In the eastern part of Simla, Barnes Court, set in forty-six acres of land, was purchased in 1879 to serve as the residence of the Lieutenant-Governor of the Punjab. The strongest recommendation of Barnes Court, a double-storeyed house, according to the *Civil and Military Gazette*, was 'that it wanted perhaps less than any other house in Simla to make it look like a country house at home.' A half-timbered Tudor structure, it grew incrementally over the years as storeys and wings were added to it.

The Punjab Government offices, like the Imperial Government ones, had hitherto occupied private houses: Craigs Court in 1871, Rockcliffe in 1878, Craigsville in 1879. In 1885, Benmore was acquired for 50,000 rupees for the Punjab Government offices. In 1902, another building, Ellerslie, which had been occupied by the Military Department, was acquired and rebuilt for the Punjab Civil Secretariat. The building now houses the Himachal Pradesh Secretariat.

The Committee of Secretaries superimposed a social hierarchy in its allocation of sites for government staff, a feature facilitated by the topography. The privately-owned and annually-rented large estates on the upper terraces of the hill were taken by the higher *varnas*. The flank was reserved for Anglo-Indian clerks; the lower peripheral regions of the bazar for the Indian clerks. The former merited small cottages, the latter, who were not expected to bring their families, single rooms in barracks.

In 1880, the clerks complained of the rising rents of small private houses, and sites were recommended at Kaithu, situated above the Jail and on the main road to Annandale, for the construction of cottages for 'European and Eurasian' clerks. But with few exceptions, the new houses were not favoured.

Since the locality indicated the caste in the official hierarchy, officials annually rented houses of their choice. It was thought *infra dig* by 'European and Eurasian' clerks to use government accommodation. As one clerk explained, 'An Englishman's house is his castle, but when the house happens to be a Government building occupied by a Government clerk . . . it is a castle in the air.'[22] The cottages, the clerks complained, were built too close together; there was no privacy and the occupant could not choose his neighbours; there was a risk of quarrels and misunderstandings; furthermore, the choice of locality was restricted.

The Committee sanctioned a four-storeyed block of a hundred single-room barrack-shaped quarters for Indian clerks on the Cart Road below Lower Bazar. But the Indian clerks also disliked their quarters 'with inter-communication from one end to another, and involving the segregation of all sorts of people in one locality.'[23] Many claimed they preferred to take up accommodation in the bazar.

In the middle of the town, the Lower Bazar spread haphazardly. A hotchpotch of construction, it rose tier upon tier from the Cart Road to the top of the Ridge. Many of the large European estates above and below the Cart Road were bought up and built upon to provide additional accommodation. The new landlords probably took advantage of a by-law according to which the municipality had to compensate an owner when it prohibited the erecting or re-erecting of a building on a private estate. The municipality could ill afford to pay compensation for new constructions.

There was a 40 per cent increase in the Indian population, most of which found refuge in the Lower Bazar. Val Prinsep described the Bazar by night: 'It is most thickly inhabited; and at night, coming home from dinner, one is astonished at the number of inanimate bundles lying on step, shelf, or roof, all of which represent so many sleeping men.'[24]

The Lower Bazar housed Indian clerks and camp followers, shops and shopkeepers; charcoal burners, wood carriers, carpenters and masons from the surrounding hills; cloth merchants, dealers in miscellaneous goods, cooks, bakers, and artisans from the plains. There were also the discharged sepoys of the East India Company's forces who served as *khidmutgars* and domestic servants on the large estates. The coolies and porters, never less than 500 during the season, lived in squalid wretchedness. There was a considerable demand for job horses and ponies, and syces stabled their animals all over the Bazar. There were no drains, although liquid waste sped downwards along the natural inclines. Not surprisingly, therefore, the Bazar was deeply contaminated by sewage and other organic matter.[25]

With the growth of the town, the Bazar had gradually spread over the hill side to cover the southern slope and squatted inconsiderately atop the European estates along the Cart Road.

Simla was until 1875 divided into an Upper (the Ridge), a Main (the Mall), and a Lower Bazar. Over thirty Indian and several English shops extended on both sides of the Upper Bazar. The three bazars were viewed as the antithesis of the British town. In 1861, the Deputy Commissioner proposed the removal of Indian shops from the Ridge and the Mall:

> My idea is to give Simlah as much an European tone as possible. . . . I look forward to the gradual removal of the Bazar at Simlah which is at present occupied by natives and to substitute European traders in their stead, in improved buildings. [26]

In 1875 a cholera epidemic in the town and a fire in the Ridge Bazar in quick succession provided the occasion to shift shops from the Ridge. An inquiry and report into the manifold problems of water supply, sanitation, sewage disposal and the location of the Bazar resulted. A grant of 5,00,000 and a loan of 7,00,000 rupees were sanctioned by the Government of India to the Simla Municipality for the town. An Improvement Committee, with Colonel Crofton as President, proposed drastic measures to dismantle, replan and rebuild the Bazar.

The Upper Bazar at the Ridge was removed and shop owners compensated by cash or grants of alternative sites for shops. Most Indian shopkeepers preferred cash, and 29,613 rupees were disbursed for the purpose. The Jubilee Theatre and the Assembly Rooms above the Cart Road, which had lost their popularity through being too close to the Bazar, were selected to house the new market place. As the old structures were destroyed in a fire in 1889, the market was rebuilt, to provide accommodation to the purveyors of food in ordinary daily use at European tables. These included ten bakers, eight butchers, eight beef butchers, fifteen poulterers and egg dealers, sixteen greengrocers, one fishmonger and three buttermen. [27]

The Colonel's Committee furthermore suggested that there be channels of through communication and air shafts from the upper to the lower part of the Bazar. The Committee thereby hoped also to impose a façade of geometrical coherence on the Bazar: one street, twelve feet wide, was to be made longitudinally through the Bazar from east to west, and six streets, twenty feet wide, to be driven vertically from north to south. 2,00,000 rupees were recommended for the cost of the required demolitions of which only 50,000 were actually spent.

A second Committee of 1877, headed by Lepel Griffin, reviewed the work of the earlier one. By then, the funds allocated for re-ordering the Bazar were running out. The compensation paid to traders on the Ridge had far exceeded the estimates. The water-supply scheme originally estimated to cost 7,00,000 rupees threatened to cost 11,00,000 rupees. Lepel Griffin believed that the Bazar could well stay as it was, since the introduction of a 'new system of conservancy' obviated the necessity for wholesale demolition. The Bazar was divided into six blocks to facilitate the construction of V-shaped wooden drains to carry all liquid drainage to the bottom of the ravine.

It was possible to widen the existing Lower Bazar road. It branched off from the Mall below the Telegraph office, coursed through the length of the Bazar to join the Mall again at the point below Lowrie's Hotel (Ladies Park after 1937). Between the Mall and the Lower Bazar an irregular lane, the Middle Bazar, was formed. A municipal resolution in 1884 restricted extension of the Bazar along the Mall over its entire length, including the road around Jakhu.

Residential houses between the two bazars accommodated the influx of Indians, landlords adding four, five and six storeys to existing structures. Often the topmost floor opened on the Mall as a shop, with the ground floor, facing south, a shop on the Lower or Middle Bazar. The residential accommodation was sandwiched in between. After the 1890s it became impossible to implement Crofton's plan of creating twenty-foot wide intersecting streets through the Bazar. Instead of streets, a jigsaw puzzle of stairways connected the various alleys.

In 1878, Edwards Gunj, the principal wholesale grain market and the preserve of commission agents and middlemen, was

rebuilt as a 'first class' grain market. By the close of the nineteenth century, a temple, patronized and maintained by the
leading commission agents, stood sentinel above the Gunj. A
small area adjacent to it was left unbuilt. In 1914, it was earmarked as a site for a town hall for Indians. Although the proposal
for a building never fructified the site itself became a 'town
hall'. In the twentieth century, the 'Maidan-i-Gunj' became
the site for political meetings, where processions and marchers
assembled. From the vantage point of the projecting balconies
and the windows of the Bazar, many, especially women,
observed the meetings below.

The Lower Bazar, cascading in untidy irregular layers down
the hill, irked successive city fathers. The Annual Report of
the Simla Municipality of 1877–78 summed up the problem.

> If you want to improve Simla knock down the Bazar. The
> removal of the whole bazar at a very moderate estimate for
> compensation would cost sixteen lakhs of rupees. When you
> have removed the present native population, where do you find
> a more suitable location for the native inhabitants who are
> essential to the existence of Simla?[28]

A local paper in 1894 lamented that the summer capital had as
a blot on its very face, 'an ugly overcrowded bazar occupying
the very portion of the site which should have been noblest
and handsomest.'[29]

Demolition of the Upper Bazar at the Ridge, however,
provided a flat stretch of land in the centre of the town. It was
the second-largest level piece of land, the largest being Annandale. It became the city centre and served as a piazza as well as
the site of all ceremonial functions. Its western corner was
dominated by Christ Church, a sturdy building in Tudor style,
designed by Colonel J. T. Boileau.

The cornerstone of the church was laid in 1844. The estimated
cost was 12,000 rupees, but costs mounted; by 1851, 28,000
rupees had been collected as private contributions but the
building was still incomplete. The Government, initially 'chill
and aloof' to attempts by the Church Committee to secure

grants for the building, relented in 1851 and contributed 5,000 rupees on condition that the right of property be so vested as to make the church a part of the ecclesiastical establishment of the country. The church was taken over as a Government building in 1856 and consecrated in 1857. The tower and clock was added in the 1860s and the porch in 1873. [30]

It appeared fitting that a Town Hall, that monument to Victorian civic energy, be built in the heart of the town. The proposal for a Town Hall on the Ridge came in 1880 from several English residents. 'Any other town in the world of the same size or importance', they petitioned, 'would not be without a public Hall as Simla is.' [31] A large building, they felt, would serve all the purposes which a town hall did in England and Europe. There had been a spurt of such buildings in England in the 1860s and 1870s, a time of steadily increasing prosperity; they were the symbol of the civic pride of a town and its municipality. Town halls were places where large assemblies could meet to exercise their right of discussing public questions, while the town halls of large cities housed the session courts and the assizes. The size varied according to the wealth and prosperity of the city. The exterior was usually not highly decorated but combined simplicity with majesty, as it was an index of the affluence and importance of the people for whose use it was erected.

In Simla the Town Hall reflected the social milieu of the 'upper five hundred'. It included all that British society needed: a theatre, a library, a large hall for suppers, balls, exhibitions and durbars; and a police station and weapons for protection. The ground floor consisted of the Gaiety Theatre, a Masonic Hall with a vaulted entrance, the municipal offices and the police station. The first floor contained the gallery of the theatre, the library, two reading rooms and a hall for holding public meetings. A European volunteer Rifle Corps was constituted in Simla after the 1857 Uprising in 1861. The Town Hall housed the volunteers' armoury in two large rooms and a basement. The armoury was meant to store two light machine guns and 700 rifles. The second floor consisted of a large ballroom and two retiring rooms. This floor also had a drawing room, a bar and card room. Viewed by most English residents as a not very striking symbol of civic pride, the Town Hall was completed in 1888. Designed by Henry Irwin in the Gothic style, a bitter controversy accompanied its construction.

To Lady Dufferin who visited the incomplete Town Hall in 1887, it looked 'something like a cathedral, but which inside is a collection of places of amusement.' The local guidebook ten years later described it as 'bastard Gothic'. Curzon thought it a 'gaunt protuberance' and hoped an earthquake would knock it down to provide the excuse for rebuilding it.[32] Eventually, the use of inferior stone and a defective design made it imperative to dismantle the upper storeys to the level of the Ridge. It was never rebuilt.

Although the main structure was defective, the Gaiety Theatre on the first floor endured and grew in popularity. The *Thackers Guide* of 1902 mentions that the plan of the theatre won the first prize offered by the Dramatic Society in London for the design of a *bijou* theatre to form part of the Dramatic College. It was eventually used in Simla. The theatre and club attached to it have survived a hundred years and are now earmarked for conservation.

From below the Town Hall, westward to Viceregal Lodge and eastwards to Chhota Simla, stretches of road were widened and linked to create the Mall. At Lytton's behest the Mall, including the road around Jakhu Hill, via Combermere Bridge was widened and its gradients levelled so as to make it 'as pleasant a riding or driving road as the Simla and Kalka road'.[33]

The Mall became one of the best cared-for of roads, watered daily, and oiled before ceremonial functions. In the 1880s, seventy-two oil lamps were erected on the Mall between Benmore and Peterhoff and lit twenty nights each month for the seven months that Simla was capital. There was hardly another road of such uniform width and easy gradients. Most of the other roads were the original village tracks which house owners had widened or extended from time to time as the need arose.

The Mall, as envisaged in 1861, had in the central part European-style shops. Milliners, clothiers, dressmakers, hairdressers, jewellers, chemists, saddlers, restaurants, and general provision stores, many owned by British traders, catered to the needs of Simla's European population. Some of the shops had a typically British façade. In 1904, Buck wrote with pride of the bank buildings near the Post Office as structures 'which would be a credit to any English town.'

'Taking the air' in the evening was a British custom. In the civil lines of most towns in the plains the wide roads, bordered by stretches of green, had served as suitable promenading areas. In deference to the custom, Captain Kennedy had in 1831 decreed that 'no led horse or other cattle be taken for exercise during the hours generally set aside for Europeans to take the air.'[34] In Simla, once the central part was cleared of the Indian bazar, the Mall became a promenading area.

It became the practice to clear the Mall of sweepers, coolies, mule leaders and workmen every evening between four and seven. Laxity in enforcing this in 1883 was regarded as a grave aberration. A letter in the *Pioneer* complained:

> The good old rule which forbade the presence of coolies and porters, and loafers generally (as distinguished from promenaders), upon the Mall between the hours of four and seven of the afternoon has lately fallen utterly and miserably into abeyance. In former days, up to the present season that is to say, the one road of Simla was vigilantly kept clear during these hours by the police, and the gangs of labourers and hill men relegated to the Cart road below.[35]

Some residents compared abeyance of the rule with the proposed Ilbert Bill which permitted Indian magistrates to try Englishmen. In the summer of 1883 both measures were hotly resented.

> Just as in regard to a certain Bill . . . the whole European community of Simla is to be subjected to extreme discomfort rather than one coolie or coolie's employer should suffer an imaginary wrong, by his being kept from going on the Mall when his betters are taking the air. . . .

The grievance may seem a small one to the Lieutenant-Governor who never goes to the Mall. The Viceroy, however, walks, and when His Excellency does occasionally honour the Mall with his presence, the spectacle of the Queen's representative trudging through the dust, jostled at every turn by swarms of stinking coolies, which may be seen this season for the first time, is the reverse of edifying.[36]

'The good old rule' was soon restored and it became a practice to post police inspectors at most points where lanes and stairways intersected the Mall.

By 1905 a tunnel was constructed under the Ridge, running from near the Blessington tennis courts in the north and opening on to the Lower Bazar below the Jami Masjid in the south. It was to serve as a supplement to the Sanjauli–Kaithu road and diverted all coolie and mule traffic which used to pass over the Mall.[37] The European character of the Mall was thus reinforced. It gave rise to the belief that Indians were not allowed to walk on the Mall.

One of the features of Simla was its forest cover of deodar, rhododendron and oak. In the early years of Simla's growth there was indiscriminate felling, but after 1832, trees could be cut only with the permission of the Political Agent. Builders then turned to the deodar stands of the Mahasu range and the range running from Shali to Narkanda. According to an official report of 1885, the denuded forests were to be found in 'the beams, roofs, floors, doors and windows of the vast habitation which now constitutes the city and suburbs of Simla.'[38]

The arcadian setting of Simla was maintained. In 1870 a forest survey was conducted and working plans made in 1882–3. Forested areas near roads and private estates were classified as amenity areas, which meant that all woods within fifty feet of a road or a public path, uphill or downhill, and forests bordering house compounds, were excluded from felling. The cutting of trees on estates required permission from the municipality.

The devising of sanitation suitable to Simla's rugged and wooded topography, together with the spontaneous growth of the town, was one of the civic challenges faced by the Simla planners. The adoption of sanitary measures was one of the outstanding socio-technical achievements of nineteenth-century industrial England. A continuous piped water-supply, an underground network of pipes, drains and sewers emerged as one of the unseen revolutions in town planning.

Simla was dependent for her water supply upon over seventeen natural springs and baolis. Once it became the summer capital, steps were taken to conserve water for the growing town. One of the principal measures was the construction of tunnels in order to channel underground sources of water.[39] In 1860, it was surmised that Jakhu, well-wooded and deeply covered with soil, rose more than 500 feet over the point where water was most needed and, was therefore, a possible site for tunnelling. The Combermere ravine, where several springs existed, was considered the most suitable. In 1861, under the supervision of the geologist H. B. Medlicott, a tunnel was made to the depth of 800 feet where 'sufficient' supply was obtained.[40]

The results of this experiment were confirmed in 1869 by a geological appraisal of the Simla tract conducted especially with reference to water supply. It was observed that while the upper beds of Jakhu were fairly pervious, the lower ones were comprised of impervious rock and formed a trough-like basin below. Water percolated into the interior and oozed out as springs along cracks and faults in the rock. The ravine at Combermere lay on a large fault and was the main outlet of the basin of percolation formed by the beds at Jakhu. Since the densest habitation was located near Combermere, it was considered the most suitable site for tunnelling for an enhanced water supply.

The water from Jakhu springs was channelled into four tunnels varying in length from 800 to about 350 feet, bored into the hillside. However since the soil was porous, much of the water seeped away. In 1863, a proposal to lay nine-inch pipes inside the tunnels was made. Only one tunnel was laid with pipes when it was discovered that the cost was prohibitive, and further work was abandoned. Water from the tunnels was piped to a large reservoir with a capacity of 32,000 gallons at Combermere Bridge. A pipe carried this water to a tap in the bazar.[41]

There were also efforts to conserve spring water. For example, it was observed that the roads, paths and artificial water courses on the upper part of the Jakhu Hill considerably reduced the flow water from the springs. Accordingly, a municipal resolution prohibited further house building and clearing of forests on sites above the sources of the principal springs. By 1875 the tunnels had caved in, but were cleared again in 1877.

The experiment of tapping spring water at Jakhu by shafts bored into the hill had sufficed for Simla when its population was below 10,000; it became inadequate when it crossed 13,000. A new plan, to pipe water by gravitation from the springs on the southern slope of Mahasu hill, fourteen miles away from Simla, was devised. It was reasoned that the Mahasu springs were fed by snow and rainfall on the hillsides above and this absorbed water found its way through cracks and fissures into the body of the hill where it formed, as at Jakhu, a storage reservoir.

The thickly forested tract known as the 'Catchment area' was rented at 2,250 rupees per year from the Rana of Koti by the municipality. Work on laying iron pipes to these springs commenced in 1877. By December 1879, masonry work connecting the springs, and a road connecting them to Simla was complete. By 1883, two reservoirs had been built: one below the Ridge and another at Sanjauli to hold 1,20,000 gallons. It was calculated as twelve days' water supply for the town. Distribution lines were laid to Lower Bazar, Kaithu, Observatory Hill and Chhota Simla. A decade later, water could be pumped up to estates on Jakhu hill. Hydrants were erected at several points and water was carried as before by *bhistis* to individual houses.

Crucial to the stability of a hill town is the drainage. Bad drainage could cause water to seep into the foundations of houses, find subterranean passages and erode soil. Storm water normally rushed down the natural ravines on hillsides. Drains were made to channel the water away from pathways and houses to the natural ravines. During these years V-shaped wooden drains were laid along the roads, especially at Lower Bazar. But they were porous and rotted within a few years, and were therefore, gradually replaced by stone and cement ones.

The more intimidating task, however, was that of sewage collection and disposal.[42] There was no uniform system until the 1870s, though the dry earth system was sometimes followed. Dry earth was added to liquid refuse and the semi-solid mass thrown by sweepers into infrequented ravines and localities. With the fourfold increase in the number of houses and a population that had doubled, the 'infrequented' localities became fewer. The large Indian labour population tended to use the edges of ravines and open land behind houses as latrines. Several methods of night-soil disposal were tried and abandoned.

The pit system, whereby all sewage was drained into a septic tank dug near the house, was rejected as unsatisfactory, since water could percolate to the interior of the hill and pollute spring water. Burning sewage in kilns was not practicable because of the prolonged monsoons. At Chhota Simla, the trench system was tried. The municipality purchased culti-vated land and sweepers deposited night soil in trenches dug for the purpose. This was not practicable for the other parts of Simla.

There was a proposal to transport night soil by bullock cart to be buried at Badai Ghat below the Lower Bazar, but the estimated cost of 40,000 rupees per annum was beyond the municipality's means. The laying of sewer pipes for all streets and connecting them with one main which would discharge sewage into the bed of a ravine below the Lower Bazar was recommended. In 1877, a large tract of land was acquired at Badai Ghat for disposal of sewage and refuse. However, doubts were expressed whether a single system of conservancy was possible for a town scattered across the length of the Simla ridge.

Finally, the disposal of sewage by gravitation down the hillside at various parts of Simla was considered. The experiment of shooting sewage through iron pipes down ravines was considered the best and most economical, and was the system finally implemented. Night soil from latrines, private and public, was carried by sweepers in iron receptacles which were emptied into pail depots. The distance to the pail depots was sometimes great, and it required constant supervision to ensure that sweepers did not empty their receptacles into the nearest ravine. The pail depots, flushed out by water, were connected to sewage mains that carried the sewage to septic tanks. Before it entered these tanks the sewage was diluted with nullah water, partially purified, and run over the hillside.

By the close of the 1880s, five nine-inch sewage mains below Kasumpti, Lower Bazar, Snowdon, Kaithu and Summer Hill carried sewage down the hillside. It was far more difficult connecting individual houses to the mains. In 1905, it was recommended that the sewage mains be extended within a hundred feet of all compounds, but the cost was calculated at a prohibitive 4,00,000 rupees.

Water closets and underground sewers were harbingers of a new urban order. But most mid-nineteenth century houses required structural changes to install water closets, and in 1914 such an installation cost 755 rupees. By that year, therefore, only thirty-five private estates and nine of seventy-two public latrines had flush toilets. Sewage disposal, therefore, remained largely dependent on human labour.

Ceaseless inspection, not only of the bazars but also of the compounds of large estates in Station Ward, was required to keep Simla clean. In 1876 it was thought indispensable to maintain an establishment of European sanitary inspectors for house-to-house inspection. 'Native officials', according to the Deputy Commissioner, 'do not possess the moral courage requisite to deal successfully with breaches of Sanitary laws, especially when their work brings them into contact with English residents and ladies.'[43] The conservancy staff employed by the Simla municipality numbered 231 in 1879, almost as much as that of Allahabad which had double the population. It rose to 312 in 1905, and 437 in 1937.[44]

Refuse and litter was removed in baskets (later in gunny bags), and burnt in incinerators located in various parts of Simla. Almost 400 additional hill cleaners and litter carriers were employed by the municipality every year. The municipal sweepers, to earn the extra rupee, lined up to serve as hill cleaners and litter carriers during their 'off time'. Despite the appurtenances of a modern sanitary system, meant to reduce human scavenging, every increase in population was accompained by an increase in the conservancy establishment at Simla. An army of sweepers, both private and municipal, was required to give Simla its legendary cleanliness.

By the close of the 1880s, the makeshift arrangements which had so irked Lytton were ended. The impress of Government influence was apparent in every aspect of the town's development and in Simla's skyline. The town plan as it emerged was simplicity itself, ill-suited even to the age of the rickshaw, with congestion guaranteed in the bazars. The canvas on which the new buildings were accommodated had been studded with everything from cottages to tin sheds; the new structures gave the impression of a hurriedly mounted English stage set. Aesthetically, they were often disdained. When Edwin Lutyens inspected Simla in 1913, his reaction was: 'If one was told the monkeys had built it all one could only say, what wonderful monkeys—they must be shot in case they do it again...'

The 'improvements' had reshaped the town to suit imperial needs. A continuous water supply had been ensured. The essentials of a drainage and sewage system had been traced out. The Ridge was cleared of shops and the European-style shops on the Mall were visible. The bazar had been stacked away, somewhat untidily, behind and below the Mall. The Government offices had new buildings, all bearing the stamp of Henry Irwin's adaptable genius. And radiating satisfaction, Dufferin could boast 'that a decent Viceregal residence has been erected... where Simla maidens will have better opportunities of displaying both their graces and their pretty frocks. . . .'45

The changes, taken together, fortified Simla's image as something of a cross between Olympus and an English enclave. The formative urban design forged during the decade of the 1880s was, with a few changes, to serve Simla until 1947, for the sanatorium and holiday resort had been overlaid with the Imperial form.

CHAPTER FIVE

The Men Who Mattered

Each man depends on his position in the public service, which is the aristocracy; and those who do not belong to it are out of the pale, no matter how wealthy they may be, or what claims they may advance to the consideration of the world around them.[1]

THE Viceroy and his family held the same position as royalty in England. Their presence at social gatherings at Simla, at balls, plays, concerts, investitures as guests of honour added pomp to the festivities, and they themselves gave endless parties. As Emily Eden had observed, 'I dare say we are an amusement to them. They liked our balls and parties, and whatever we did or said was the subject of an anecdote, and if we said or did nothing they invented something for us.'[2] British official society consisted of a rigid hierarchy with fixed boundaries of social intercourse. The officials of the 'heaven born' Indian Civil Service were at the apex of the social pyramid with those officials of the other covenanted services a close second. Of the same social rank as the civilians were the military officers of the British army posted at headquarters. Then there was the mercantile community; the ones in commerce were socially acceptable while traders who owned or sat in shops were regarded as distinctly inferior. The Eurasians or Anglo-Indians, and the Domiciled Community—people of British stock who settled in India— manned the senior clerical positions. These formed the fringe of British society.

Like oil and water, Simla's social classes did not mix. A clear-cut caste system framed British social attitudes and behaviour, based on European taboos and snobberies. Nearly all the senior officials had the common background of an English

public-school education: Eton and Harrow supplied the civil
services, while Rugby, Marlborough and Wellington were the
schools of prospective Indian army officers.

The term 'covenanted civil service' emerged in the late
eighteenth century as a result of the covenants or contracts
rendered to the East India Company by British recruits for the
civil service. Between 1833 and 1855 the term applied only to
graduates of Haileybury. After 1855, successful candidates at
the annual competitive examinations were considered covenanted members. After the Queen's Proclamation of 1858, the
covenant was drawn up with the Secretary of State for India.
Bradford Spangenberg has shown that by the late nineteenth
century, civil servants came largely from the British professional
classes. The aristocracy regarded Indian appointments with
disdain, as an enterprise for 'second-rate minds and middle-
class citizens.'[3] But in India, the aristocracy was the official élite.

A verse in *Punch* in 1919 portrayed the exemplary civil servant
at Simla: austerely dignified, hardworking, efficient, indispensable.[4]

> Along a narrow mountain track
> Stalking supreme along,
> Head upwards, hands behind his back,
> He swings his sixteen stone.
>
> Out of the tinsel and the glare
> That lit his forebears' lives,
> His tweed-clad shoulders amply bear,
> The burden that was CLIVE's.
>
> A man of few and simple needs
> He smokes a briar—and yet
> His rugged signature precedes
> The half an alphabet.
>
> Across these green Elysian slopes
> The Secretariat gleams,
> The playground of his youthful hopes,
> The workshop of his schemes.

He sees the misty depths below,
Where plain and foothills meet,
And smiles a wistful smile to know,
The world is at his feet.

There was some dispute over this in the local Simla newspaper on two counts: that bureaucrats were generally not sixteen stone, and that the Secretariat was not located on Elysium Hill.

Secretariat posts were generally more highly coveted than the dull, dusty district posts in the plains. They were prestigious because secretaries to Government were pivotal figures in the formulation of policy; the Secretariat offered the most promising gateway to the highest executive posts both in the provincial and central Government. Securing a Secretariat post at an appropriate point in one's career was a crucial step in advancement beyond the common level of achievement.

Conrad Corfield was posted in 1924 in the Punjab Secretariat as Under-Secretary to an I.C.S. Secretary in charge of departments under Indian ministers. At Simla he got to know an officer of the Political Department who dealt with the selection of candidates and recounts: 'I then started to pull strings, but it was some time before they had any effect.' After a summer at Simla 'the strings' began to work, and he was assigned to the department of his choice—the Political Department.[5]

The cream of the civil service was posted in the Secretariat. 'The highest appointments went to the secretariat staff', a not-so-privileged civil servant was to point out, 'and that staff was selected from those whose family influence, clever noting and city speech attracted promotion.'[6] The divide between the privileged 'Secretariat man' and the civil servant in the field was always wide.

Simla society was considered 'superior' because of the officers at the Secretariat. A subtle difference between 'senior' and 'junior' officers (the latter majors, under-secretaries and below) marked social relations; yet the bond of service and class knit them together, for as Walter Lawrence wrote: 'The youngest civilian knew that he might one day become a Lieutenant-

Governor or a Member of Council.'[7] Socially aloof anywhere in the country, civil servants were doubly so in Simla, for while other towns afforded some scope for the diffusion of social divisions, in Simla they were more sharply etched.

For officials on leave, Simla was a sort of refuge: 'After seven years of somewhat lonely life, to find oneself in the midst of a cheerful English family and the refinements of home life was a delightful experience. . . . It was pleasant to find one's own kind once more, turned out tidily in English clothes, and still pleasanter was the crowd of pretty, well-dressed women.'[8]

It was possible at Simla to revive old school ties and rivalries: Dufferin attended an annual dinner to meet old Etonians; there were sixteen of them. During World War I, the Etonians received a belligerent message from old Harrovians, and allegedly shot back a telegram, 'Gott strafe Harrow.'[9] At Simla, such things didn't seem incongruous.

Simla's official society bristled with inter-service rivalry. There was, for instance, the controversy that raged between Curzon and Kitchener over civilian domination of the military. As Commander-in-Chief of India from 1902 to 1909, Kitchener had reorganized the army and was determined to secure complete authority, executive and administrative, over military affairs. As Viceroy, Curzon disagreed and opposed abolition of the post of War Member. There was a bizarre off-shoot of the controversy. As Kitchener battled with Curzon for control over military administration, his official residence, Snowdon, was being enlarged and renovated. As a soldier he regarded the clerical systems of the military department as so absurd that he directed his aides-de-camp to pound up their files into papier mâché to be used for the mouldings on the ceilings of the new dining hall at Snowdon.[10]

One of the most obvious features of life in India was the social distance between the two races. In Simla, Indian opinion could be ignored or overlooked because of the absence of a local population, except for those that had settled there after the creation of the hill station. The bureaucracy toed the line.

The epitome of the maverick official who stepped out of

line, lent an ear to Indian aspirations and moved away from the safe and sensible paths chosen by mainstream British official opinion, was the Scottish Allan Octavian Hume (1829–1912).[11]

Hume, after an erratic career in the civil service spanning thirty-two years, resigned and settled in Simla. Son of the radical politician, Joseph Hume, he had joined the civil service in 1849 at the age of nineteen. After a spell at Haileybury, he was sent to Meerut for practical training to serve first as *muhrir*, then *naib-daroga, peshkar* and *naib-tehsildar*, until he was ready to hold independent charge. He spent until 1857 as Assistant Magistrate and Deputy Collector in Etawah, a small town in present-day Uttar Pradesh. In the 1857 Uprising, Hume escaped narrowly and had to leave Etawah for several months. He was ever after haunted by the spectre of revolution and devastation and apprehensive of the future of British rule, which he had seen 'shrivel up in a single month... like some emblazoned scroll cast into a furnace.' In later years it led him to work for a safety valve—the Indian National Congress—whereby Indians could voice their aspirations on a constitutional platform.

After a two-year stint as Commissioner for Inland Customs of Allahabad, Hume was transferred to the Home Department in the Government of India. In July 1871, he was promoted Secretary to the newly-created Department of Revenue, Agriculture and Commerce.

As Secretary to Government from 1870 to 1879, he came to Simla annually. And as was the established practice amongst British officers, he bought a large estate on Jakhu, called Rothney Castle. It was one of the oldest houses of Simla, built by a Colonel Rothney in 1838, which had housed the Simla Bank Corporation for about a decade after 1844. After 1867 it passed to a P. Mitchell who then sold it to Hume. Hume rebuilt the house into a virtual palace with enormous reception rooms and spacious halls, and extended the grounds and gardens. He had hoped it would be bought by the Government as the Viceregal residence, but it was not considered suitable because of its situation above the centre of the town, on the steep slopes of Jakhu Hill, which made it inaccessible to carriages.

Hume's fellow officers found him eccentric, mischievous, arrogant—impossible as a colleague—and ganged up against him. He had trouble with two successive Viceroys, Northbrooke and Lytton. A serious difference of opinion led Lytton to get rid of a 'very troublesome Secretary' by abolishing the Department altogether. Hume was demoted and expelled, in Wedderburn's words, from 'the official paradise' of Simla, and sent back to Allahabad as a member of the Board of Revenue. Thwarted and frustrated in the struggle for promotion, combined with failing health and disappointment at not having a son, Hume resigned from the civil service. In 1881, he returned to live at Rothney Castle.

In retirement Hume busied himself with other activities, especially ornithology. With characteristic zeal, he employed an army of collectors to catch bird-specimens from all over India, and Rothney Castle was converted into a veritable ornithological museum. He then found refuge in theosophy, propagated by Colonel Henry Olcott and Madame Helena Blavatsky. They were frequent guests at Rothney Castle in the summer and performed several well-publicized miracles—the digging up of a lost brooch belonging to Mrs Hume from under a bush; the materializing of a spare tea cup, once again, from under a bush at a picnic at Mashobra. He was attracted, perhaps, as much to its eclectism and its belief in the universal brotherhood of man, as by its miracles and occultism.

Hume was also drawn back to an interest of his youth–politics. For two years, he directed his organizational ability on the Simla municipal constitution. He then concentrated his energies into linking the various Indian associations to shape the Indian National Congress in 1885. His colleagues believed that he spent his time and money to energize the non-official intelligentsia of India into political hostility to the state.

Non-conformists were always unpopular, but there were few men so disliked as Sir Guy-Fleetwood Wilson.[12] Finance Member on the Viceroy's Council for five years from 1908 to 1913, he was the antithesis of the 'sun-dried' bureaucrat. A bachelor of solitary habits, he disliked the social life and the holiday atmosphere of the summer capital with its tendency to divert attention from working efficiency, and attributed many of the Indian difficulties to Simla where the Government of India went 'to sleep'. He delivered lengthy speeches on finance in the Council. (During one such speech in 1909, it was observed that all the twenty-one members of the Council fell asleep, one by one.)

He drew up a deficit budget and took measures to enforce economy and cut official spending. There was a ripple of disbelief when, in his attempts to prune extravagant expenditure, he declined to sanction funds for the construction of an official country house at Mashobra for the Punjab Lieutenant-Governor. Louis Dane, in 1909, had moved the Punjab Public Works Department to acquire a camping ground at Chhrabra on the Hindustan–Tibet Road. The Department acquired the land and constructed a pavilion and a rose pergola. Fleetwood Wilson's refusal to sanction funds halted work on the main building, prompting British residents to name the two structures 'Dane's Folly'. For his tight-fistedness the Finance Member was nicknamed 'not-a-bob Wilson'.

Wilson's political views were in advance of his time. He had none of the prejudices of the high British official and was something of a phenomenon; he deplored the lack of camaraderie between Englishmen and Indians, and stirred up a controversy when he invited and entertained G. K. Gokhale for a week at Simla. He then broke with tradition by giving a dinner to all members, including the Indians, of the Legislative Assembly.

When the incumbent Viceroy, Hardinge, was injured in a bomb explosion at Delhi in 1912, Fleetwood Wilson, as senior member of the Executive Council, was made acting Viceroy. Unfamiliar with Anglo–Indian headgear, he committed sacrilege by wearing his topee back to front at the formal investiture ceremony. Officials gleefully murmured that 'his head had quite turned.' Fleetwood Wilson admitted that he was like a red flag to his colleagues. He dedicated his reminisicences of his Indian years to his 'good friends, the Simla monkeys whose entertaining companionship stemmed many a wave of over-whelming depression.'[13]

The Simla season commenced in April once the officials came in from Calcutta or after 1911, from Delhi, and Lahore. It took about a month to be fully launched; the officials, convalescents and holiday-makers settled in by the end of May. This coincided with the week-long celebrations connected with the Emperor's birthday. An elaborately planned durbar in the Town Hall, a parade at the Ridge in the centre of the town, special services at Christ Church, and illuminations by night marked the public functions. They were the 'manifestation of the magnitude of the empire'. The 'Birthday Ball' at Viceregal Lodge was the highlight of the celebrations. Then came the monsoons, lasting from July until mid-September, confining people to indoor entertainments.

If Simla provided an escape from the heat and a refuge from Indian problems, amateur theatre took audiences 'for a time out of India'.[14] Amateur theatricals were one of the most popular informal entertainments of Simla. It had Viceregal patronage; Lytton himself produced and directed a play he had written. Plays were staged at the residences of the Viceroy and Commander-in-Chief, and in the nineteenth century, in build-ings with large halls which included the Assembly Rooms and the Royal (now Thakur) Hotel. With the opening of the Gaiety Theatre in 1887, the fledgling group acquired a proper theatre and the Amateur Dramatic Club to organize it.

The Amateur Dramatic Club was open to all those who were 'dramatically or musically useful' to the club and had as members 'most of the leading Princes and Gentlemen and Ladies who form the society of the summer capital.'[15] By 1937, its members 'ranged democratically throughout the social scale from band masters to field marshals, from assistant secre-taries to viceroys, clerks, authors, lawyers and governesses.' Its active executive committee appears to have been largely composed of military men, colonels and majors. In the 1890s they held their weekly meetings at 8 o'clock in the morning. Money for productions was raised by auctioning boxes. While civil servants, especially those serving as judges and magistrates, were not expected to act, Corfield recounts with pride of having acted in three plays one summer season. 'This kind of activity was not looked on with great favour by my service superiors, though no one actually suggested that it had interfered with my work.'[16]

The Amateur Dramatic Club produced, during the Victorian period, as many as twenty different plays in a season that stretched from April to mid-October. They dwindled to six or seven by the 1930s, the result both of a diminished British population and the advent of a rival form of entertainment—the cinema.

The occasions when the Viceroy, the Governor and the Commander-in-Chief were present were brilliant functions at which everybody who was anybody in official and social Simla was to be seen. 'Everybody came in full evening dress, usually after dinner parties which they'd got up before the show. The rickshaws all roared up and down outside the theatre and it was very gay indeed.'[17] The plays selected from the club library suited the mood; they were usually farces, satires, comedies, burlesques, and musicals—never Shakespeare or serious drama.

'A watering place gone mad', is how Val Prinsep described Simla life. It perplexed a young civilian who wrote:

> Work and play were inextricably mixed up. As part of the former and yet, apparently, wholly the latter, one was expected to go everywhere and do everything. One had to shew oneself at Viceregal Lodge and at the Commander-in-Chief's and Lieu-tenant-Governor's residences. One had to call on everyone in the station; to ride and play tennis; to dance, to picnic and generally have a thoroughly good time—all, as part of one's job.[18]

If social life was important for senior officials at Simla, for the others, it was a struggle to be socially accepted. A visitor in 1870 was surprised at the resentment over this issue felt by non-officials.

Ian Stephens, a civil servant and later a journalist, described the British social hierarchy in terms of the Hindu caste system. The upper *varnas* were members of the civil service and the Indian Army. The British businessmen were

> analogous to the wealthy but also low caste mercantile and money-lending, caste, the *Vaisyas*. . . . They might be merchant princes of the very highest quality but were quite inferior to the covenanted services and the military caste. This mercantile class subdivided willingly, even strongly—into two. The upper people said that they were in commerce, the lower people said that they were in trade and there was a hard division between them. A member of the trade sub-caste, for example, would find it impossible to get elected to the best British clubs. They were inferior, they were people who actually traded and worked in shops, which was very demeaning.[19]

The social gap between those Englishmen in trade and commerce and the officials can be illustrated by a history of their clubs.[20] Clubs provided not only places for social intercourse and sports, but also residential accommodation to unmarried officers or those living without their families. The officials had since its inception in 1844 patronized the United Service Club which restricted membership to officers holding a permanent commission in the civil, military and naval services of Government. The club did not take as members non-officials, however wealthy or influential.

In 1886, the non-officials started the New Club, situated in a large building on the Ridge at a site now occupied by the Grand Hotel. The Club was constructed on relatively modern lines, for the benefit of those who were not in the covenanted civil or military service and, therefore, not eligible for full membership of the United Service Club. It admitted members of 'the learned professions' as well as government officers above the rank of registrar. The management was in the hands of wealthy bankers and affluent non-officials. The New Club became very popular for several years and attracted the clientèle that normally frequented the United Service Club. The rivalry between official and non-officials manifested itself in the annual elections to the Club management; non-officials, lower down the social scale, were elected members. As the president of the New Club explained it, 'the class of members for whom the New Club was intended gradually ceased to seek election, one or two cases of black balling deterring them.'[21] The officials then revived the older United Service Club where, in 1890, the committee added a new block of quarters and renovated the old public rooms. Thus the New Club languished, and was purchased by Peliti where he opened a hotel. The officials' view of this rivalry was reflected in the history of the United Service Club, compiled in 1905. 'The New Club really did Simla a great service; during its short life, its example compelled the U.S. Club to throw away worn-out clothes and to put on a new garb; while its death bequeathed to Simla the first of the really good hotels that now adorn this station.'[22]

The United Service Club was reorganized as a private limited company, and expanded into a large institution. Spread over twenty-eight acres, it had eighty-three fully-furnished residential units with running hot and cold water, five lawn-tennis courts, two squash courts, a soda water factory, extensive wine cellars, and stables for seventy horses. In 1901, it installed its private electric plant.

It was a male preserve, women were not permitted even as guests. In 1890, the Chalet was constructed to enable members to entertain ladies. In 1909, Bendochy with twenty-four acres of land was rented at Mashobra as a weekend resort. Later another property, Carignano, was also acquired. The U.S. Club was the most exclusive and wealthiest in Simla.

Russell, who visited the club in 1858, described it as a scene of revelry, drunkenness, gambling for high stakes and inter-service rivalry. It was the picture of ritual thirty years later: the Honorary Secretary sat at one table at the head of the dining room, from which vantage point he was able to command a view of most of the club's diners. Alongside was the 6,000 rupees table, reserved for the Viceroy's executive councillors, when they visited. Inter-service rivalry was quelled by alternately electing a major-general and a senior civil service official as president for two-year terms. It is illustrative of the social divide in Simla society that by 1946 there were only ten Indian members.

In 1945, because of the exodus from Simla, the Club ran into a loss for the first time in its history. The committee tried to sell the Club's assets profitably the following year, advertising the sale of its properties for 30,00,000 rupees. There being no offers, the committee decided to sell the property by lots, but by then it was September 1947. The Punjab Government of free India requisitioned the property, which was valued at 1,00,000 rupees. The Chalet was sold to Loreto Convent, Carignano to the Simla Municipality. The library was sold to the House of Commons, the Empire League Hand the Punjab Government. The Club was finally liquidated in December 1947 and its cash assets divided amongst its members.

In a town with limited trade, and bereft of industry, it was only an occasional banker who edged his way socially to the top bracket. Joseph Elston in 1904 was one of the Directors of the leading Alliance Bank of Simla. The bank had been started in 1874 with a capital of 50,000 rupees, and by 1904 it possessed a capital of 15,00,000 rupees, a reserve of 19,00,000 and a working capital of over 3,00,00,000 rupees. It had branches at Agra, Ajmer, Bombay, Calcutta, Lahore, Darjeeling, Mussoorie, Murree, Ambala and Rawalpindi. Since 1874, Elston had published one of the local papers at Simla; in 1886, he became ex-officio member and trustee of the non-official New Club established in 1886, and was a member of the Simla municipal committee in 1879–84. Property was a standard form of investment, and Elston owned about thirty large estates which he let out annually to officials. Until his death in 1919 he was an influential property owner.

British traders who owned the European-style shops on the Mall were the most conspicuous of the non-officials. In the 1870s, these shops, numbering a little over twenty, supplied the European goods so much in demand at Simla. Although most traders were based in Calcutta or Lahore, Simla became a seasonal centre of commercial activity. The British traders on the Mall were affiliated to the Punjab Trades Association with its headquarters at Lahore. Aggressive, energetic businessmen, they reaped handsome profits supplying imported goods.

So expensive were these goods that in 1882, some officers, both covenanted and uncovenanted of the Government were driven to form a club called the Simla Co-operative Association,[23] which supplied its shareholders with English goods at little more than cost price. The Association started with a capital of 10,000 rupees, the following year its capital was raised to 50,000 rupees. The tradesmen therefore made a representation that the Association had been established for the purpose of carrying on a general mercantile business, while the officers claimed that theirs was an ordinary club, with new members being vetted by the committee. However, after the complaint, the club had to be closed down.

A. M. Jacob was a trader with a difference.[24] He became a celebrity as an antique dealer. With a shop on the Mall and a house at Belvedere, Jacob was known for his tea and dinner parties. He could speak English, French, Urdu, Persian and Arabic fluently. A handsome man with a compelling and magnetic personality, he has also been described as having occult powers, being a conjurer, a mesmerist and having achieved levitation. In addition, he was said to be an invaluable aide to the political secret service.

Jacob was believed to be a Polish or Armenian Jew, who became at the age of ten a slave to a rich Pasha. On reaching manhood, he worked a passage to Bombay and obtained a clerkship with a nobleman at the Nizam's court in Hyderabad. After a profitable deal in precious stones, he moved to Delhi and set up business at Chandni Chowk. In the 1870s, he shifted his trade in antiques, precious stones and jewellery to Simla, which offered the prospect of a captive market. Jacob's unrivalled knowledge of precious stones gave him a remarkable clientèle of notables. Belvedere, his Simla home, was furnished in the most lavish 'Oriental' style, and filled with priceless ornaments. It was thronged with wealthy visitors, yet his own habits were simple, almost ascetic: he was a vegetarian, a teetotaller and non-smoker, and it was said that with excellent mounts in his stable, he rode only a shaggy hill pony.

His nemesis came with an attempt to sell a diamond for 46,00,000 rupees to the Nizam of Hyderabad. He received a deposit of 23,00,000 rupees, but the Nizam declined to honour the agreement, since a Government of India commission brought pressure on him to renounce the transaction. In the sensational 'Imperial Diamond Case' of 1881, Jacob was sued to return the money and indicted on a charge of cheating. After a fifty-seven day trial at the Calcutta High Court he was acquitted, but the expense of the case ruined him. He left Simla at the age of fifty-five, a broken man, to live out his life in Bombay as a dealer in old china. He has provided a ready-made character for three novelists—to Rudyard Kipling, as Lurgan Sahib in *Kim*; to Marion Crawford as Mr Isaacs in a novel of that name; and to Newnham Davis as an occult ascetic in *Jadoo*, yet his real life was perhaps more fascinating than his fictional ones.

There were many lucrative businesses at Simla.[25] George Corstorphan, for instance, was a successful property agent with several large estates waiting to be sold. He also owned 'Corstorphan's Hotel', a popular hotel in the heart of town where he let out rooms for the season to families. Corstorphan's wife, 'a charming old lady who had all the gossip of the place at her fingers' ends,' was the proprietress of the Simla Fancy Repository, a long wooden shop with a range of glass windows opposite the Telegraph Office. The Corstorphans imported general goods of every description, including stationery, artists' requirements, books, toys and perfumes. In 1897, the Corstorphans purchased the printing press and business of the *Simla Times*, and renamed it the *Simla Times Advertiser*. The weekly paper, as its name implied, carried advertisements from shops on the Mall together with a few columns of news.

The British non-officials, numerically and socially insignificant, were an assertive and vocal section of society. Many of them were bankers, house owners, estate agents and traders.

Others had made their fortunes as contractors, supplying materials required in the hectic construction which took place once Simla was formally established as the summer capital. House owners and traders regarded Simla as being in many ways an English town but resented the official dominance. There was little competition from Indian businessmen, initially; by the turn of the century, however, Indian shopkeepers drove several European traders out of a profitable business by underselling.

Outside the pale of British society, but under its uneasy protection, were the 'poor whites' and Eurasians. The former were Britons who could not afford to return to England, or had opted to stay in India, and were called Anglo-Indian. Eurasians were of mixed European and Indian blood. On representation they too after the 1911 Census, were termed Anglo-Indians. They were largely the offspring of army men and civilians who had taken Indian wives or mistresses. For the greater part of the eighteenth century, the Eurasian offspring of influential fathers joined the Company's service as officers. But as the covenanted services became more coveted and exclusive, Anglo-Indians of both kinds were excluded from the service.

The growing abhorrence of misalliance and mixed blood crystallized in the form of an order issued by the Court of Directors of the East India Company in 1791. Indian-born sons of British parentage were denied employment in the civil, military and naval services of the Company, thus excluding both categories of Britons, the domiciled and those of mixed blood. The order was modified in 1795, restricting employment of all persons not descended from European parents on both sides in the army, except as fifers, bandsmen, drummers and farriers.[26] The Company's Charter of 1833 was more liberal and provided that religion, place of birth, descent or colour would not be a bar to official employment. However, by then the Anglo-Indians were neither sufficiently qualified nor affluent enough to send their children to England to avail of these opportunities. But then as English supplanted Persian and Urdu as the official language of courts and Government offices, the Anglo-Indians were able to secure posts in the middle and upper levels of the subordinate services.

Both classes of Anglo-Indian, the domiciled and Eurasian, served as clerks in Government offices. They were usually grouped together, for the white were also suspected to have traces of brown. Numbering about a 1,000, by census counts, they formed the fringe of white society at Simla. They lived in the smaller cottages scattered across Simla, but a large number were housed in Kaithu and Bemloe, in Government housing.

At Simla, uncovenanted clerks were not invited to Viceregal Lodge. In 1837, Emily Eden observed, 'I see how it would be impossible to ask a "white" Mr and Mrs Smith, though they are better looking than half the people we know, without hurting the feelings of half-black Mr Brown.'[27] Another note in her diary in Simla reads, 'We had a meeting of ladies, to settle about the fancy sale, which was easily done. . . . The only novelty I suggested was to ask the wives of the uncovenanted services (the clerks in public offices) to send contributions. This was rather a shock to the aristocracy of Simla, and they did suggest that some of the wives were very black.'[28] The main objection of officials to the advancement of Anglo-Indians was that the Indians also despised them because of their mixed birth, and that it detracted from the prestige of the official élite.

After the 1857 Uprising, the utility of these classes to the Empire in India was perceived. As one army officer wrote: 'Those classes might, perhaps, ere it be too late, be worked up into the defensive system of a landwehr or reserve sub-vexillo.'[29] The backward educational state of the Anglo-Indians was the first barrier to any such scheme. This concern spread to the ecclesiastical and government establishments and led to the creation of public schools in India.

The ethos of the English public school had been idealized by Thomas Hughes in his *Tom Brown's School Days*, published in 1858. The book gave a romantic account of the zeal with which the headmaster of Rugby, Thomas Arnold, inculcated what were seen to be the essentially English qualities into his boys.[30] The public schools served as a breeding ground for the civil services. The Right Reverend C. E. L. Cotton, Bishop of Calcutta, had been assistant master at Rugby under Dr Arnold. He planned three public schools in India which he hoped would 'not be less secure and by God's blessing not less useful than Winchester, Rugby, and Marlborough.'[31] In 1866, Bishop Cotton was drowned a fortnight after the foundation stone of the school he had envisioned had been laid at Simla by John Lawrence.

Bishop Cotton School, meant to be a replica of an English public school, was founded in 1863 at Jutogh as a thanks-offering to God for His deliverance of the British people in India during 1857. It was shifted to its present site in Simla three years later. The school was designed to bridge the educational and social gulf between the children of officials who came from England, most of whom sent their children to English schools, and the domiciled Europeans and Anglo-Indians.

The school was founded by public subscription and with financial assistance from the Government, which also had an active interest in the successful running of the school. On the Board of Governors, the four ex-officio members were the Lieutenant-Governor of the Punjab, the Bishop of Lahore, the Commissioner of Delhi, and the Deputy Commissioner of Simla. There were also four elected governors who were to be residents of Simla. The Viceroy was the school's Visitor. The parents of the boys were largely clerks in Government service, and there were also many who belonged to the non-official classes. An official report proclaimed, 'A European or Eurasian lad brought up and educated at Simla is, generally speaking, immeasurably superior to a lad brought up and educated in Calcutta or indeed anywhere in the plains.'[32] The Simla school was reputed the best.

The education in Simla might have been superior to any other in India but the social prejudice against the domiciled British continued. An office superintendent at Simla pointed out the crux of the problem: 'After spending a considerable sum on the education of my son at Christ-Church and at Bishop Cotton's School, Simla, I was obliged when he arrived at the age of sixteen years to consider his future. I sought the advice of a gentlemen of standing, experience and influence in Calcutta. He wrote, "I could have no doubt got him apprenticed in either Burn and Co. or Jessop and Co.'s engineering works, which would be good training for him . . . (but) managers of mills and factories here do not like country trained men." '33 Indian-born and Indian-trained were not considered suitable officer and manager material.

The local newspaper, the *Simla Times*, the mouthpiece of Anglo-Indian opinion at Simla, provided a ready outlet for the community's views. After the outbreak of World War I, it agitated for an Anglo-Indian regiment, a project that had been shelved by Curzon. An Anglo-Indian Empire League was formed in 1915 to press for this demand, which it did success-fully. 'Up till now the community had been treated as a child, to be disciplined, snubbed, corrected and kept in its place, a child they were somewhat ashamed of. That night things were altered.'34 The euphoria was temporary. It did nothing to enhance employment opportunities or status. In 1922, a *Simla Times* editorial lamented, 'On the one hand the Government make every use of them (as witness the Indian Mutiny and the Great War), and relegates them to subordinate positions; while on the other, the non-domiciled Europeans treat them with disdain.'35 The disabilities of the Anglo-Indian community, however, became more acute as the twentieth century wore on.

The threat to their position in the upper echelons of the clerical services came from the western-educated Indians. In the nineteenth century, Indians had begun to replace Anglo-Indians in the uncovenanted services, and in 1880, some posts in the provincial civil services were reserved for Indians. By 1921, with the implementation of the Montague-Chelmsford Reforms for the Indianization of the services, the Anglo-Indian community felt it had been ousted from its special preserve. Most Anglo-Indians viewed the Indianization of the services with apprehension, for it could mean the virtual end of their dominance at the clerical level. In 1922, in a mood of optimism, the local paper said, 'It was once said that the Anglo-Indian clerk ruled India. If the Anglo-Indian community wishes to retain its place in the sun, it must orientate afresh its outlook.'[36] The move to Simla proved crucial to Anglo-Indian fortunes, for as an urban group their stability was linked with government service. The Government of India Act of 1935 made provision to safeguard the community's continued employment in three services—the railways, posts and telegraphs and the customs. By 1942, however, the Anglo-Indian Conference in Delhi noted with alarm that while upto 1921, they could count only 1,000 unemployed, in the wake of Indianization of the services the number had mounted to 20,000. In Simla, Anglo-Indians were swamped by the increasing numbers of Indian clerks, though they retained their positions at the upper levels of clerical service. It was symptomatic of the changes taking place at Simla.

CHAPTER SIX

Property and Prestige

OLD maps of Simla always showed large houses marked by name, while the smaller ones had numbers against them, explained in a key. The Simla guidebooks detailed the conditions under which houses were to let. Edward Buck devotes about one-third of *Simla, Past and Present* to narrating the pedigree of old houses—each had a tale to tell of a Viceroy, or a Secretary to Government at least, who had owned or tenanted it. One of the characteristics of nineteenth-century Simla was the private ownership of houses by British officials, serving and retired. Over 400 of the estates of Station Ward were built, owned or tenanted by British officials. The pattern gave Simla its tangibly official and English atmosphere.

The Public Works Department bungalows in the geometrically laid-out civil lines in the plains were uniform and impersonal, while Simla's cottages were individual and personal. For British officials, each one bridged the distance in space and time to an English home, and for seven or eight months a year it was theirs.

Architecturally, houses in Simla were a mixture of the spacious bungalows built in the plains of India and nostalgic, sentimentalised memories of English cottages. A rectangular plan with a wide veranda and a porch in front (for parking rickshaws), was typical of the bungalow. On to it were grafted stylistic features like pitched roofs, gables, chimney stacks and fretwork eaves. This façade, however, concealed the traditional local hill techniques of construction utilized. Charles French, in 1839, had described a house being erected:

> A brittle kind of stone resembling slate, and which is procured in great abundance in the hills, is in the first instance shaped into squares or parallelograms by chipping off the ends and sides. These stones are then adjusted or laid down in layers of about

two or two-and-a-half feet in thickness, and this they do so
regularly and neatly without the aid of lime or mortar, that the
outer and inner surface appear sometimes like one piece with
slight crevices running over them.... At every two, three, or
four feet of the height of the wall, the adjusted pile of stones is
bound down with long pieces of timber laid horizontally over
the edge on each side, and connected by cross bars of wood.[1]

Hill temples and large houses are still built in this manner.
When stone is not available, another method known as *dhajji* is
used. A wooden frame is erected and filled with a mixture of
close-packed earth, gravel and pine needles to a width of upto
two feet. The ceiling and floors are made of panels of wood.

There was some experimenting with roofing material. Some
of the early nineteenth-century houses had flat roofs covered
with layers of beaten earth. This was not very successful since
muddy droplets streamed in after a sharp monsoon shower.
Emily Eden recounts that gentlemen sometimes dined with
umbrellas held over their heads and their dinners.[2] Wooden
shingles or slates, the latter most commonly used in the Simla
hills, were then tried. However, a roof could leak if the square
or triangular pieces of slate were not precisely formed.

Most houses were eventually roofed with corrugated,
galvanized iron sheets painted red and sometimes green. The
galvanizing process was patented by Craufurd in 1837 and
galvanized sheets were mass-produced a few years later in
England. Large quantities were shipped to the colonies.[3] This
sheeting could be transported to the hills with relative ease and
consequently crowned most Simla structures.

The larger, more favoured houses were situated on the
summits of ridges with the lower terraces forming the compound. They had beautiful views and were built to let in light
from all directions. However, the disadvantage of being surrounded by precipices struck Lady Dufferin forcibly: 'At the
back of the house [Peterhoff] you have about a yard to spare
before you tumble down a precipice, and in front there is just
room for one tennis court before you go over another.'[4] It was
more usual to have houses set back against the hill, so that the

rooms at the rear tended to be dark and gloomy.

Houses were either single or double-storeyed and had compounds of one or more acres of hillside attached to them. The veranda usually led into a lobby and then into a drawing room. Adjacent to it or behind was the dining room, while the bedrooms and dressing rooms were normally upstairs. Kitchens were several yards behind and separate from the house. Eight or ten, sometimes as many as twenty-five, single-roomed servant-quarters were within calling distance of the house; they accommodated the cooks, bearers, *masalchis*, ayahs, syces and *jampanis*. An ice pit in a shady corner stored snow for use during the summer months. An overhanging terrace with beds of English flowers would form the garden. Lastly, a slope would be levelled out into a tennis court.

In 1894, Constance Cummings described Simla houses as 'a good deal like Swiss chalets with a strong family likeness to each other'. Individual tastes accounted for the varying interior and exterior embellishments. The main entrance of Torrentium, for instance, was reached by crossing a small artificial pool surrounded.with weeping willows; a later owner replaced the lake and willows with a tennis court. Yarrows (now the Indian Audits and Accounts Training School), was built on the plan of a South African cottage, with a black timber-roof and a low-raftered ceiling with black and gold decor inside. There was a fountain in the paved courtyard at the entrance.[5]

Houses were a lucrative investment especially when new estates were built to accommodate the offices and residences required by the government after 1864. The estates meant for officials were usually large, fully-furnished and well-maintained, for they had to be commensurate with their status, and therefore the rents and values were always high. Houses were generally let for a season which commenced in spring on the first of April and ended on the thirteenth of November. It thus covered the varying dates of government residence at Simla.

There was hardly a house-owner more quarrelsome than the burly Major Samuel Boileau Goad. A retired officer of the

First Bengal Light Cavalry, Goad was one of the more influential property-owners of the 1850s.[6] Speculation led him to buy thirty-three large estates in Simla; these included the prestigious Barnes Court and Kennedy House, yielding an annual rent of 3,000 rupees each; and fifteen other properties which brought in between 1,800 rupees and 1,200 rupees each.

He also owned an assembly hall and a popular racquets court used by army and civil officers.[7] Yet for one reason or another, his litigious temper or aggressive ways, disputes would arise and Goad was always in hot water. He even maintained several armed gurkhas for his personal protection. One day, a Lieutenant Hill dismissed a court marker at Goad's racquets court calling him an 'impertinent pig'. Goad tried to prevent Hill from using the court, and when Hill insisted on playing, Goad sent for his private retainers to throw him out. Hill and the Simla Deputy Commissioner's brother, Frederick Hay, severely beat a gurkha retainer with a riding whip. The case went before the Deputy Commissioner, William Hay, and both were fined. The fracas occurred during the tense uncertain days of September 1857, and Goad was asked by the Deputy Commissioner to disband his armed retainers. When he obstinately refused to do so, the Deputy Commissioner called a contingent of the army from Sabathu to force him to do it.

Despite the clash with officialdom, five years later, in 1862, Major Goad because of his 'intelligence and wealth' and 'his experience of natives' had conferred on him the office of Justice of the Peace and Honorary Magistrate. Major Goad had in the meanwhile disposed of his racquets court, only to repurchase it six years later in 1863.[8] Once again he debarred from membership an officer he considered 'obnoxious', an incident which cost Goad his honorary magistracy. However, he retained his authority as a large property owner, and wielded enough influence to become President of the Municipality for five different years between 1856 and 1875.

Owning or tenanting a house in the village of Mashobra was a sign of status. It was more thickly forested than Simla and lay about six miles along the next ridge. The British brought with them their passion for the country—in England a retreat into the country would have been from the smog-filled industrial city; in Simla it provided an escape from the 'dust and dirt with which the bazars filled the Simla atmosphere.' Many found these bungalows an excellent rendezvous for picnics, others a refuge from the merrymaking of Simla. Some found reasons similar to the ones that had led them from the plains to the hills. Edward Buck found the environment both more salubrious and more conducive to work and official conferences, than Simla.

Edward Buck, Secretary to the Department of Agriculture, recounts how he purchased the Retreat with its 300 acres of attached forest: 'My introduction to the Retreat was in May 1869. . . . I sat on the bank opposite the house, half intoxicated with the beauty of the scene, [and] registered a vow that if ever fate should bring me to Simla those woods would be mine. Fate did lead me there in October 1881, and within a month those woods were mine.'[9] The house was let by the Rana of Koti for a petty annual rent of 100 rupees, which was raised to 200 rupees by Buck. The Rana tried in vain to cancel the lease. In 1896, Elgin, the Viceroy, spent several weekends there. After Buck's retirement, it was leased permanently as summer residence for the Viceroy.

The official élite at Simla lived like aristocrats. Houses acquired distinction from the civil servants who owned or tenanted them. For example, Stirling Castle, perched on the summit of the thickly wooded Elysium Hill was owned originally by a Mr Stirling. In 1838, Emily Eden described it 'as a bleak house that nobody will live in, and that is generally struck by lighting once a year.' But its location, commanding views and large grounds ensured it a succession of noteworthy occupants. Buck lists the owners and tenants. Between 1844 and 1850, it became the residence of Sir Fredrick Currie, Foreign Secretary to the Viceroy, Hardinge. He relates that in 1865 Stirling Castle became the property of Mr Moore, a solicitor, and in 1870 was bought by Mr Cotton, a well-known Simla merchant, who sold it to S. T. Berkeley in 1873. Seven years later W. W. Hunter purchased the house and resided there for several years. It was in Stirling Castle that he wrote his *History of the Indian People*. It then became the residence of Colonel Ian Hamilton, and later passed into the hands of Colonel R. M. Jennings, C.B., after which a Mrs Meakin lived there in 1896–8. Stirling Castle then belonged to General A. S. Hunter.

Sometimes officials acquired more than one house. In the 1860s, General Peter Innes owned several large houses, including Snowdon, Chapslee, Peterhoff, Inveram and Innes Own. Edward Buck, then Secretary for Agricultural Development, owned North Bank at Simla and the Retreat at Mashobra. Officials who bought houses during a Simla posting usually sold them at as high a profit as they could when they retired or returned to England.

Here lay the rub. The eager buyers of such properties or those who could be inveigled into purchase were the Indian princes. The princes formed almost a 'caste' within British society. Regarded, together with zamindars and *jagirdars*, as the 'natural' leaders of Indian society, they had been absorbed into the imperial system. Besides, their lavish style of life made them welcome figures in British society.

In the nineteenth century, most Indian princes, especially those from northern India, had some acquaintance with Simla on account of the numerous durbars held there. Until the 1880s it was felt that there should be increasing social intercourse between the native chiefs and the higher European officials as this would promote a good understanding between the two sets of 'natural' leaders.

Theodore Hope, a member of the Executive Council, expressed the desire to see the chiefs on a visit to Simla 'assuming gradually the position of noblemen coming up to town for "the season" or for short periods when "the court" was there.'[10] The princes were therefore to be permitted and encouraged to buy houses at Simla.

In the 1880s, several Indian princes and zamindars had purchased estates in Simla. They bought them not only to live in when they spent the summer at Simla, but like some British officials, as an investment, to rent out annually. Simla then threatened to be inundated by ruling princes who could be relied upon to buy up houses at exorbitant prices from wily estate agents. This was a trend not viewed with equanimity by officials who found it hard to get houses on rent.

, Estate agents and officials selling property sought out the princes as customers. In 1891, George Corstorphan, an estate agent, queried the Home Department, 'I have the charge of several large Estates in Simla with instructions from the owners to sell, some of these Estates are so highly priced that I think it is improbable any one but Rajahs will purchase.'[11] In 1890, the Nizam of Hyderabad had been persuaded by the retiring Commander-in-Chief, Fredrick Roberts, to buy his Simla house, Snowdon. 'I had an offer for "Snowdon" from the Nizam', Roberts divulged to the Home Department. 'It is unlikely that my successor, or indeed any European would buy the house, and as the Nizam is less likely than any other Native Chief to come to Simla, I think I had better sell it to him.'[12] In 1894, A. O. Hume, on his impending return to England, sought permission to sell his house, Rothney Castle, to an Indian ruler.[13] Both applications were rejected. Roberts was told: 'I think it is objectionable to have the Nizam owning a house in Simla where he is not likely to come and indeed is not wanted.' Snowdon was acquired by the Government as the official residence for the Commander-in-Chief.

Government discovered that the princes owned thirty-four of the large houses (with rentals of above 1,500 rupees per annum) in Station Ward.[14] This was one-seventh of the large houses available in Simla. The Raja of Cooch Behar, for instance, owned four properties: Rose Bank, Kennedy House, Kennedy Lodge and Guard House. The Maharaja of Faridkot owned Knockdrin and Ravenswood.

The Raja of Nahan topped the list with fourteen prize estates, which included Torrentium, Retreat, and Yarrows. Nahan acquired importance since it lay *en route* to Simla before the Simla–Kalka road was built. Emily Eden, passing through

Nahan in 1839, wrote of the ruler, 'He is one of the best looking people I have seen, and is a Rajpoot Chief, and rides, and hunts, and shoots, and is active . . . and if the rajah fancied an English ranee, I know somebody would be happy to listen to his proposal.'[15] The Maharaja of Nahan, entitled to a salute of only eleven guns, was relatively unimportant in the hierarchy. But he had light blue eyes, was reputed to be civilized and gentlemanlike—socially an acceptable figure in Simla.

By the end of the 1880s, it was decided to check the trend of Indian rulers buying property at Simla. It seemed 'impossible' to issue any positive prohibition to officers buying, selling or renting houses belonging to Indian princes. The Foreign Secretary wrote to the Chief Secretaries of all British administered states that 'The Viceroy has, therefore, decided that Native Chiefs should in future be discouraged from owning houses in Simla. . . . His Excellency does not wish to compel or press Chiefs who already own houses here to get rid of them. The object is to check the growth of the practice in future. At the same time, if there are any Chiefs who wish to part with their houses in Simla, it is desirable that they should avail themselves of any suitable opportunities which may offer for so doing.'[16] The reason given was the possibility of unsatisfactory dealings between officers and princes. It was apprehended that the princes would be unable to distinguish between their position as rulers and their position as houseowners and difficulties could arise about municipal taxation. Above all there was apprehension that the way might be opened to undesirable dealings and transactions with Government officers.

The Government at first considered imposing the rule which applied to military cantonments for special municipal regulations regarding ownership of houses. Finally, an Order-in-Council decided to withhold administrative permission to rulers to buy property at Simla and to block individual cases when they arose. No general order was ever issued but permission to sell to Indian rulers was seldom sanctioned.

The rule was extended to sales between two rulers. For instance, the Maharaja of Cooch Behar was denied permission to sell his two properties, Kennedy House and Rose Bank, to the Raja of Kapurthala.[17] Sales to British buyers, on the other hand, were usually encouraged. The comparison of princes with 'noblemen coming up to town' receded. Lansdowne, Dufferin's successor, wrote that the 'Government was strongly opposed to allow chiefs as a rule to hang about Simla.'[18]

And then came a precise set of rules formulated by the Foreign Office.[19] A formal visit by a chief or 'high officials of a native State' had to be preceded by permission from the Government of India. This meant outlining the object of the visit, the duration of the stay, the house in which he proposed to reside, and the names and degree of relationship of the members of his retinue. 'There is a great feeling against permitting native Chiefs to congregate at our sanatarium, as they bring up a quantity of followers, who have to be huddled together in close quarters, and are apt to bring cholera and all kinds of sickness with them.'[20]

A chief with a more than ten-gun-salute was treated to the ritual of *Mizaj Pursi* or a social call by an aide-de-camp, followed by the *Peshwai* or presentation to the Viceroy. The Simla visit together with gun salutes and procedures at official receptions, became one of the techniques manipulated to inculcate a habit of deference to Imperial authority.

No rulers were more frequent visitors and more controversial than those from Nabha and Patiala, who both owned property in Simla. A running feud, that had begun with their ancestors, continued over boundary disputes and matters of *izzat*,[21] and sharpened in the 1920s when they vied with each other for leadership of the Sikh community through the conduct of gurdwara politics. There were mutual complaints and recriminations, extensively reported by the nationalist press, which became entangled with growing nationalist opinion. In nationalist eyes, Nabha emerged as a patriot who paid the price by abdication; Patiala was branded as the one who resorted to illegal practices.

The rulers of Patiala, with an unbroken tradition of loyalty to the British, commenced their connection with Simla in the wake of the Gurkha Wars. They traced their ancestry back to the time of Babar. The title Maharaja was conferred in 1816 by Akbar II on the recommendation of General Ochterlony for services rendered during the Gurkha Wars. Apart from the title, the East India Company had rewarded Patiala (at a price) with substantial portions of hill territory won from the less pliant hill states of Keonthal and Baghat. At each subsequent crisis, the Sikh Wars, the 1857 Uprising, the Kuka uprising of 1872, the reward for loyalty had been an augmentation of territory or conferment of a title. Patiala, the largest of the Phulkian states, enjoyed a seventeen-gun-salute and was entitled to be received by the Viceroy. By 1882, the Patiala ruler had visited Simla several times and purchased three estates, Oakover, Rookwood, and Cedars, along the Mall.

Until the railway was constructed up to Simla, it was thought 'better not to run the risk of hurting his feelings' since the Patiala chief was one to whom every Viceroy was 'indebted for a certain amount of hospitality at Pinjore on the way to and from Simla.'[22] Patiala's espousal of causes affecting the Empire were an index of his frequent visits to Simla. During World War I, he had provided a contingent of 28,000 men and had served as India's representative in the Imperial War Cabinet. In 1916, the Maharaja handed over Oakover to the military authorities as a home for convalescent British officers.[23] In 1925 he represented the Indian princes at the League of Nations and was elected Chancellor of the Chamber of Princes.

The Patiala ruler's loyalty made the Government over-look many of his other misdemeanours. Of Rajinder Singh (1882–1900), it was said, 'He was a loyal chief, but his many good qualities were marred by a fatal weakness of will with the result that the affairs of the State have fallen into confusion.'[24] The name of his son, Bhupinder Singh (born 1891, succeeded 1900, died 1938), was popularly associated with the Scandal Point. His notoriety owed much to a highly denigrating and publicized pamphlet, *The Indictment of Patiala*, assembled by the All India States People's Conference in 1929, which charged him with turpitude, corruption, and maladministration. The Maharaja countered these allegations by requesting an official inquiry by J. A. O. Fitzpatrick, the Agent of the Governor-General for the Punjab State. The inquiry generally exonerated the Maharaja. His unswerving loyalty and shrewd foray into Sikh politics blunted criticism of his extravagance and bankruptcy. At Simla, where his six-foot frame and dazzling appearance fascinated the Viceregal staff he was a welcome figure;[25] his lavish hospitality enchanted officials and their wives; his polo team, the Patiala Tigers, received approval.

Patiala's rival Phulkian state, Nabha, also entrenched itself firmly in Simla. In the early years, a quarter of the Nabha territory had been confiscated during the Sikh wars. In the post-1857 period, Nabha had fallen in line and given repeated proof of his desire to contribute to the power and prestige of the Empire. Consequently, he was offered a seat in the Legislative Assembly, his salute was raised from eleven to thirteen guns in 1874, and to fifteen in 1898. Predictably he had acquired a large five-and-a-half acre estate, Innes Own. Val Prinsep mentions it as being furnished with colourful glass lamps and globes.

But, according to the Commissioner of Delhi Division, the Raja was possessed of a 'building craze'. As a calculated investment, he built seventeen houses with sixty-eight sets of quarters. The houses were leased annually to Indian clerks, who found them conveniently located below the Government of India offices. Nabha Estate, despite remonstrances and notices from the Municipal Committee, sprawled into a 'huge colony' with a summer population of 393 in 1907. Since relations with the Government were cordial, it was felt that 'the high character of the Raja is a guarantee that the settlement will in his time be properly managed.'[26] But Nabha Estate was princely property and hence outside municipal jurisdiction; although by 1928 the population on the estate had swelled to about a thousand, most parts of the estate had no sanitation and no drinking water facilities.

Nabha's eccentric behaviour, attributed to senility, vexed Simla officials. On two occasions he bought up a large number of animals being brought to Simla for slaughter, and sent them back to the plains, so that the town was deprived of its meat.[27] But British officials were mollified by his formal manners and undeviating observance of protocol. His period of rule was referred to as 'Nabha's Golden Age'. The ageing Hira Singh could boast of having driven twice within a period of four years in his carriage along the Simla Mall.

His·son, Ripudaman Singh, however, alienated the authorities by supporting a nationalist resolution, and his refusal to allow rituals at his installation durbar. In 1923, the Government's displeasure took the form of an inquiry, and the Commission found that charges of maladministration and other misdemeanours warranted abdication by the ruler. Ripudaman Singh was deprived of his title and his allowance was reduced. He was at first exiled to Dehra Dun, and then in 1928 ordered to reside in Kodaikanal. Though he could never visit Simla, his family continued to live at Nabha Estate, a constant reminder of him for the scores of Indian clerks who lived there as his tenants. The property with small houses was acquired by the Government in 1937.

A prince's visit to Simla thus became a symbol of official approbation and one to be given with care. In 1891, the honour of a holiday at Simla was bestowed on the Raja of Kapurthala because he had 'taken so much pains to educate himself, and is in every way such a creditable representative of the class to which he belongs, that he deserves special encouragement.'[28] A princely visit to Simla was in effect an index of the ruler's standing *vis-à-vis* the Raj.

While the British had divested Indian rulers of political ambitions, they were not equally successful in creating the enlightened, pliant ruler, dedicated to his subjects' welfare and to his work. It was an ideal which Curzon, the disciplinarian task-master, sought to instil. He pointed out: a 'prince's gaddi is not intended to be a divan of indulgence but a stern seat of duty.'[29] A mixed marriage for instance could be regarded as 'misconduct' and a 'disgrace'.

When the Raja of Jind secretly married Olive, the daughter

of a Bombay barber called Monalescu, Curzon was appalled. Olive had accompanied her mother, who was acting as parachutist to an American balloonist, Van Tassel, to Simla. The Raja and his newly-acquired wife were denied the privilege of attending a polo tournament, for for 'the Government of India to allow him to come up to Simla to amuse himself is rather to condone his folly. It will probably do the young man good to learn in the practical form of refusal of permission to come to Simla, that the Government of India are displeased with him,' an official noting stated.[30]

Similarly, the rulers of Cooch Behar and Dholpur, two frequent visitors, were denied permission to visit Simla in 1904. 'Cooch Behar and Dholpur are pleasant to meet in society . . . but both have now spent more than they can afford.'[31] The former was not able to finance a length of railway-line in his State; the latter had to take a loan of 3,00,000 rupees to avert bankruptcy.

When the princes were permitted to buy property, elaborate conditions were laid down. In 1921, for instance, the Nawab of Malerkotla was given permission to acquire Maisonette at Mashobra with the proviso that he could not transfer it, or create encumbrances, and would divest himself of the house when called upon by the Government to do so. It also became normal to exercise a 'little procrastination' every time there was a princely request.[32]

The princes continued, however, to be potential buyers of large estates at Simla. In 1930, an advertisement for three properties, Chapslee at Simla, and Sherwood and Cosy Nook at Mashobra, were described as 'eminently suitable for the summer residence of a Ruling Chief'.[33] Chapslee, with an impeccable history of owners and tenants, was one of the oldest houses of Simla. Constructed as Secretary's Lodge in 1838, it accommodated the offices attached to three Governors-General, Auckland, Ellenborough and Hardinge. It was bought by General Peter Innes who named the house Chapslee. It was the residence of an array of official notables such as Courtenay C. Ilbert, General Pemberton, General Sir C. E. Nairne, Surgeon General A. F. Bradshaw, Surgeon General J. Cleghorn, General

N. Arnott, and General Sir A. Caselee.[34] The house, a large double-storeyed structure, was sold in 1930 by the heirs of A. M. Ker to the Kapurthala family. It is preserved by the family till today, together with its Victorian decor. A panelled hall has painted escritoires from the Doge's palace in Venice; there are Venetian chandeliers and tapestries of Watteau scenes. In the bedrooms lace-covered taffeta quilts are set on brass bedsteads, while ewers and basins with floral designs stand in the bathrooms. It is a living museum.

Simla's pattern of distinctively British house ownership in the early years gave the town the air of one big family circle in an English town. By the turn of the century, British officials were seldom given permission by the Government to buy or sell property in India thus putting an end to the purchase of houses by them at Simla; nor could non-officials be prevented from selling to Indians. However, the prestige attached to owning property in Simla and the influence this commanded paved the way to large-scale purchases of houses by Indians.

While it had been possible to effectively discourage Indian princes from buying property, it was difficult to check all Indians, and large-scale property purchases by them eroded the influence of the non-official British houseowners. It was the landed aristocrats and affluent middle-class Indians who bought the prestige by closing in on Simla's property owner-ship structure.

CHAPTER SEVEN

Experiment in an Elected Municipality

O! for a business government, as John Bull has it.

Simla is essentially a European town, and should be administered by Europeans and Europeans of independent mind, elected by the tax payers.[1]

FOR British non-officials, Simla was an extension of John Bull's island. They believed it should have local, representative self-government that safeguarded personal freedom and fostered and protected trade and private enterprise. A strong local government was seen as a barrier or defence against an all-powerful central government: thus it would help to diffuse political power and result in a more efficient civic system. Since Simla resembled an English town as nearly as was possible in Indian conditions, it was assumed that it would have a local government elected by the tax payers. Who were these tax payers? In this context it is worth while examining the term 'interest'.

'Interest' is a word frequently used in Simla's municipal records till 1947. A Whig concept, it connoted that the quantum of tax paid to the municipality by individuals or institutions, including government, as houseowners or tenants, entitled them to a proportionate right in the running of local affairs. The owner of a number of properties had a proportionately higher number of votes than the owner of one.

Thus 'interest', not mere numbers, was the basis of representation. The idea reflected the conditions of mid–eighteenth century British society where local affairs were in the hands of a landowning gentry towards whose property and activity the State pursued a policy of non-interference.[2] It thus adopted the liberal predilection for constitutional advance by representation, and ensured the propertied a pivotal role in local affairs. At Simla, somewhat paradoxically and disconcertingly, the concept served to strengthen Government's hold over the town. The value of government property highlighted its stake in Simla.

As its tentacles spread and its imperial grip tightened, Government establishments grew in size, complexity, and influence, creating an expanding Government 'interest' in the town. Its infrastructural requirements also made property a lucrative investment. Many of the structures built for Government occupation and use as offices and residences, were large, with high rents and values. Houseowners, consequently, formed a significant interest in municipal affairs. The tussle for control over municipal functioning between Government and private interests began with the setting up of the municipality.

Simla's Municipal Committee was first constituted according to the provisions of the Government of India Act of December 1850. According to this, the government of any province was given the power to set up a municipal committee in any town where it was satisfied that the inhabitants of the town wanted one. Government was, in that case, authorised to appoint the magistrate and the requisite number of local inhabitants on the municipal committee. The Act conferred large powers for making civic regulations and levying taxes upon the committee.

William Edwards, Simla's Deputy Commissioner, was anxious that the Act be brought into operation in Simla because of the deteriorating civic conditions there. He informed the Secretary of the Board of Control of Calcutta:

> It is impossible for a magistrate in a place like Simla to enforce cleanliness or order of any kind within the limits of Private Establishments, his authority, decried and oftentimes resisted by European occupants, his Police, if they enter a compound, are in all probability forcibly ejected and strictly official interference has hitherto been of no avail.[3]

British houseowners resented official interference with their private property, and Edwards feared that the 1850 Act would be rejected. However he believed that if they worked in cooperation with the official magistrate, new taxes could be imposed to maintain a larger conservancy establishment.

He convened a meeting of property-owners at the Kutcherry in June 1851. There were then fifty European property-owners who, apart from the bazar shops, owned the 150 houses at Simla. They were serving or retired officers of the East India Company, private traders, businessmen, and widows who ran boarding houses. These houseowners agreed that the existing funds were inadequate to provide the necessary sanitation but challenged the magistrate's authority to enforce cleanliness. Above all they asserted doggedly that the local fund was one that he didn't have the right to 'control and direct'.[4]

At a subsequent meeting held in the Assembly rooms, two-thirds of them consented to introduction of the Act, provided that the Simla local fund was entrusted to a committee composed partly of houseowners' nominees. At a meeting held in July 1852, seven were elected commissioners, while the Deputy Commissioner was nominated ex-officio Chairman. When other ex-officio members were added, outnumbering the private houseowners, there were protests over the official infiltration into the committee, which had altered the representative character of the municipality.

Thirty-six houseowners submitted a memorial with an alternative code of rules and regulations decided at a meeting convened on 18 September 1854. As a result, a new constitution was framed in 1855. According to this, although the Deputy Commissioner was an ex-officio member of the Committee, the Municipal Commissioners were all elected by houseowners. In 1864, when the offices of the Government of India moved formally to Simla, membership was increased. Three ex-officio members were added—an Executive Commissioner, a Medical Officer and a Senior Commissioner—all nominated to represent the interests of the Government.

In 1871, Simla was given the status of a first-class municipality, one of the categories created by an Act in 1867. A first-class municipality was to enjoy independence with regard to expenditure, subject only to a government audit. The Committee was reconstituted again to consist of seventeen to twenty members. Seven of these were officials, nominated to the Committee. Between seven to ten houseowners, of whom three were to be Indians, were elected. Three representatives of the summer visitors were chosen by the Committee from a list of six submitted by the Deputy Commissioner. The newly constituted Committee was weighted so that the houseowners of Simla could exercise a preponderating influence.

By 1876, when Simla's status as summer capital seemed assured, extensive plans for its development were afoot. The system of municipal elections was abandoned to facilitate implementation of these plans by Government officials. The Committee was once again reconstituted to ensure official control. The Deputy Commissioner served as ex-officio President, and the Committee was limited to five nominated members, two salaried government officials and two houseowners.

Simla's private houseowners rekindled the controversy on the unrepresentative constitution of the municipality in 1881.[5] The attack on the 'despotic and arbitrary tendencies' of the Simla Municipal Committee was launched by Allan Octavian Hume.

He organized a meeting of houseowners at Benmore, and followed it by a memorial to the Government, criticizing the functioning of the Committee. Hume directed his censure towards the proposed construction of a Town Hall on borrowed money and without the tax-payers' approval.

Other memorialists were provoked to protest against the by-laws which interfered with the rights of private property owners. The *Pioneer* thought that the 'surest spot' of the whole controversy was the restriction on felling trees which residents found unnecessary and irksome. 'The Englishman in Simla cannot regard his house as his castle if he is not allowed to alter an outhouse or cut a branch of a tree in his compound, without having agents of the Municipality down his throat with injunctions and fines.'[6] Hume felt that an elected element in the Simla Municipal Committee would act as a brake on such arbitrary tendencies. To achieve this, he organized a Reform Committee of which he was secretary.

As a representative of the Liberal Party in England, Ripon, in the early months of his Viceroyalty, was anxious to promote local self-government throughout the country. It is not unlikely that he viewed Simla as a place where a model vigorous municipal government could function. That he was sympathetic to the municipal agitation spearheaded by Hume in 1881 is apparent from the following comment in the *Pioneer*: 'The Simla municipal agitation, like all other sweet hill-flowers, is budding out into renewed existence under the genial rays of the Viceregal sun.'[7]

Ripon's Resolution of 18 May 1882 on local self-government paved the way to a fresh experiment in municipal government in Simla. Since Simla was considered an English town where the electors and municipal commissioners would largely be British, it was assumed that there would be few problems in actualizing the ideal.

Charles Aitchison, Lieutenant-Governor of the Punjab, was also a warm supporter of the liberal experiment, and had unbounded faith in the public spirit of the official classes. He considered Simla a place in which there would be little difficulty in bringing into practical operation the principles of self-government.[8] Once the initial resistance of officials was overcome, 'there seemed no place so good, for nowhere else have you so intelligent a public to work it.'[9]

In Bombay, discussions about the constitutional framework extended for several months.[10] In Simla, in June 1882, a memorandum of fourteen points spelled out the basis on which the new municipal constitution was to be framed. It included issues of membership, the manner of election or nomination, qualifications for holding office, qualifications for voters, conditions for voting if a voter had more than one vote, division of the town into wards for the purpose of election, the election and position of the President, the role of the elected municipality, and the special precautions necessary to ensure representation and protection of the interests of the government.

A seven-member committee which included A. O. Hume, Edward Cullin, a lawyer, and J. Elston, a houseowner, was appointed by the Government to draft a suitable constitution for the Simla Municipal Committee. By September 1882, the Committee had submitted its recommendations. Despite four dissenting notes, the Committee favoured a wholly elected Municipal Committee.

The Committee's recommendations were based, predictably, on the concept of enfranchising 'interests' and 'classes' rather than individuals. Differences arose on the extent to which these different groups should be given the right to vote. The over-riding idea was that 'votes are apportioned to house proprietors and tenants not in proportion to their intelligence, but in proportion to the amount of taxes which they pay.'

The longest dissenting note came from Hume, the architect of the 1881 agitation for a reformed municipality.[11] Paradoxically, he cautioned against the sudden introduction of a purely elective system, since 'successful institutions are generally the growth of time—they develop slowly—evolution is the law of the entire universe.' Hume preferred a committee of which only two-thirds was elected, raised to three-fifths of the total within five years.

Hume advocated enfranchising a mixed bag of six interests. These included the Government of India and Punjab as landlords and tenants, European and Indian landlords and tenants; European professionals such as barristers, doctors, dentists, photographers, brewers; Indian lawyers and traders, including stall keepers, and all clerks drawing upwards of thirty rupees a month. After careful reflection, he added to the list magistrates of the Jutogh cantonment and *vakils* of ruling princes whose territories adjoined Simla.

The controversy affected another major 'interest'—government officers resident in Simla. Thirty officials held a meeting at the United Service Club to protest against the recommendations of the Reform Committee. The officers disliked the idea of playing at politics and submitting themselves to the indignity of an election. *The Civil and Military Gazette*, reflecting the views of such officials thus sarcastically described an At Home at the Lieutenant-Governor's: 'So all Simla arranged itself in *jampans*, in rickshaws, and saddles, and went off, rejoicing in the prospect of a fine afternoon, to play badminton and to give Sir Charles valuable and interesting suggestions on Local Self-Government and other matters affecting his province, which, being a Lieutenant-Governor, he of course enjoys discussing in public.'[12] But their views were not unmixed, and there were strongly differing opinions.

Charles Aitchison, the Lieutenant-Governor, was enthusiastic about local self-government in Simla, and a nucleus of officials held a meeting to lend support to the new constitution. *The Pioneer* sardonically commented on the 'ardour with which the apostles and advocates of the self-government policy are casting off the traditions of official life in the desire to manifest their zeal in the cause.'[13] The controversy was finally stilled when the new constitution was promulgated.

The Municipal Committee was to consist of thirteen honorary members, including the President, who was elected by the Committee. Members of the Committee had a three-year term, but one-third were to retire each year. All voters had to be resident at Simla for five months. Government officials as a class were not barred from contesting the election, although the Punjab Government could remove any salaried officer whose continuance was inconsistent with the proper discharge of his official duties.

There were two categories of voters: property owners and tenants. Different qualifications were prescribed for the Station and Bazar Wards. The first consisted of houseowners: male or female; resident or non-resident. In Station Ward they had one vote for every 1,000 rupees of rent on which house tax had been paid. In Bazar Ward, one vote was allotted for every twenty-five rupees of house tax or frontage tax paid. Male tenants in Station Ward had one vote for every 500 rupees of bona fide rental paid and in the Bazar Ward one vote for every quarter of it. A houseowner living in his own house qualified for voting as both houseowner and tenant.

The Government's voting power in Simla was measured in

proportion to the taxes it paid to the municipality as property owner or tenant. Such votes were exercised through persons nominated by Government from time to time on its behalf. Persons residing in Government houses qualified as tenants.

The Government vote was divided into three: the votes of the Government of India, the Punjab Government, and the Viceregal establishment. The Government interest in the town, therefore, rose with each new office and residence constructed. In 1882, government property was valued at 6,10,000 rupees; it was entitled to one-sixth of the total votes. By 1890, when the Army Headquarters, the Secretariat, the Foreign Office, and the Viceregal Lodge were built, its properties were valued at 25,50,000 rupees of a total of 76,00,000 rupees. Government therefore commanded one-third of the total possible votes. The principle eventually justified government take-over of the municipality.

In a similar manner, the interests of the two sections into which the town was divided were justified. In 1882, for the purpose of municipal elections, the town was divided into two wards—Station Ward and Bazar Ward—signifying not only the residential and commercial areas of Simla, but also the European and Indian. Bazar Ward covered all the five bazars of Simla—Lower, Chhota, Boileauganj, Lakkar and Kainthu. Shops on the Mall were, until 1900, included in Bazar Ward, thereafter in Station Ward. The interest of each ward in municipal affairs was established on the basis of the income they yielded to the municipality.

The interests of the two wards (see Table 1) was calculated in 1882. Since the Bazar Ward paid about one-quarter of the total taxes it was represented by three members on a municipal committee of twelve.

Table 1[14] *Taxes Paid by Wards (in rupees)*

	House tax	Conservancy tax	Frontage tax	Total
Station Ward	44,000	11,000	–	55,000
Bazar Ward	3,000	–	11,000	14,000

Elections under the new constitution were held on 1 August 1883 under a cloud of apprehension. On the eve of the elections, Hume wrote that 'in consequence of the principle involved, and in view of the widely spread diverse opinion that exists, it is extremely desirable that the new purely elective committee... prove a success.'[15]

In Simla, the divide between municipal and Government jurisdiction was often blurred. The efforts of non-official members to stay free of Government control on the one hand, and the reliance on large Government loans as well as the Government 'interest' in the municipality on the other, often led to a conflict. The first election, held in 1883, changed the complexion of the Municipal Committee. There were several surprising election results. C. L. Tupper, Under-Secretary in the Punjab Government, an advocate of local self-government in Simla, was defeated. A. O. Hume was elected, and became Vice President of the Municipal Committee. James Walker, a wealthy banker, became the Committee's President.

The conflict between Government and private interest and between officials and non-officials focused on the question of apportioning funds for any project in which a large expenditure was anticipated. There is the example of the Town Hall. The story of its construction illustrates the delays, deviations and distortions which made local self-government suspect in Simla.

The project of the Town Hall was enthusiastically initiated by the newly elected municipality of 1883. A subcommittee consisting of Hume, James Walker, Benjamin Franklin, the Surgeon-General, and R. G. Macdonald was assigned the task of overall responsibility for the construction. The new Town Hall planned in 1884 was to be completed by the summer of 1885. It was to cover an area of 1,602 square yards and cost 1,50,000 rupees. In September 1884, Government permitted the municipality to issue debentures bearing an interest of 6 per cent per annum and repayable at periods varying between three to eighteen years,[16] to part-finance the project.

Irwin, the architect and the Superintendent of Works, Simla Imperial Circle, was requested to 'gratuitously' design a Town Hall within the budget. F. B. Hebbert, Executive Engineer of the Simla Imperial Circle, was deputed to assist the municipality to 'supervise in a general way our Town Hall project in his leisure moments.'[17] Hebbert was co-opted as a member of the Town Hall subcommittee in October. It was to be constructed by contract and daily-paid labour. A PWD sub-engineer was appointed clerk of the works.

The estimates drawn up were grossly inaccurate since they were made on the basis of incomplete drawings,[18] but, construction began on 22 October 1884, even before the working plans were completed or subsoil tested. A tramway was laid from Lakkar Bazar to Sanjauli to carry away the rubble masonry. Labour was imported from Ajmer, Jaipur and Agra.

Within two months it became apparent that, owing to the weak foundations, a tower, planned to be the architectural focus of the building, would have to be shifted from the centre to the north-west corner. This, according to Irwin, upset the architectural balance of the building. He therefore recommended that an additional storey be built to restore the balance. The additional space, he pointed out, would afford extra accommodation for a volunteer's armoury and corridors around the theatre, all at a comparatively trifling extra cost of 18,000 rupees. The altered design was readily approved by the Municipal Committee. Hebbert further assured Committee members that the new design would be juxtaposed 'in such a way that most of the new walls coincide with the old ones.'[19]

In October 1885, when a newly constituted subcommittee comprising James Walker, James Craddock, Benjamin Franklin, Captain Litster and Hebbert examined the accounts, Hebbert discovered a miscalculation, 'an oversight which should now be rectified.' The additional sum of 18,000 rupees had been calculated on the basis of incomplete detailed plans, and the actual cost of the structure was now projected at 2,37,997 rupees. The miscalculation forced the Municipal Committee to raise a loan of 75,000 rupees to cover the cost of the additions.

By June 1886, a need for further funds was forecast. Despite 162 drawings and two framed elevations, the final design was still incomplete. However, a police reporting room had been added, and the upper storey above the theatre was designed as a drawing room. Extra funds were required because of expenditure on earthwork, on wages paid to labour and on the foundations and construction of the tower. The total sum required rose to 3,23,000 rupees.

A memorandum by the Vice-President laid the blame for the yet incomplete Town Hall and for the escalating expenses, on Hebbert, the engineer, for having 'either . . . willfully or recklessly misled the Committee.' Hebbert shrugged off responsibility by blaming the architect whose designs, he claimed, had become more and more ornate. Irwin, the architect, countered with the plaint that his designs were 'entirely a work of love'. The Committee could have rejected them. Amidst the welter of mutual recrimination, an inquiry was held by the Punjab Government.

Charles Aitchison fixed the responsibility for 'the deviations from the sanctioned plan . . . primarily on the Engineers-in-Charge and secondly on the Committee'. But as the file filtered through the departments of the Punjab Government and to the Central Government and then to the India Office, the responsibility of the engineers came to be rated second, the blame falling squarely on the Committee. In 1889, the Secretary of State fixed the seal of censure on the elected municipality in a communication to the Governor-General regarding the construction of the Town Hall:

> It is hoped that the history of this transaction to which I think full publicity should be given, will induce the rate-payers in the future to look more closely into the proceedings of the Municipal Committee and to elect as their representatives none but persons who will adequately protect the interests entrusted to them.[20]

The task of completing construction was then handed over to the Punjab PWD, and a loan of 25,000 rupees was given towards the additional expenses, bringing the total cost of the building to 3,50,000 rupees. The controversial eastern wing with its additional storey was ready, speedily and economically, the following year, in time for Queen Victoria's Jubilee celebrations.

It was not the most durable of structures. In winter, it was discovered that its hastily completed roofing leaked after a heavy snowfall. A cryptic note to this effect reads: 'Large Hall in at least 80 places... East gallery where the band used to play, in at least 30 places.'[21] This was ascribed to the fact that snowflakes had drifted under the tiles and they then melted and seeped through the wooden ceiling. A corrugated iron roof replaced the leaking tiled roof in the eastern part.

In the early twentieth century, officials recorded that the building had been 'badly bungled', the stone used was of the 'worst', and the design was faulty. Longitudinal cracks in the concrete vaulting and an inward movement of the walls, noticed in 1902, were attributed to the design of the trusses. Attempts to strengthen them led to the conclusion that they were 'radically wrong in design'. A part was dismantled.

By 1911 the cracks had widened and the cause was traced to the use of 'soft and friable calcareous rock' which was unsuitable as building stone. It was apparent that the more durable but expensive Kalka stone had not been used. H. H. Hayden of the Geological Survey reported that the stone had been obtained from the Kareru quarry on Prospect Hill between Jutogh and Simla.

A committee of experts in 1912 made three recommendations: first, dismantling of the upper floors; secondly, for a temporary roof to be installed above the theatre; and finally, that no part of the existing structure be incorporated in a new building since the trusses could not be strengthened. A. A. Begg, the consulting architect of the Government of India, rejected any plans to reconstruct the dismantled storey. 'If we were able to retain enough of the structure to be worthwhile from the point of view of economy, we should be tied to the rather egregious architectural style of the present building with its banal and tasteless pseudo-gothic details.'[22] New municipal offices were constructed, but the old dismantled Town Hall was preserved, housing the Gaiety Theatre.

The construction of Ripon Hospital likewise created tremors. A hospital contemplated in 1863 to replace an earlier 25-bed charitable hospital located in Lower Bazar, attracted Hume's attention. He took the initiative of reviving the plans and interesting the Viceroy, Ripon, in the scheme. The foundation stone for Ripon Hospital was laid in October 1882.

Hume headed the Hospital Committee which was to oversee its construction. With characteristic zeal he persuaded the visiting princes—Patiala, Dholpur, Jodhpur, Kotah, Travancore, Darbhanga, Kashmir, and Bahawalpur to make donations and subscriptions for its construction. Ripon Hospital was designed, like the Town Hall, by Henry Irwin during his leisure hours and in his private capacity.

Once again, friction arose over its construction. According to Act XIII of 1884 of the municipal by-laws the management, control and administration of every public institution maintained out of municipal funds vested in the Committee. However, since the Government of India and the Punjab Government had contributed 30,000 of the 1,47,000 rupees required, they disputed the Committee's right to total control of the hospital.

The Hospital Committee headed by Hume worked in connection with all matters relating to the collection of subscriptions and preparation of building plans. The conflict arose soon after construction began, when the Deputy Commissioner asserted his prerogative of checking the work of the Committee, and found that it had sanctioned rates higher than the estimates. An irate Hume retorted:

> Don't bother to write about rates to anyone, for *we* have sanctioned the estimate after a most careful consideration. . . . It is our business and no one else's. . . . Your letter clearly indicates that you fancy you have some responsibility in the matter; whereas you have none.[23]

Despite such clashes, the building was completed in three years and declared open by Dufferin on 14 May 1885. Ripon

Hospital was Hume's lasting service to Simla, before his resignation from the Municipal Committee in July 1884. In 1888, he declined to be the Life Visitor of the hospital declaring that he had consistently declined honorary titles; and if it involved duties, he could not find the time for them. He also fell out of grace at Simla—the officials hated him and Dufferin publicly criticized him.

Meanwhile, despite the fact that it was a municipal institution, the management was vested in a body of twelve Governors, of whom only three were members of the Municipal Committee. In 1910, when the municipality was an official body, the management of Ripon Hospital was entrusted to it again. The Committee would provide in bulk the money required for the upkeep of the hospital as sanctioned in the annual budget. The detailed allocation of funds under different heads was vested with the Civil Surgeon in his capacity as Superintendent of the hospital.

The manner of construction of the Town Hall and Ripon Hospital furnishes two examples of Government interest in operation. The Committee tried to modify Government's control over its functioning in various ways. One was by advocating the distribution of votes amongst various departments of Government. However, within the framework of the constitution, it appeared more logical for the Government to nominate its representatives than elect them. The novelty of an elected Municipal Committee waned, and little interest was evinced in the elections—in 1889, there were only seven candidates for five seats.

In 1889, Aitchison, the champion of local self-government retired. The following year there was a battle of memorials by the officials on the one hand, and the Committee on the other.[24] On 1 August 1890, a memorial signed by numerous officials and property-owning non-officials of rank was presented to the new Lieutenant-Governor. Amongst its signatories were tenants of several of the larger houses of Simla.

At the root of Simla's problems—the incomplete and defective sanitation, the open drains and the fact that the hill-sides were covered with garbage—was the failure of the representative system, the memorial pointed out. 'There is almost as much reluctance on the part of voters to exercise their right of voting for candidates as there is on the part of respectable residents to ask the voters for their votes.' Secondly, the diffused public vote was overshadowed by the solid Government one.

The Municipal Committee was roundly discredited for all the defective and incomplete civic arrangements as well as for the inadequate water supply. The fact that Simla's population had almost doubled during the 1880s and outgrown the civic amenities planned for it in 1879, was overlooked.

Despite a spirited defence by private houseowners and several traders, it was apparent that the conflict of interests made the smooth functioning of an elected municipality unlikely. The Government's dual role as an active partner in an elected Municipal Committee and as the guardian of effective municipal functioning contributed to the failure of the experiment.

The dominance of government interest in Simla was mirrored in the subsequent re-constitution of the municipality, the elected municipality of the previous decade having been declared by official opinion to be inadequate. The men who had conceived the constitution set up in the Ripon era as a model of local self-government in India were no longer at the helm of affairs, and many ardent supporters of the experiment had resigned or retired.[25] The local paper, referring to the sharp exchanges between officials and non-officials wrote: 'I am afraid that the committee as at present constituted is not "a band of brothers". There is a playing off of element against element, and when cliquism sets in, fraternity, and with it, usefulness takes flight.'[26] For this, the constitution of the Committee, combining official and non-official members, was held mainly accountable; on the other hand, a municipal committee dominated by the non-official British—estate agents, bankers, houseowners and traders—in a predominantly official town, seemed untenable and unworkable.

In 1891, the Committee was reconstituted to consist of four

nominated and six elected members. Of the latter, the two Wards were represented by three seats each. As before, the nomination of Government officers and the redistribution of seats tended to erode the influence of the British non-officials.

The Indian representatives from Bazar Ward were non-controversial, virtually ciphers, who did not understand English. In 1883 the Municipal Committee passed a resolution saying that, 'with a view to the expeditious dispatch of business a majority of the Committee shall decide what matters are proper and necessary to be explained in the vernacular to the Indian members.'[27] This was meant to include all questions in which general principles were involved, expenditure of money, and other matters relating to the Bazar. However, it seemed 'inexpedient' to appoint Indian members to a subcommittee even for the special inspection of the Bazar,[28] and they were doubtless induced to cast their votes in favour of Government resolutions. With such a composition it was possible for Government to effectively control municipal functioning.

In 1900, the elected seats were reduced to five. In 1908, the façade of elections was removed and for reasons affecting the 'public interest' the Municipal Committee was reconstituted to consist of seven nominated members, of whom only four were ex-officio Government nominees. The Deputy Commissioner served as President. Three 'interests', those of houseowners, traders and the Indian communities were represented by three nominated members.

The 1880s had however laid a precedent: the Committee met weekly to confirm proceedings and take fresh decisions. In 1884, two permanent subcommittees, one for finance and the other for executive and general affairs, were appointed. From time to time various *ad hoc* committees were set up to inquire into complaints, the construction of large buildings, etc. Each Municipal Commissioner was given field duties, one of the four Wards into which the town was divided. The Ward Commissioners were authorised to grant permission on the spot for routine or trivial matters, reporting them for formal confirmation by the Municipal Committee.

The experiment with a wholly elected municipality bequeathed a lasting mistrust of democratization. The enfranchising of interests based on the quantum of property tax paid as owner and tenant, made the Government, since it dominated the town with its offices and officers, the single predominating interest. Government became both an active partner and umpire in municipal matters, in cases of disagreement and conflict with non-official interests. The elected officials, though trained in a system of paternal rule, were expected to usher in a model system of local self-government.

CHAPTER EIGHT

The Official Impress

THE kingpin of Government 'interest' was the Deputy Commissioner. Simla town had the only first class municipality in the district, although the Deputy Commissioner also exercised the function of the Municipal Committee in the suburb of Kasumpti and those of the District Board throughout the district. The Simla tract was *nazul* land, held in trust for, and under order of, the Government. The proceeds of all land sold was invested in Government paper while the Municipal Committee was entitled to utilize the interest for current expenditure. After 1902, the Deputy Commissioner served as ex-officio President of the municipality. He was the spokesman, and supervised its civic functions. He also reported on the functioning of Municipal Commissioners.

A member of the Punjab cadre of the Indian Civil Service, Simla's Deputy Commissioner functioned under the watchful eye of both the Imperial and Punjab Governments. His authority extended over Simla District of the Delhi Division (Ambala Division after 1911) of the Punjab. The district included the town and nine small tracts adding up to about 101 square miles. It included the sub-tehsils of Kotkhai and Kotgarh. Another sub-tehsil included the Bharauli tract, a narrow eight-mile strip of British territory stretching from Sabathu to Kiarighat. Besides these, the cantonments of Jutogh, Sabathu, Solan, Dagshai, and the Lawrence School located at Sanawar, came under his jurisdiction. The Deputy Commissioner maintained law and order and as District Magistrate was responsible for the criminal justice of the district, civil justice being administered by the District Judge; his other important task was collection of land revenue. Land settlement implied a contract between Government and cultivator or agent. A series of settlements in 1834, 1856 and 1882–3 achieved their purpose—a substantial increase in income from land revenue.

From 1858 to 1935, the Deputy Commissioner was also ex-officio Superintendent of twenty-eight small hill states, known as the Simla Hill States. As the Crown's representative, he was entitled to show the imperial flag, and to a fifteen-gun salute, two more than the largest of the hill rulers. Curiously, in independent India, states such as Haryana, Punjab and Himachal Pradesh, continue this practice:all deputy commissioners and police superintendents are entitled to fly a flag, presently a black one with the words D.C. or S.P. embroidered in white, on their vehicles.

The Deputy Commissioner was assisted by two Assistant Commissioners, one of whom remained at Simla the whole year round as Assistant Superintendent of Hill States. The other was attached to the district during the summer months and was in charge of the jail and treasury.

Despite this awesome list of duties, the office of the Deputy Commissioner at Simla was a 'light' charge. The tenure was often for a fleeting few months: in the seventy-six years from 1859 to 1935, there were eighty-four incumbents.[1] Officers requiring a spell of convalescence were often posted there, especially during summer; in winter the charge was often given to accommodate an officer pending orders or in between assignments. It gave rise to doggerel like the one below that appeared in a local newspaper:

> It is hard we know
> In a place so slow
> To earn advancement and promotion.
> A bomb or two,
> Would be welcomed by you,
> Just to give you a chance, I've a notion.
> But sedition you know,
> In Simla doesn't go;
> So you've got to look around you s'what I say.[2]

The verse pinpointed one reason for Simla being a comfortable assignment. Besides, the routine civic administration of Simla was entrusted to a municipal official—its paid Secretary.

Simla's first Secretary to the municipality, Horace Boileau Goad, left the stamp of his personality on the office. During his tenure it was said that few may have known of the existence of the D.C. but everyone knew Goad. To European Simla he represented the active principle of Government.

Goad became a legendary figure in his lifetime. He was the son of Major Samuel Boileau Goad, a large property-owner, notorious for his cantankerous outbursts against officers. Horace Goad, unlike his father, distinguished himself as white Simla's *alter ego*. He was a genial hearty man, and the picture of bustling activity in his navy-blue serge suit and a thick stick in his hand.[3] 'If a landslip came down, if a tree fell across the road, if a roof fell in, a drain got itself blocked, or anything went wrong, in a few minutes Mr Goad and his alpenstock was sure to be on the spot seeing things put right, while his pony and dog looked on critically at their master's proceedings.'[4] He was known for not leaving work to his juniors and could be counted upon to be strict with his subordinates.

Buck writes that he kept the market *banias* and dealers in better control than any man had done before, and that ayahs quietened children with the threat of handing them over to 'Goad Sahib'.[5] A newspaper reporter in 1894 commented that he was a household word all along the route from Ambala to Simla, describing how the driver of his tonga cautioned each stable where they changed horses that 'Goad Sahib' was coming behind them.[6] His knowledge of Indian languages and customs, combined with a genius for disguising himself, made him a ready-made character for Kipling to use in some of his stories.

Goad served the Simla municipality in an honorary capacity for three years, and later as paid Secretary for seventeen years, from 1877 until his retirement in 1895. He was a Deputy Superintendent of Police in the North-Western Provinces when he was recommended for appointment, at a time when 12,00,000 rupees was allocated by the Punjab Government for the improvement of Simla. In an official noting, his superior commented that 'he was a much better officer for outdoor work than for office work,' and to put him in charge of the treasury or ordinary judicial business would be a 'great loss of power'.[7] Likewise, the Lieutenant-Governor of Punjab thought him 'the best man available'. He was thus assigned the work of supervising changes outlined by the Simla Improvement Committee of 1877, which included the task of removing the bazar adjacent to the church on the Ridge and ordering the Lower Bazar into a more 'sanitary' habitation.

Goad earned commendation in several annual reports of the municipality for his 'interest' and his 'knowledge, experience, aptitude for the work and zeal in the discharge of his executive duties which render him a peculiarly valuable officer to the municipality.'[8]

Goad's otherwise successful career came to a tragic end. He shot himself on 12 February 1896, a little over two months after his retirement, in October 1885, the very day that the PWD office went up in a fiery blaze. (Many Indians saw this as Goad's funeral pyre since he had foretold a disaster on the day of his death.) Contemporary newspapers reported that his suicide was the effect of melancholia and depression brought about by ill-health,[9] while a local story goes that it was caused by depression at the fine of two annas imposed by the municipality he had served so faithfully. (It was the practice to impose fines only on Indians for violation of municipal directives.) The municipal records however do not substantiate any action against Goad.

During Goad's tenure, the municipal administration was structured to suit the needs of Simla as summer capital. The Secretary exercised general control over the whole municipal establishment, and, with the approval of the President, had wide powers to appoint, dismiss, reduce or fine subordinate employees. The municipality had various departments; the tax and octroi departments, which earned the major income; a medical officer who was in charge of the medical department managed Ripon Hospital and the dispensaries; a public health officer covered conservancy, registration of births and deaths, the market and slaughter houses; and a public works department, manned by an engineer of roads and buildings and assisted by a staff of supervisors, overseers, building inspectors and draftsmen, maintained buildings, roads, and supervised street watering, while a municipal engineer looked after the water works and drainage. The municipality added an electricity department in 1914. Lastly, an education department of which the Secretary was ex-officio head, provided Simla with its schools.

Simla became one of the most highly-taxed towns in India. In 1890, the rate of municipal taxes per head was Rs 7–8–0 as, against Calcutta's Rs 7–11–4, or Bombay's Rs 4–6–4. The average in Punjab towns was Rs 1–1–0.[10] Over the years hill stations generally paid higher rates than metropolitan cities, and Simla continued to be the highest taxed town: in 1914 its per capita tax was Rs 15–2–0 while Mussoorie ranked second at Rs 10–1–3, and Darjeeling third at Rs 8–6–9.[11]

There was a continuous need to augment municipal income, and this was achieved in a variety of ways, often to the detriment of the interests of the local people. A study of the municipal balance-sheet reveals that the tax on property formed the largest single source of municipal income.[12] In 1890, house and ground rent from both wards amounted to about 30 per cent of the total. The residences of Station Ward were charged ground rent according to the built-up area of the estate. In 1855, the municipality charged a house tax as well, which was assessed on the basis of the rent which an estate could realize per annum. House tax was calculated in 1855 at 3 per cent of the rental, in 1871 it was raised to 5 per cent, and in 1879, in order to defray the cost of the water supply scheme, it rose to 10 per cent.

Indian traders in Lower Bazar were subject to the annual payment of one rupee, called *teh zamini*, for land from six to sixteen square feet, depending on the location. In addition to the ground rent paid on the Mall, traders were assessed for frontage tax according to the frontage they occupied on the Mall. In 1886, this tax was also imposed on the Lower Bazar at the rate of two rupees per running foot.[13]

Some of the earliest large European estates had been built

above and below the Cart Road and consequently were assessed for both ground rent and house tax. When some of them were split up and built upon, the new occupants, mostly shop owners, continued to be assessed for ground rent. In 1906, in order to standardize calculation, the distinction between ground rent and *teh zamini* was eliminated, with grantees of the latter being treated as tenants in perpetuity. [14]

The second largest source of municipal income was octroi. When the Punjab Government framed the rules for levying octroi in 1871, it divided towns into two categories: those which were centres of trade or were situated on trade routes, and towns through which little or no trade passed. Simla fell into the second category since re-exportation from Simla to the hinterland was negligible. [15] Octroi was levied for the first time at Simla in 1875 only when the municipality required additional funds to provide for civic amenities. Four years later, in 1879, the rates were revised to help the Municipal Committee to liquidate the loan raised for the water supply scheme of Simla. Thereafter, it remained, except for a gap of a few years, a remunerative source of municipal income.

Octroi was collected at check posts set up at the municipal boundaries. It was levied on food, articles for fuel, lighting and washing, articles used for house construction, tobacco, spices, perfumes, etc. The tax irked the trading community which believed that there was a tendency to throw the burden of direct taxation on trades people, and that their interests were ignored because they were numerically insignificant. The local newspaper, *Liddell's Simla Weekly*, provided the main forum for their views.

Octroi was a perennial source of friction between them and the Government. According to the Punjab Government ruling of 1871, Government of India and Punjab Government establishments were exempted from paying octroi for all items they imported. The Municipal Committee in one of its annual reports commented:

> Though the presence of these governments greatly increases the local burdens, yet they do not bear their fair share of taxation

with the other rate payers, being wholly exempt from octroi charges.[16]

Subsequently, octroi for the Viceregal establishment was compounded for an annual charge of 150 rupees, and the Punjab Governor's and Commander-in-Chief's residence at 25 rupees per annum each. For well over a quarter century British trades-men agitated against these figures. A letter in the local weekly stated 'Surely there is some ridiculous mistake in these figures. They have left some noughts out. It is not much to say that these households get things out by the ton, and make a regular trade of it. Yet they compound for these ridiculous sums.'[17] They accused influential Government officials of evading octroi by importing items directly from England through the post.[18]

It was always a problem raising funds for municipal expenses. A tax was devised on vehicles drawn by men, horses and mules. The burden, therefore, was spread evenly on illiterate mule drivers, rickshaw *chaudhris* and houseowners wealthy enough to maintain vehicles and own animals.

Employers were taxed on the menials and domestics working for gain. The returns on animals and vehicles amounted to 3 per cent of the total income, and the servants' tax yielded, by 1890, 4 per cent of the total, only a little less than the frontage tax. Additional sources of income were the 1,150 acres of forest attached to the municipality, and the rent realized from buildings such as the theatre attached to the Town Hall, the market, etc.

The cost of maintenance of the water supply formed 25 per cent of the total expenditure. Since Simla functioned as a sanatorium, the second highest expenditure, about 20 per cent, was on public health and medical facilities; street lighting and road maintenance and watering took up about 7 per cent; and police charges about 18 per cent. The expenditure on education was only 5 per cent.

Towards the close of the nineteenth century, Government interest in Simla steadily increased. The concern for provision of civic amenities is evident from the plethora of official reports initiated at the highest level. While officials of the Government of India and the Punjab Government sketched out the overall development plans and the priorities for Simla, the routine civic work was handled by the Municipal Committee. The funds for these larger projects were sanctioned partly as loans and partly as a grant by the Government. For instance, the vast amounts spent on the gravitational water supply scheme and the compensations to be paid for removal of the bazar from the Ridge in 1877, were met by a grant of 7,00,000 rupees, and a loan of 5,00,000 rupees, for which the Municipal Committee had to find sources for repayment.

Successive reports detailed the civic needs of the town—water supply, sewerage, drainage, roads, electricity and street lighting. They outlined the manner in which they were to be financed and the additional municipal taxation required. A series of extension and improvement reports—the Report of the Simla Extension Committee, 1898, Report of the Simla Improvement Committee, 1907, Report of the Simla Improvement Committee, 1914, provide an insight into official plans and priorities. The Report of the Simla Extension Committee of 1898 laid the foundations for future development, pinpointing possible areas for expansion and the sources which could be exploited to increase the water supply. The Report also surveyed the composition of the Indian population living in the bazars. The subsequent Improvement Reports of 1907 and 1914 assessed the progress made on the plans outlined in 1898, and drew up fresh plans for the future. These broad plans were supplemented by specialized reports on the technical feasibility and other details of such plans. These included the Report of the Simla Water Works Committee of 1904, and Report of the Simla Sanitary Investigation Committee of 1905.

The composition of the committees which drew up the reports is an excellent index of the official interest taken in these plans. The chairman was invariably the Home Secretary in the Government of India, and of the five to eight members drawn mostly from the civil services, the leading ones were secretaries to the Government of India and the Punjab Government in the finance and public works departments. The Sanitary

Commissioners of both the Government of India and the Punjab Government, and the Deputy Commissioner of Simla, completed the team of government officials; only one member was nominated from the Municipal Committee.

The official impress was amply evident both in the proposals and the priorities laid down for implementing and executing the civic plans. Not every proposal and recommendation fructified into a tangible road or sewer, but the ones that did had the weight of official authority behind them. For instance, a road from the church to the convent along which lay several large estates, and 'a new driving road around Summer Hill', were given precedence over others.[19] 'These monuments of municipal sycophancy' were resented by non-official British residents, who would have preferred to have priority given to roads to Khalini or Bharari where they lived.[20] The municipality, as everything else, had become an adjunct of the Government.

CHAPTER NINE

The Problem of Numbers, 1898–1921

Simla is overcrowded, and was really very unhealthy this year, it will never be a good hill-station. However, we should do what we can to make it bearable.

Memorandum, 1871

I regard Simla in a general way, as vastly overbuilt and overcrowded in the summer season. . . .

Sanitary Commissioner, 1898

A paranoic fear of overcrowding underlay official decision-making about the urban growth of Simla. There was a dread that the hill station, cool, clean and disease-free, would become 'unhealthy' and 'insanitary'. The fear had materialized in 1875 when cholera claimed 184 lives.[1]

The popularity of hill stations as sanatoriums never failed: 'whatever the ailing, low fever, high fever, "brandy pawnee" fever, malaria caught in the chase of tigers in the Terai, or dysentery imbibed on the banks of the Ganga, there was only one cure, the hills, and the chief hill station was Simla.'[2] Each visitor hired a retinue of cooks, bearers, *masalchis*, ayahs, *bhistis*, *jampanis*, rickshaw coolies, syces, all seemingly necessary, yet potential typhoid, cholera and enteric-fever carriers. 'The dung of this score thousand human beings is daily scattered over the neighbourhood in every direction, and . . . is a much more fertile source of sickness than the jungle or damp or dryness or any other local cause,' an adjutant had fumed in 1851. Simla would 'soon become a Pestilentarium instead of a Sanatorium'.[3]

It had been assumed that visiting Indian princes with their large entourages were the culprits. In 1905, it was suspected that Nabha's entourage was the origin of enteric fever. In 1915, the remedy to overcrowding at Patiala's Oakover took the form of a regulation, applicable to all houses, limiting the number of servants who could be accommodated on the premises.[4] In view of the restricted funds and the high cost of civic amenities, the answer to the problem of overcrowding was simplistically logical: to restrict the population and urban expansion of Simla. It was a solution which found expression in late ninenteeth-century policies.

Fanshawe, the Commissioner of Delhi Division, likened Simla to a cantonment,

> the outcome of our rule and the peculiar conditions of that rule, and there is no reason why we should admit persons to be residents of the place except upon such conditions as we consider necessary with regard to the peculiar conditions of it. Sentimental reasons of freedom of movement and politico-economic reasons of liberty of trade do not apply to such a case.[5]

The conviction grew that Simla derived its existence from the Government, that Simla, being the summer capital, was built primarily for the needs of Government officials. Two further assumptions followed: firstly, that Simla's population, and hence also its physical expansion, could and should be checked. Secondly, that such a policy was essential to maintain its official and British character.

The concern over Simla's physical expansion and increasing population led to frequent monitoring: the all-India decennial census, taken in February or March when Government employees and holiday visitors were not present, was considered less representative than the figures of a summer census for planning civic amenities. At a municipal summer census, a preliminary head count was finalized on an assigned census day, when all residents were required to stay indoors and keep their houses lighted until the census enumerators had filled in their returns. Such a census had its pitfalls: the accuracy of the summer census of August 1898 was doubted since a storm and heavy downpour at night might have deterred the census staff

from making house-to-house checks of residences lying along
slippery hill paths. Censuses were taken in September 1904,
August 1907, June 1911 and July 1914.

A predictable demographic feature was the wide divergence
between the summer enumeration, when the Government
was stationed at Simla, and the winter count. In 1911, for
instance, the summer population was 37,895, almost 20,000
more than the winter one, whereas by 1931, it had increased by
25,000 over the winter one, which had remained stationary.[6] Till
1911 the winter population was about half that of the summer, although it stabilized into a permanent population of
about 18,000. This was a familiar hill-station pattern; Nainital's
population doubled; Darjeeling's increased by two-thirds.

Functionally, Simla could be described as a migratory and
service town, as the occupational break-down of the Simla
summer population reveals. In 1904, of the total working
population, 26.4 per cent were in government service, and 33
per cent in domestic service. Unskilled labourers constituted
16.8 per cent and artisans, mainly carpenters and tailors,
accounted for only 8.6 per cent of the population, while 14.8
per cent of the population consisted of traders and shopkeepers.[7]

The racial characterstics of Simla's urban population were
spelled out in 1898. 'Simla consists of a European and Eurasian
colony, mainly in government service, the army or in commercial dealings supported by those classes, with a peculiarly
large proportion of children, and the native population is, as
a rule, attracted by the service of the colony, and not being
permanently domiciled in the place comprises a remarkably
small population of women and children.'[8]

The statement reflected the British perception of the town.
The most important part of the population, the officials, represented only a little over one per cent of the actual workers.
Another significant feature was the proportionately high
number of European women; the summer census of 1911, for
example, shows that for every 100 European males there were
98 females. The highest female ratio, 109 to 100, was amongst
the Anglo-Indians, who were employed as clerks in government

offices and European firms. The report gave as the reason for the high proportion that, in addition to their immediate families, Anglo-Indians took up female relatives to the hills as well.[9] In sharp contrast, the Indian ratio was 27 females to 100 males, reflecting the fact that traders, artisans, and labourers especially, left their families behind when they came to Simla.

The municipal summer census of 1898 confirmed suspicions of a marked increase of Indians in Simla. To the collective dismay of the hierarchy of officials, the Indian population had risen from 20,779 in 1889 to 29,048 in 1898, an increase of forty per cent. It was felt that the increasing Indian presence could easily swamp Simla's European and salubrious features, raising the bogey of an overcrowded and built-over Simla.

There was an official consensus, from Curzon downwards, that expansion of the town was 'extremely undesirable'; it was essential 'to restrict and retard' it and to find ways and means to prevent any large-scale influx of population, particularly Indian. This view was reflected in two of the five terms of reference of Simla's Extension Committee Report of 1898:

> Whether it is desirable or possible to take any measures for preventing or limiting the extension of Simla.
>
> Whether there is any method by which the influx of unemployed persons into Simla can be regulated and controlled.[10]

The second clause had been included on the recommendation of the Governor-General-in-Council as one in which the Government of India were 'greatly interested' since it was closely linked with the former question. The Simla Municipal Committee resolved that if Simla expanded beyond the capacity of the water supply the probable result would be 'shrinkage, followed by loss of capital to those who have invested in house property and by other forms of disaster.' The resolution echoed the interests of British private property owners. It was left to Simla's official planners to devise a method of curtailing its population and thereby growth. The Extension Committee of 1898 had reported that although expansion was 'undesirable' it was 'difficult or impossible to prevent', and had accordingly earmarked areas for expansion for a projected population of 60,000.

The Committee apprehended that, as the building of the railway to Kalka in 1891 had stimulated a sharp increase in population, extension of the railway to Simla would result in a further spurt in population. Since the agreement for construction of the railway had already been signed, the Committee rightly assumed that the company would object strongly if extraordinary measures were suddenly taken to restrict the normal growth of the town. It therefore recommended suitable legislation and a massive tax on persons visiting or residing in Simla, except those in government service. Several expedients on many fronts were attempted.

One of the most publicized measures to check overcrowding was Curzon's proposal of removing the summer headquarters of the Punjab Government from Simla to Dalhousie. It was surmised that every official who came up to Simla brought with him, directly or indirectly, six to a dozen followers: clerks, servants and labourers, and these in turn required additional shops and shopkeepers. In 1898, detailed investigations were made to determine the reasons for overcrowding in the bazar areas, inhabited primarily by traders, government servants, artisans and labourers who provided essential services to the town. It was reasoned that a reduction of Government officials would automatically reduce the number of other categories of population. Curzon made a public statement about shifting the Punjab Government out of Simla, however, without consulting the Lieutenant-Governor of the Punjab, Mackworth-Young.[11] The proposal exacerbated the already strained relations between them. At a Masonic Lodge banquet on 11 June 1901, Mackworth-Young gave vent to his irritation regarding the proposal:

> In regard to this matter I can only say, I have received no communication to this effect. I do not mean this is any reason against such a possibility, but I presume we shall at all events have three months to quit. I hope it may not be taken amiss if I say that a hill-station where the full glare of the Supreme Government may be softened by distance would possess some fascination for a Lieutenant-Governor and his hard-worked satellites.[12]

The speech was given wide publicity.

The Punjab Government held two departmental surveys, in 1901 and 1902, to determine the exact strength of its employees and their dependants in Simla. The results were counterchecked in the municipal summer census of 1904. The census figures indicated that the Punjab Government was responsible for a population of less than 1,000, and occupation-wise, contributed 13.4 per cent of the officers, 28.9 per cent of the clerks, 20.3 per cent of the peons and office servants, and 37.4 per cent of the domestic servants in Simla.[13] The *Pioneer* commented: 'The revised Census figures have come as a surprise to those who thought that several thousand persons were "dependent" on the Punjab Government.'[14] The transfer of the Punjab Government was never pursued, for the census results were announced when Curzon was away on leave in England, and the Punjab Government continued to come annually to Simla.

As for the influx of unemployed vagrants and mendicants, while officially, they could not be checked, in practice, the erection of a plague post at Tara Devi, where the name and address of every visitor was noted, proved useful.[15] The health authorities forwarded a copy to the superintendent of police, and thus a dual purpose was served: of excluding the afflicted and acting as a check on undesirable visitors. The system enabled the police to exercise surveillance over nationalist agitators and political workers, especially after 1921. (The rule was rescinded in 1950.)

There was a steady increase in the number of Indians, especially coolies, who now 'crawled' into Simla annually. In contrast, Simla's early history had been marked by a comparative reluctance on the part of Indians to live there. In 1858 it was noted that 'the natives of the plains detested the climate of the hills, and are induced to come up by nothing but by the hope of the huge gains to be made there.'[16] Labour had been difficult to procure. The petty agriculturists of the surrounding sparsely-populated hills were invariably reluctant to work as human beasts of burden. Yet thousands of labourers were required for road and house construction, for porterage, and domestic service—the Viceroy alone needed about 2,000 on hunting trips. In the 1880s, enterprising contractors began importing load-carrying labour from Kashmir, and labour for house construction from Ladakh, while rickshaw-pullers and coolies came from the arid regions of Bilaspur, Hamirpur and Hoshiarpur.

It was estimated by the Municipal Committee that 300 additional coolies employed in and residing in the Lower Bazar had entered Simla after the construction of the railway in 1903. A ropeway was then constructed connecting the railway goods terminus with the Lower Bazar, a distance of about three-quarters of a mile,[17] to reduce the number of labourers required for transporting commodities. It was assumed that diminishing work would also reduce the coolie population of the Bazar. It is not very clear if the ropeway enabled the Municipal Committee to reduce overcrowding, but it did prove convenient to the grain-dealers. The ropeway broke in 1932 and was dismantled.

From the point of view of the Indian residents of the Bazar, one of the problems was the location of the red light area. In most cities, brothels are situated in the heart of the commercial centre; Simla was no exception. The earliest nautch girls had been brought up in the trail of the first traders who set up the bazar on the Ridge. In 1832, Kennedy had debarred nautching (dance shows), after nine o'clock. A few years later, Emily Eden had noticed them in the bazar and wrote: 'Some of the nautch girls in the bazar are very pretty, and wear beautiful ornaments but it is not lawful to look at them even for sketching purposes. Mr N–, one of the magistrates has removed them all from the main street, so the bazar is highly correct.'[18] In 1839, it had been possible to shift them out of sight over the hillside; but as each area of the bazar in turn became a residential and respectable one, there were representations and protests. In the 1880s a *chakla* or prostitute quarter was set up at a house called Charleston. When the Municipal Board School was shifted to Mayfield nearby, the quarter moved[19] to houses on the Gunj Road and Alleys number 2 and 6 in Middle Bazar. On a representation from residents, a Municipal Resolution of

1915 prohibited the nautch girls from residing within the municipal limits of Simla except below the Cart Road,[20] but the resolution was not acted upon and in 1921, when the Gunj became a venue for political meetings, the legality of permitting them in the Bazar was questioned. The *Tribune* proclaimed that Gunj Road was a 'respectable quarter inhabited by respectable people'[21]—public opinion prevailed, and the prostitutes moved to a compound of Gusain on Jakhu. It was then the turn of the Europeans to complain to the authorities, so the prostitutes vacated Jakhu and shifted below the Cart Road. This in turn incensed the Sikh community, since the house was near the Singh Sabha.[22]

There were efforts to restrict the urban sprawl in Lower Bazar. The bazar areas formed enclaves surrounded by Station Ward, and to ensure that they would not steal into Station Ward, for 'Natives are too fond of encroaching and stealing a little of their neighbour's fresh air by putting up boards and walls or other forms of obstruction,'[23] the boundaries of the former were now clearly defined. Consequently, Lower Bazar grew vertically rather than horizontally; till a municipal resolution of 16 March 1904 restricted the erection of new buildings or the enlargement of existing ones. In the next two years, about seventy applications for extension of the bazar area, or of existing houses, or the erection of new houses within the Bazar, were rejected. However, the 1904 municipal census revealed that Lower Bazar had the highest population density in the Punjab, with an average population of 17.4 per house, in startling contrast to the average of 5.7 in the province. The policy of restricting the physical expansion as well as population of the Lower Bazar met with some success. The population in the bazar stabilized at about 7,000, registering a return of 6,672 in the 1911 census. The diminished population in 1911 was attributed partly to a fire which in 1907 had burnt down a section of Lower Bazar. In part, it was attributed to the camel and mule stand near the Gunj being abolished in 1907 after construction of the railway.[24]

However, the problem of inadequate sanitation and overcrowding in the Bazar was never solved, although the Victorian fetish about cleanliness had driven British planners, convinced of the dirty degenerate ways of natives, to pen Simla's Indian population as far as possible within the confines of the bazars.

The zeal to restrict the expansion of Simla was applied to Station Ward as well. Extension of the railway line to Kalka had led to an increase in the number of houses from 440 in 1891 to 544 in 1898. The official view was to be found in *1907 Report*: 'Simla is similarly circumstanced to a cantonment as regards (a) the limited house accommodation, (b) the obligatory residence of officials on limited salaries, and (c) the absence of any necessity on the part of non-officials to reside there.'[25]

Private houseowners, on the other hand, looked forward to the prospect of increasing numbers of visitors who would need houses to rent. The officials viewed this as part of the larger question of checking the growth of the town. They feared that extension of the railway line to Simla would be accompanied by even greater efforts on the part of houseowners and others to build more houses. A judicious rejection of applications, or procrastination until the validity of the application lapsed, helped to check this. The policy was outlined in 1907:

> We consider, however, that every application to construct new buildings, or to enlarge buildings now existing, even in the Station Ward, should be most carefully scrutinized, and that permission to build should only be given when it is quite clear that the building is not open to objection.[26]

Between 1898 and 1907, largely as a result of policy, only eighty new buildings were constructed in Station Ward. It became easier to enforce the official policy of restrictions on fresh constructions when in 1902 the Deputy Commissioner of Simla also became the ex-officio President of the Municipal Committee. The close scrutiny of all applications concerning the erection of buildings on private estates left little scope for the fragmentation of large estates into smaller ones.

British houseowners hoped to see measures such as the construction of new roads in Simla—at Summer Hill, Mount

Pleasant, the Elysium, as well as in the suburbs near Jutogh, Mashobra and Mahasu—to facilitate house construction. The Secretary of the House Proprietors Association represented that this would have the 'desirable effect of opening access to building sites on which erection of houses, cottages and villas should be encouraged rather than discouraged by irritating Municipal restrictions and interferences on the pleas of ventilation, pollution, etc; which except in the Bazars, is generally provided and cared for by the owners or tenants for their own sakes.'[27] The plea was not heeded.

In 1898, 109 sites for new houses had been selected by a committee which framed the recommendations for Simla's extension, sites whose remote location made it unlikely they would be of any use to the Government. In 1907, nine years later, only fifty-four had been demarcated, for it was noted that there 'was not sufficient demand for any systematic arrangements for demarcation and sale of sites.' In 1912 Jai Lal, an Indian municipal commissioner, suggested that these sites be auctioned since there was a 'great demand in Simla for small houses with moderate rentals'. Yet only fifteen were auctioned in the three ensuing years. By such means was construction in Station Ward discouraged during the first two decades of the twentieth century.

Finally, measures were taken to restrict squatter settlements outside Simla's municipal limits, on land belonging to the states of Koti, Keonthal and Patiala. The treaty with the Rana of Koti, who owned Sanjauli, a suburb of Simla, contained a proviso that no building would be permitted within the limit of one mile of Simla. However, traders along the Hindustan–Tibet road found Sanjauli a convenient camping place where they could avoid paying octroi and other Simla taxes. The pressure for accommodation in Simla bazar led many to search for accommodation at Sanjauli. Denouncing it as a 'pirate colony', an official noting said: 'The Rana of Koti has, however, deliberately set Government at defiance in the way in which he has permitted new houses to be built at Sanjauli, and is, I consider, deserving of no consideration at the hands of the

Government.'[28] In 1907, Sanjauli had a population of over 700, and, restrictions notwithstanding, the area continued to grow.

By 1907, it was noted with satisfaction that extension of the railway to Simla had not resulted in any appreciable increase in its population of about 36,000. By constant vigilance and checks on expansion, Simla's planners could look back with satisfaction on the early years of the twentieth century when the Indian population had grown only marginally.

World War I marked the beginning of an increase in Simla's Government population beyond the bounds sketched by its planners. The creation of the Munitions Board in 1915 led to the doubling of personnel in the offices attached to Army Headquarters. It was, however, felt that the end of the war would see a redistribution of the new staff in other offices. The forecasts plotted for the next fifty years envisaged only a marginal increase in Government personnel,[29] but the war proved in fact to be the beginning of large-scale recruitment to Government jobs in the lower echelons.

Making Indians eligible for Government jobs had been one of the demands made by the nationalists. The war-time need to reconcile every shade of opinion led Government to reconsider its recruitment policies, and in 1917, Montague, the Secretary of State, announced the policy of increasing association of Indians in every branch of administration. In 1919, as a first step, the formula of a 33 per cent increase in the number of Indian employees was accepted. Since the ratio of officers to clerks was one to three, this meant a massive intake of clerical staff. A glance at the census figures of Simla for the subordinate service clearly indicates the relative increase in their numbers: the number of officers increased from 308 in 1911 to 575 in 1921, while the number of non-commissioned officers trebled from 1,573 to 4,149.[30]

The summer census of 1921 showed a 20 per cent increase in the total population of Simla, now over 45,000; Government and municipal employees showed an increase by 48 per cent.

The problem of numbers also stemmed from another source. British private ownership of houses had been a unique feature of mid-nineteenth century Simla, and there were efforts to perpetuate the pattern well into the twentieth century. The Government, in addition to limiting expansion of the town, also endeavoured to confine ownership of all available.estates to British hands.

In the first quarter of the twentieth century, three factors altered the precarious property-ownership pattern which the Government sought to impose on Simla; firstly, there was the increasing tendency of the non-official British and affluent Indians to buy large estates for their own use during the summer months; secondly, the shortage of accommodation for Government personnel, combined with inflation caused by the war, resulted in spiralling property values; and thirdly, the increased staff in the Army Headquarters permanently stationed in Simla during the war led to an increased demand for estates.

By far the most 'disconcerting' trend noted after 1905 was the number of houses being bought by Indians in Station Ward. While it was possible to hinder the purchase of estates by the Indian princes, it was more difficult to check purchases by the landed aristocrats from the Punjab and affluent middle-class Indians. The number of Indian-owned houses once again showed an increase; in 1903, only sixteen houses of Station Ward were owned by Indians; in 1907, the number had risen to twenty-nine, of which only seven belonged to the princes and the rest to 'native gentlemen'. The rapidity with which large houses in Simla were passing into the hands of wealthy Indians became a matter of 'some concern', about which statistics were collected.

For example, Mir Mohammad Khan, a local pleader and nominated member of the municipality, owned four houses— Firgrove, Springfield, Winscottie and Yarrowville. Firgrove was one of the estates rented by civil servants annually. Its annual rent had risen from 1,300 rupees in 1891 to 2,000 rupees in 1916. In 1916 the house was bought by another Indian pleader,

Rai Bahadur Mohan Lal, as his residence. Hoosain Buksh, the owner of a large general store on the Mall, had purchased six properties on Elysium Hill—Belvedere, Battesley, Elysium Hotel, Rookery, Rook Nest and Sylvan Hall. Dr Rash Behari Ghose had bought a house, Grasmere, from a British trader.

It was thought that Chhota Simla would soon become 'useless for Europeans' on account of the large number of houses occupied by Indians,[31] many of which were bought by landed aristocrats of the Punjab. Sardar Sir Jogendra Singh (1877–1946), a *taluqdar* of Kheri district was Home Minister in Patiala State and later Member of the Council of State. Literary and religious, he had written several books, was editor of the journal *East and West*, and associated with the Singh Sabha. In 1919 he bought a house, Morefield Grange, in Simla East and renamed it 'Aira Holme'. Gagrain House, Bagrain House, Majithia House— the names of such re-christened estates in Simla East betoken their ownership. The Bagrain family were the spiritual guides of the Malwa Sikhs. They were the office-bearers of the Chief Khalsa Diwan and founders of the Singh Sabha movement. Sir Sunder Singh Majithia was also associated with the Chief Khalsa Diwan from its inception in 1902, and was Revenue Minister to the Punjab Government. A Parsi visitor in 1924 commented that many well-to-do Punjabis owned bungalows on the hill, where they went for a change of air.

Table 1. *Number and value of Indian-owned houses in Station Ward*[32]

Year	No. of houses acquired by Indians	Total property value (Rupees)
1879	2	57,000
1880	4	1,25,000
1885–9	–	–
1890–4	5	49,260
1895–9	10	1,72,100
1900–4	8	1,52,750
1905–9	20	4,41,300
1910–14	23	6,39,150

As Table 1 indicates, the purchase of houses by Indians was carefully vetted. Officially, it was declared that purchases by Indians as 'commercial speculation' were not to be viewed with alarm, especially if the houses were tenanted, as before, by Government servants. But affluent Indians often preferred to live in Station Ward; the rising price of real estate was attributed to this factor. The tax superintendent of the municipality observed that wealthy Indians were generally prepared to pay higher prices if the house was purchased for their personal use. He concluded that such Indians were 'prepared to pay any price in order to have a residential house in Simla, balancing this with the advantageous European amenities, and the opportunities they obtain for the advancement of themselves and their friends.'

By 1916, the Municipal Committee had drawn up a list of seventy-nine houses which were habitually occupied by officers and subordinates, charting the increase in rents for each house over a twenty-year period.[33] For instance, Torrentium in Chhota Simla, a house bought by an Indian, had an annual rental value of 2,000 rupees between 1891 and 1901, which rose to 2,500 rupees in 1911, and 2,900 rupees in 1916. The rent for Harvington, located on Elysium Hill, rose from 2,000 rupees in 1891 to 2,700 rupees in 1911, and 3,500 rupees in 1916. Bairdville, a large house on Jakhu Hill, let for 2,520 rupees in 1891, had a rental of 4,000 rupees in 1916.

It was reasoned that the increasing property values and rents led to speculative purchasing of houses, resulting in a further increase in rents. This and shortage of accommodation, however, made officials pressure the Government into taking remedial action. It sometimes also led to exacerbated landlord–tenant relations: a complaint by an official in 1916 to the municipality about the insanitary conditions of a house known as Marleyville, led to an acid exchange with the landlord. The landlord felt that the suggested changes were 'unnecessary' and demanded an enhanced rent for the following year. Narayani Gupta has shown how British residents living in houses owned by Indians at Delhi were chagrined to find

Indian landlords laying down their own terms.[34] Clearly, at Simla the prospect of such landlord–tenant clashes were undesirable if the former were Indians.

Meanwhile, official committees like the Simla House Accommodation Committee of 1917 juggled with figures:

> Only 271 houses suitable as residences for officers and 148 suitable for subordinates to meet both official and non-official requirements. Of these, numbers 54 and 18 respectively were, in 1917, occupied by non-officials, leaving 217 and 130 available for the housing of 395 officers and 800 European clerks. The balance had to fend for themselves in hotels, clubs and boarding houses, the congestion in which has consequently been very considerable.[35]

The question often raised was whether the Public Works Department should acquire or construct houses for its employees or whether officials should follow the practice of renting them for the term spent at Simla.

To meet the additional requirements for houses, another phase of construction of smaller cottages was undertaken. The 'junior military officers' were accommodated in apartments in the newly-acquired Longwood Hotel and Craigdhu. The local papers wrote: 'The accommodation for the Government employees of all grades seems likely to be a grievance of the past when one sees the number of houses—great and little, beautiful and ugly—springing up on all sides.'[36] Thirty-two residences were built for the European clerks and registrars at Bemloe, and for Indian clerks and superintendents below the railway station, at Dhar and at Tutikandi. The Punjab Government then built a series of houses and cottages at Brockhurst.

In 1917, the Punjab Government passed a bill to freeze rents to rates before World War I. Convinced that Government officers required to be protected against rack-renting landlords, the Government also decided to acquire houses in Simla. Anxious not to acquire only Indian-owned houses, the facts and figures of rent increase were shown to the Viceroy, Reading, who advised that 'the racial aspect of the case [be reduced] as far as possible. This we may do by making it a question between officials and non-officials.'[37] A Punjab Government notification of 1919 named forty-nine houses, covering an area of 100 acres and valued at about 30,00,000 rupees.

The notification came as a 'bombshell' to many Simla house-owners. There was intense indignation amongst non-official British houseowners, for although the Government had restricted rents in 1917, it acquired these houses on a value based on old rentals. According to Buck, 'the Government certainly secured some bargains at the market rates then prevailing, for one owner offered the 'Sirkar' Rupees 15,000 to be left in possession of his property, and more than one law suit was threatened.'[38] The *Simla Times* commented: 'If Government is going to purchase house property it is hoped they will pay actual market value for it and not pre-war prices. . . . Demand is, all the world over, recognized as regulating the value of supply. The demand for houses in 1919 is twice or three times that of 1913 in Simla. The Government 'should give even the landlord his due.'[39]

The acquisitions ended a phase when private property was largely owned by Europeans. Thereafter, acquisition of houses by Government for residential accommodation became an accepted feature, and several estates were acquired and built upon in the next two decades. Thus, by the end of World War I, Simla's characteristics as a bureaucratic enclave were reinforced.

The summer census showed Simla with a population of over 45,000. The Report of 1921 indicated a 20 per cent increase in population. Its verdict was that the 'station practically exists solely on Government service; all other occupations exist for supplying Government requirements or the requirements of Government servants.'[40] Simla's European character, however, had undergone a change. While British ownership of private property gave way to large-scale acquisition of houses by Government for its staff, the purchase of large houses by wealthy and aristocratic Indians could not be checked.

CHAPTER TEN

The Horizon from Lower Bazar

Every effort had been made to restrict economic activity in Simla to simply fulfilling the requirements of the Government and its employees; the commission agents, traders and shopkeepers were merely necessary appendages for the town being kept supplied with essential provisions. Only about a seventh of Simla's population was dependent upon trade and shop-keeping for its livelihood, of whom four-fifths lived in Lower Bazar.

The community that captured the lion's share of the trade and business of Simla was the Sood; they were the principal moneylenders, commission agents, traders, and shopkeepers; the bazar had been their domain since the inception of the town. The three S's, 'Sarkar–Simla–Sood,' were in fact interdependent. The Soods considered themselves partners with the Government in the building of Simla; and knew that their fortunes were linked with the Sarkar that had established Simla as summer capital.

Traditionally moneylenders and traders, the Soods were known for their business acumen. There was a saying: 'If a Sud is across the river, leave your bundle this side.'[1] The *newandia*, Soods from the plains, and the *uchandia*, the *pahari* (hill) Soods, migrated annually from the lower hills of Kangra, and Hoshiarpur and the adjoining districts up to Amritsar in Punjab. The *newandia* Soods controlled the extensive sugar trade in Ludhiana and moneylending in the richest agricultural parts of that district. The *uchandia* were not as wealthy though they owned much of the land in the arid parts of the Kangra hills near Jwalamukhi, and controlled both trade and moneylending in the region.

In Simla there were both *newandia* and *uchandia* traders, but the majority came from the two villages of Garli and Pragpur in Kangra, for whom the growth of Simla, and the opening up of channels of communication to the hill states beyond it, ushered in an unexpected era of prosperity. (Their now deserted large houses at Garli and Pragpur bear witness to the money invested then.) The menfolk would set out for Simla after the spring festival of Holi, on foot, covering ten to fifteen miles a day, and arrive as the first batches of Government departments steamed in. With the close of the Simla season, most returned home to celebrate Diwali in early November.

Robust and hardy, the Sood trader accompanied on foot his pack animals, generally bullocks and mules, sometimes camels, loaded with sacks of grain and bales of cloth. He bought his goods from the *mandi* (wholesale market) at Hoshiarpur and took the route to Simla past Amb, halting at Nadaun, the chief mart of the Kangra valley and a favourite resting place of merchants for the night.[2] He then crossed the river at Dehar, passed through Arki, and finally climbed the ascent to Jutogh and Simla. He thus traversed the hill states of Kangra, Suket, Bilaspur and Baghal.

At Nadaun and Dehar the crossing was made on inflated buffalo skins known as *senais*. The ferryman lay across the inflated skin, balancing himself by a rope strapped across it, using a paddle in his left hand; the passenger sat astride the ferryman's back. A *charpoi* strapped across two skins served as a seat for special customers. Heavy and bulky articles were also strapped onto two skins, while the bullocks, horses and mules were led across the river. Some travelled from the *mandi* at Jagadhri across Nalagarh, via Pinjore and Sabathu to Simla.

The rigours of the journey were the least of the Sood trader's travails. There was pillage along the highway, and duties imposed at *chowkies* erected by the hill rulers. In 1832, two traders from Kangra, Needha and Surdha, stated in a petition to the Political Agent that they had been compelled to leave silver ornaments in lieu of duty at Bilaspur before they could bring eighty bullock-loads of flour to the Simla market.[3] In Simla, they lived in makeshift structures set up in the bazars.

As the town grew the numbers multiplied, and the more affluent bought property in Lower Bazar.

By the close of the nineteenth century the 'rich men who could be counted on the fingers of your hand' and owned most of the Lower Bazar property, were, it was said all Soods.[4] The rest, petty traders, also mostly Soods, owned property which was 'mortgaged up to the chimneys' to a handful of their rich kinsmen.[5]

The wealthy Soods were largely commission agents, wholesalers, and moneylenders, who operated from Edwards Gunj and dominated the foodgrains trade. As commission agents (*ahrties*), they procured commodities such as food-grains, oils, and pulses, for re-sale to wholesalers or retailers, charging a commission for the procuring, weighing and selling. They served in fact as middlemen for the dealers who bought their goods in bulk from the *mandis* at Hoshiarpur and Jagadhri. They also relieved, by fraud or persuasion, the villagers who descended upon the town from the surrounding hills with *kilta*-loads of surplus produce—grain, corn, ginger, seasonal vegetables—anything they could sell. Produce from the more distant villages was brought on sheep-back, each sheep with several pounds strapped onto its back. Sometimes the pressure of the commission agent's foot on the weighing scale was communicated as so many *maunds* or *seers* of weight, and while it is unlikely that the villager, dressed in his coarse woollen coat, was duped, he didn't have a choice.

Commission agents also became wholesalers, re-selling these commodities to retail shopkeepers. In the process, they made advances of money both to the traders who sent their goods for sale, and to the shopkeepers who purchased them. Most successful commission agents extended their activities to become moneylenders and bankers as well. As commission agents, wholesalers, and moneylenders, they were in a position to manipulate prices and the availability of their goods.

One of the 'rich men' who established himself at Edwards Gunj was 'Rai Sahib' Nidha Mal Puran Mal (1842–1932) of Garli, who by the turn of the nineteenth century, came to own much of the property of Lower Bazar. Astute management and the ability to drive a shrewd bargain made him the wealthiest and best-known commission agent and moneylender in Simla. Puran Mal had a hand in every potentially paying business, whether it was promoting and financing potato growing or forest contracts. He served as *modi*, supplying goods to the Thakurs and Ranas of the surrounding hill states. It was whispered that he (like a merchant out of the Arabian Nights) loaned mule-loads of currency to them. The story was probably close to fact. Money was preferred in silver coins; since each one-rupee silver coin weighed one *tola* (11.2 grammes), a sum of 5,000 rupees would weigh 1.5 *maunds* (54 kilograms), which together with the packing material, would make a full mule-load. Puran Mal was a respected figure amongst the Simla Soods; he provided loans at easy rates of interest to needy Sood retailers, and made donations to the Sanatan Dharam temple near the Gunj.

The Simla commission agents also supplied commodities to the small bazars at Kufri, Theog, and Matiana which had sprung up near the dak bungalows along the newly-built roads. The injunction to the Simla Hill States to construct twelve-foot-wide roads throughout their territories had converted former pathways into mule roads, and the construction of the Hindustan–Tibet road connected Simla to the northern hill states, making it into a focal point where several routes converged. Little was sent out to the surrounding hill villages, but hill products such as opium, honey, borax, and ginger passed through the Simla market. Some Simla commission agents served as *modis* to the Ranas and Thakurs of the hill states, supplying foodgrains, piecegoods and other commodities ordered by them.

Promoter, usurer and manipulator—these were some of the faces of Simla commission agents. They made potatoes into a profitable cash crop in the villages lying along the new roads, especially the Hindustan–Tibet road. They provided loans to local village traders who in turn advanced them to the farmers for potato seed, to be recovered at harvest time. At Dhalli and

Sanjauli, on the outskirts of Simla, middlemen such as Durga Das Pyare Lal set up a *kachchi arhat* where they installed weighing scales. The potatoes were procured, graded and repacked in gunny bags for onward transmission to markets, the wholesale price of potatoes being declared by the commission agents at Simla. By 1939, eighteen of the twenty Simla commission agents dealt in the expanding potato trade.

Individually, a commission agent had the power, by a timely loan or the withdrawal of credit, to make or mar a small trader; as a group they made a truly formidable combination when in 1931 they organized the 'Ahrties Association of Simla'. Two factors led to the formation of the association. The increase in the number of competing commission agents pointed to the need to prevent undercutting into one another's profits. Secondly, the introduction of a 'Bill to Prevent Accumulation of Interest' in the Punjab Legislative Assembly was viewed as a threat to their trading and moneylending methods. The 'Sahukar Bill' as the commission agents called it, had been framed to prevent the accumulation of credit over long periods.

Twenty-two commission agents, dealing in foodgrains, pulses, edible oils and potatoes, joined the Ahrties Association.[6] Within the first year, the Association sought to formalize the accepted trading practices between them and the retailers. At a general meeting, in June 1931, it was decided that a retailer should make payment in cash by the evening of the transaction. If he failed to do so, he would be boycotted by the community of commission agents. The Association also dealt collectively with the retailers of the Simla Trades Association to settle details of trading practices such as the price of packaging material, and the rates to be paid to coolies carrying loads.

Although the Soods dominated the Ahrties Association, it included some non-Soods as well; but in 1931, of the twenty-two commission agents, only eight were non-Soods. The Sood commission agents were, consequently, the principal office-bearers of the association. However, there were some prosperous non-Sood commission agents. A Khatri firm, Messrs Chiranji Lal Gokal Chand, was a close rival of several Sood firms. Two commission agents were Aggarwals. In 1933, dissension between Soods and non-Soods led to litigation with the management of the Association. A compromise was reached by the creation of an additional senior vice-president of the managing committee. This position was held for two years by a non-Sood, and the association was controlled by Khatri commission agents. In 1935, membership increased to twenty-seven, the additional members being largely Soods. And once again it became possible for the Soods to capture the association.

The records of the Ahrties Association have largely been in the custody of the Sood firm, Messrs Sunder Lal Chowdhari Mal. The firm was one of the oldest in Simla. Sunder Lal Chowdhari Mal (1854–1947), made a humble beginning as a small-scale commission agent. His son, Devi Saran (1900–76) expanded the business and made large profits. By 1931, he was the owner of a flour mill, and a Director of the People's Bank; he was instrumental in forming the Ahrties Association and was its first secretary; by 1938, he had bought property in the Gunj and on the Mall; in 1963 he became a Municipal Commissioner. His son also was the President of the Ahrties Association.

Sood commission agents had patronized the Sanatan Dharam Sabha and its temple adjacent to the Gunj since its inception in 1892. They were not, however, office-bearers of the Sabha. In 1930, the Sanatan Dharam Sabha, with a membership of 200, had as its president and vice-president two cloth merchants of Lower Bazar and the Mall respectively. Commission agents, such as Puran Mal and Devi Saran, donated funds to the temple and to the school attached to the Sabha, both individually and collectively as members of the Association. The meetings of the Association were usually held in the precincts of the Sanatan Dharam Temple.

The contact of commission agents with the authorities was limited to requests for representation on the Municipal Committee, or to the conferring of the title Rai Bahadur on one of its members. But there were frequent demands by local politicians for funds from individual commission agents and their Association. 'The Ahrties were', as Puran Chandra, a Municipal Commissioner expressed it, 'the key to any Municipal election.' Their patronage was widely sought during municipal elections, though their influence was confined to the bazars.

Many retail traders did not have a permanent interest in their Simla shops which were often a branch of the main one in Lahore, Delhi or Calcutta. The Soods, however, had their base in Simla and operated through them most of the year. By 1925, an increasing number of Soods had acquired business interests that were once the preserve of Europeans. For instance, Bihari Lall in 1920 became an agent for a well-known gramophone company, and moved his premises from the Lower Bazar to the Mall. He also bought over Laneloss & Co., formerly a British company which rolled cigarettes. In 1930, he was elected Municipal Commissioner from Station Ward.

It was not only in the traditional areas of moneylending and shopkeeping that the Soods made their mark. The educated amongst them became *vakils*, pleaders, advocates, and doctors. One such was Rai Bahadur Sir Jai Lal.

Jai Lal (1880–1975) from Pragpur was the son of a draftsman in government service at Simla.[7] He had his schooling at Simla and Lahore and graduated from Government College, Lahore. After qualifying as a lawyer, he returned to Simla to practise, where, for almost two decades, he was the leading Indian lawyer, being President of the Simla Bar Association from 1909 to 1921. From 1901 to 1919 he was a nominated member of the Simla Municipal Committee, and represented the Indian population of Bazar Ward. Following the pattern of successful middle-class professionals, he chose to live in Station Ward and bought several estates there. He then moved to the heart of Simla, to a house known as Monastery. Later, Jai Lal became Administrator General and was the official trustee of the Punjab High Court between 1920 and 1923, Government Advocate of

Punjab in 1923–4, and finally a Judge of the Lahore High Court from 1924 till he retired in 1940.

Timber extraction from the forests of the hill states turned into one of the more lucrative avenues of high investment and returns. Rai Bahadur Mohan Lal, Rai Bahadur Jodha Mal Kuthiala and Rai Sahib Lehnu Mall Thakur Dass, had, apart from the honorary titles conferred on them by the British Government, several features in common. They were all Soods; and Simla's wealthiest middle-class Indians in the second quarter of the twentieth century. And they were all timber contractors and forest lessees.

In the nineteenth century, the forests of the Mahasu range, its spurs running from Shali to Narkanda, supplied Simla with deodar for house construction and *ban*, *kharsu*, and *mohru* for fuelwood. In 1885, the Suket ruler had been induced to construct a road through his state, and a bridge across the Sutlej at his boundary at Tattapani, to facilitate the transportation of fuel-wood. The wood was marketed by the timber merchants of Lakkar Bazar. By 1908, sixteen timber merchants were in business.

The demand for wood for construction and fuel, calculated at over three lakh *maunds*, paled into insignificance compared with the auction of hardwoods by the Forest Department of the Government. The principal hardwood was from deodar trees growing at between 5,000 and 9,000 feet. Founded in 1862, in the era of the great railway building period in north India, the Forest Department was created to ensure a steady supply of sleepers for rails. It was also meant to rescue the fast-depleting accessible deodar forests from 'hit and run contractors'. The Forest Department had to reconcile the conflicting demands of supplying wood to the railways, improving and controlling forests, and in addition to show a large profit from their operations. The trees in their custody were their 'standing capital'. They sold marked trees for felling and transportation to private timber contractors by auction, and derived spiralling profits from the business. The contractors were British in the nineteenth century, and Indian by the twentieth. Large forest tracts of Chamba and Bushahr had been leased by the Government in 1860 and 1863 respectively.

Subsequently, the hill states came alive to the value of their timber. Patiala and Keonthal, together with smaller states such as Darkoti, Mailog, and Baghat, were chary of selling or leasing their forests to the Department, because they were aware that the Forest Department, in order to show a large income from its operations, offered the lowest rents for lease, and would seldom give a lump sum for the timber. Occasionally, it turned large tracts into 'reserved' forests, exercising full powers of management over such tracts and thereby disturbing the grazing and cultivation rights of *zamindars*, including their rights over forest trees for fuel and house construction. (The smaller states also sold the autumn crop of grass required by the government Tonga Dak which employed hundreds of well-fed horses.) The hill rulers, therefore, turned to Indian timber contractors and forest lessees who offered more advantageous terms. Such business deals, especially during World War II when the demand was massive, matured into steadfast agreements, as between the Jubbal ruler and Jodhamal Kuthiala, for the deodar stands in his state.

A combination of business skills and a profession could make for great influence and power, as witnessed by the career of Rai Bahadur Mohan Lal (1890–1932) of Garli. The Rai Bahadur started his career as a lawyer in Simla and became associated with Sultan Singh, a Delhi-based firm of forest contractors. He soon became a forest contractor and lessee in Kashmir, Chamba and Jubbal with his office at Simla. Over the years he formed his own contacts as a timber contractor and became a principal supplier to the North-West Railways. During this time he invested in the Hoshiarpur Electric Company and by the 1930 he became chairman of the company. Belonging to the Gurukul section of the Arya Samaj, he was its president in 1930 and helped to open a school for girls in Simla as well as in his village, Garli. His personal dynamism and popularity led to his becoming an elected member of the Punjab Legislative Assembly. In Simla, Mohan Lal owned and lived in Gulshan Villa in the Lower Bazar. As he became affluent, he bought up a block of shops along the Mall Road; by 1919 he had built, as his residence, a house named Manorama in Kainthu, and when that was acquired by the Government, he bought another estate, Firgrove, in Simla east. By 1920 he had moved out of Lower Bazar to occupy Firgrove and thus became a householder of Station Ward, and qualified to become a member of the Municipal Committee representing Station Ward. Nominated at first, and later elected, he retained his seat in the Simla Municipal Committee until his death in 1932, and was often sought out to present local grievances. Although he never joined the Congress, he was host to Gandhi in 1931.

Men like Jai Lal and Mohan Lal popularized the Arya Samaj in Simla, having been drawn to it in Lahore. Both had graduated and received their professional training at Lahore, the cultural and educational metropolis for middle-class Punjabis. Mono-theistic and iconoclastic, the Arya Samaj sought to defend Hinduism against the inroads of Christianity and Islam. Its ethic of social service, its ideal of social reform and concept of a congregation which held a weekly *havan* or service on Sunday mornings, was one that appealed to educated men of progressive views. It provided a sense of social dynamism corresponding to the increasing wealth and influence of the western-educated professional. It also helped bridge the gulf between wealth and social status based on caste.

The publication of Denzil Ibbetson's *Glossary of Tribes and Castes of the Punjab* had fixed the seal on the British interpretation of the hierarchy of castes. Ibbetson assigned the Soods a position 'markedly' inferior to that of either the Bania or the Khatri. He described them as ancient in origin, but 'lax in the obser-vance' of religion compared to the other mercantile com-munities. He also recorded a tale he had heard: A man of low caste who owed money to a Bania after a few years settled the account. The principal was paid by the debtor, but he could not pay the interest, so he agreed to give his wife to his creditor. Her children by the Bania were called Sood—'interest'. In time the Soods began to intermarry with the higher castes and were considered to have the same status as the Banias.

These disparaging remarks led members of the Sood community to ransack the Sanskrit classics for proof of their Rajput origin. To disprove Ibbetson's findings, the first all-Sood conference was convened in 1882 at Lahore, resulting in the compilation of several Sood caste histories.[8] These histories trace the descent of the Soods from the mythical Agnikul sacrifice performed near Mount Abu, from which the progenitors of the four Rajput castes emerged. The second son of Parmar, one of the four progenitors, was named Sood. The word Sood thus meant not 'interest' but a noble person, one who would prosper easily. The traditional texts were ransacked for evidence of a Sood kingdom, discovered at Pattan in Sind. The Muslim invasion led them to disperse to Rajasthan and eventually to Sirhind. Mughal sources indicated that the bulk of the population of Sirhind was concentrated in twenty *mohallas* in front of the royal estates many of whom supplied commodities on contract. Sirhind was also a commercial centre and gateway to hill trade. The Soods believed that necessity had made a martial community turn to trade and business to earn a living.

The relatively low status ascribed to the Soods resulted in many disabilities. The Rajputs and Brahmans of a Kangra village prevented them from drawing water from the local spring and tank. In the court suit that followed, the Sood cause was supported by *Sood Vanshavali*, the first history of the community, written by the Rajguru of Jubbal state, according to which the Soods were Rajputs. (It may be pointed out that several Sood timber contractors, such as Lala Mohan Lal and Jodha Mal Kuthiala, had business dealings with the Jubbal ruler in exploiting his forests.) The right to draw water was restored to them, but the stigma of low caste persisted. Educated Soods were thus greatly attracted to the Arya Samaj.

The Simla Arya Samaj in the Lower Bazar was founded in

1882. Dr Thakur Dass, a physician with a clinic known as Medical Hall on the Mall, was its president; its secretary, Lala Manohar Lal, was a trader in Lower Bazar. The Arya Samaj appears to have been popular and active in Simla, for one of its patrons, Pandit Ram Narayan, a notable banker of Simla, sought to donate an area called Dedo-ka-nal which lay above a popular picnic spot, to the Arya Samaj. Ram Narayan's ownership of Dedo-ka-nal was not however a recorded fact, and the Simla Municipality, anxious to protect the Glen, 'the popular recreation ground from spoliation', filed and won a civil suit to recover municipal right of ownership over the area.[9]

Many educated Soods were associated with the Arya Samaj. For almost two decades after 1900, Sir Jai Lal was its president; he donated a large estate in Lower Bazar, Dilkusha, for its use. His successor, Lala Mohan Lal, was instrumental in opening a girls' school on the premises for which he secured a grant from the municipality. In 1930, the Samaj had about 250 members.

A schism in the Arya Samaj in Lahore came to the fore with establishment of the Anglo-Vedic school in 1888. The group which promoted it emphasized western science and literature along with the study of the Vedas, and the preparation of its students for examinations recognized by Government which would be likely to lead to jobs. The College group, as it was known, seized control of the managing committee. It was then represented by twenty-eight Samajes, Simla being one of them. In 1896, the College section had opened a school in Simla, and in 1903, the managing committee at Lahore provided a loan to the Simla Arya Samaj for construction of a temple in Lower Bazar. The College section school attracted Government employees while its active members included several Congress workers. In the 1920s, Dr Kedar Nath, a Sood from Ludhiana, was its president.

There was little antagonism between the two wings of the Samaj at Simla—they represented 'differing points on a continuum rather than separate categories'.[10] Both were similarly organized, and had two types of members: those who enrolled as regular members, paid the subscription fee and could be elected as office-bearers, and those who attended the *havans* held every Sunday morning but did not enroll formally. Both held an annual three-day function on their anniversary. Beginning with a *havan* in the morning, there was *kirtan* or devotional singing during the day, which was rounded off with speeches from well-known Arya Samajists invited for the occasion.

After 1920, both sections of the Arya Samaj extended their proselytizing activities into the hill states around Simla. In 1920, the Simla Arya Samaj (College section) formed the Vidya Pracharni Sabha in order to counter the activities of Christian missionaries, and turned its attention to education. A middle school was opened in Kotgarh and three primary schools at Mashobra, Kufri and Theog. The Simla Arya Samaj was able to enlist the support of and obtain donations from the princes and local businessmen of these areas. Gauri Mal Butail, a Sood commission agent and banker, and the Ranas of Theog and Dhami made handsome donations.[11] In 1930, Dr Kedar Nath organized the Hindu Orphanage Industrial School with twenty-five boys at Tutikandi and was its secretary. In 1937 he also organized the Nari Bikriamia Nirwani Sabha (Society for the Prevention of Traffic in Women). Kedar Nath secured once again the patronage of the rulers of Baghat, Keonthal and Bushahr.

In 1925, the Gurukal wing of the Arya Samaj, under the impetus of the *shuddhi* and *sangathan* movements, established the Himalaya Arya Up-pratinidhi Sabha which consisted initially of twenty members, to work 'towards the amelioration of the conditions of the Kolis and Kanets of the Simla Hill States, untouchability, polyandry, polygamy and the customs of Rit, belief in deotas, etc'.[12] The programme of *shuddhi* and *sangathan* meant conversion to Hinduism of those belonging to other religions, or re-conversion to Hinduism of those who had adopted Christianity or Islam. The Samaj aimed at raising the status of the depressed classes.

The emphasis on social reform by both wings of the Arya Samaj served to break the isolation of hill society. Simla became the springboard for ideas of education and reform, and paved the way to the political consciousness manifest in 1939.

While there were individual, wealthy, and popular non-Soods, they were too diverse to shape the character of the bazar. The Soods, as a single caste group, made a powerful lobby. A subinspector cautioned his successor thus: 'Suds in general make common cause and all Sud pleaders join hands to support when any Sud member comes into trouble.'[13] The Station House Officer was to be on his guard when dealing with this community, and especially careful when investigating a case in which a Sood was involved, whether as a complainant or accused.

It was caste consciousness and modern organization that made the Soods an effective group. They utilized to the full non-caste organizations: whether organized around economic interests, like those of commission agents, traders, houseowners and the Bar Association; or socio-religious ones, such as the Sanatan Dharam and the Arya Samaj, a Sood was, more likely than not, at its helm. They emerged as local representatives on the municipality as well as patrons and office-bearers of the various associations of the town.

If, as a group, commission agents and wholesalers had a distinctly Sood complexion, this was not true of the retail traders and shopkeepers of the Mall and bazars. The latter were a heterogenous group of various communities and castes. Jain traders constituted a small but active group, who organized the Jain Sabha in 1904 and built a Digambar Temple. But they were a small group of only thirty-one individuals in 1921. Messrs Framjee and Company, an impressive general merchandise shop, was evidence of the presence of Parsi traders, numbering twenty-five in 1921.

The Sikhs constituted another section of Simla's population, ranging from the landed aristocrats who lived in Simla east to the building contractors, shopkeepers of Lakkar Bazar, Government servants, and tailors and Ramgarhyas belonging to the lower castes. The Singh Sabha and the gurudwara built on the

Cart Road in 1886 formed a congregating point as well as a
forum for them. In 1930 there were 300 members, with 'considerable local influence among the Sikh community in Simla'.[14]
The Singh Sabha was established in 1873 at Amritsar by people
drawn from the traditional Sikh élite, noted for loyalty to the
British.[15] The object of the Sabha was to restore Sikhism to
pristine purity and to publish Sikh historical and religious books.
In Simla, the Sikh aristocrats, Sunder Singh Majithia, Bhai
Arjun Singh Bagrain, and Sir Joginder Singh, were the patrons
and donors of the Singh Sabha until the first quarter of the
twentieth century.

In the 1920s, the Simla organization came under the control
of middle-class contractors and government employees. Sardar
Dalel Singh, a building contractor, was president of the Sabha
for over a decade, while government clerks served as the other
office-bearers. In 1939, the Sabha was captured by a small group
of tailors and Ramgarhyas who became its office-bearers. A
parallel committee of contractors and government pensioners,
disputing the election, represented that the tailors and Ramgarhyas paid no regard 'to the Sikhs of high ranks and also in
government service'. The parallel committee continued. The
Singh Sabha held weekly meetings or a *diwan*, which echoed
the tangled happenings at Amritsar, Lahore and Patiala, though
the celebration of the gurudwara's anniversary was the annual
highlight. In Simla, the Singh Sabha tried to promote Sikh
interests by a plea for separate municipal representation and
reservation of jobs in the municipality.

The Muslims constituted a significant section of the trading
community, though they too belonged to different provinces.
Kashmiri Muslim merchants dealing in shawls, dry fruits,
trinkets and semi-precious stones were a small but close-knit
group, and lived in the Kashmiri Mohalla in the Lower Bazar.
They patronized the Masjid Kashmirian in the mohalla. (A case
in the Lahore High Court filed by the Maulvi of the rival Qutab
Masjid challenging its parochial name was defeated.) The
Muslim butchers had their own niche in the meat market and
congregated in the nearby Masjid.

The most affluent of the Muslim traders were the Punjabi Muslims. Messrs Hoosain Buksh and Company, the oldest and most successful Muslim firm, owned by Mir Nadir Hoosain, was started in 1842. The shop was located on the Ridge until 1875 when it moved to the Mall. Mir Nadir Hoosain bought several houses in Simla, including the Elysium Hotel. The family was patron of the Jami Masjid and of the Anjuman Islamia Trust founded in 1895. In 1922 the Jamaat-i Anjuman Insarul Muslamin was started by the Imam of Jami Masjid, with the object of encouraging conversion to Islam in the surrounding hills.

The trading community of Simla forged links with the Simla Hill States, setting up shops at the new bazars near the dak bungalows along the highways, and laying the beginnings of the townships many have now become. As *modis*, they supplied essential commodities and loaned cash to the hill state rulers. They made them collecting points for cash crops, such as potatoes, from the hill villagers whom they financed and exploited in turn. Those with capital and contacts turned to the forests, deep in the interior, to the deodar timber stands up the river valleys, and made money multiply by felling trees. Some of the profits were invested in business and some in Simla real estate to acquire the influence that wealth and property could buy. They tightened their financial grip on the town and then fanned out along the arterial roads created by the Raj to convert Simla into an entrepôt.

The Bazar, which the rulers tried to restrict and contain, burgeoned with activity that far outstripped its function of merely fulfilling the needs of Government, its employees and white Simla. Trade initiative, particularly of the Sood community, led to the rise of money power and the establishment of vigorous non-white institutions or associations which stirred Simla with ideas of reform and political awareness.

CHAPTER ELEVEN
Subordinate Service

THE Government provided employment to Indians in the lower rungs of service. The jobs included many lower level clerical positions plus those as peons, policemen, watchmen, gardeners, and so on. The Indians who manned the lower echelons of Government service not only formed a distinct group but were also a sizeable segment of Simla's population. By 1921, the clerks accounted for 23 per cent and the inferior services for 9.5 per cent of the population.

Government employees fell into three categories: the superior, subordinate and inferior services. The upper echelons, after 1910, were divided into Class I and Class II officers. The 'aristocracy' comprised the covenanted officers of the Central and Provincial Governments, while the subordinate service included the uncovenanted clerical staff. The upper grades of the subordinate service were largely filled by poor whites and Anglo-Indians, who drew salaries of between 300 to 600 rupees per month. The vast majority of the lower-level clerks, drawing salaries of less than 100 rupees per month, were Indians. A head clerk in the early twentieth century earned 75 rupees, an assistant 30 rupees, a *daftry* 10, peons between 8 and 9, and a *jamadar* 12 rupees.

In order to accommodate the large number of Indian graduates, the clerical staff of the Central Secretariat was divided into an upper and a lower division in 1908. The former was the clerical *corps d' élite*, open only to graduates who would later be eligible for promotion as assistants and superintendents. The latter were referred to as 'clerks'. Supersession and out-of-turn promotion in the clerical services were not favoured. In 1908, the Clerks Salaries Committee of the Government of India felt that such a policy was both unnecessary and one that would affect 'injuriously both the morale and the popularity of the service'.[1]

The clerical cadre of the uncovenanted civil administration was filled by British officials on the basis of influence and connections rather than merit and ability. All that an entrant required was a modicum of proficiency in English and Urdu. One newspaper commented in 1884, 'But supercilious partiality and unjust favouritism have stood in the way of the development of true merit while kinship, race, interest or love of flattery have introduced unqualified and inexperienced men into offices.'[2] Cliques formed of certain castes and families appropriated opportunities for service and soon monopolized Government positions.[3] Government service was sought after, in part at least, because prestige was attached not only to the exercise of political power but also to the service of government, even in a subordinate capacity. Additionally, the security of service until retirement at fifty-five made even a low-paid job at the bottom of the hierarchy prestigious and popular amongst Indians with an education in English.

The lowest rung of Government employees were the *chuprassis*, formerly the personal bodyguard and private armies of servants of the East India Company. After these armies were disbanded, the *chuprassis* were employed for miscellaneous menial duties, with a fixed income, but without government accommodation. Many had been employed by officers when they were posted in the district or provincial headquarters, and they were transferred when their masters moved to new stations. Depending on their seniority, officers were entitled to a specified number of *chuprassis*. Often illiterate, though some had received primary education, *chuprassis* were attached either to the office or to the residence, where they worked as orderlies, cooks, bearers or gardeners.

In a Simla office, as one writer puts it: 'The *chuprassis* . . . met trains, squatted outside offices, despatched telegrams and opened doors, carried files and cups of tea, and in their almost unlimited spare time, spun hunks of crude woollen yarn and knitted it up into pullovers.'[4] This description fits the peons belonging to the hills, especially to those of the Simla Hill States. By the turn of the twentieth century, some had obtained primary education; once literate, the hill people sought Government employment at Simla. They were increasingly in demand in offices, such as Army Headquarters and the municipal office, which functioned throughout the year. From thirty-one government and municipal employees from the Simla Hill States in 1911, the number rose to 272 in 1921.[5] Most lived in Simla during the week, but trudged along short cuts and over hill paths to spend the weekends with their families in the village. Peons from the hills who sought Government jobs were usually small landowners from the Brahman and Kanet castes. Subject to the modernising influence of the Arya Samaj in the 1920s, by the 1930s they were receptive to the message of the Praja Mandal movement. Some became spokesmen for the community in their villages.

Who were the clerks who came to Simla? During the nineteenth century, most came from Bengal. Since Bengal was one of the first provinces exposed to English education, it was convenient to appoint English-knowing Bengali clerks in the offices. The Bengali *bhadralok*, belonging to the Brahman, Kayastha and Vaidya castes, had in the early nineteenth century seized the opportunities offered by Calcutta as the commercial and political centre of the British Empire. They came to Calcutta, learnt English, and were employed in large numbers by the East India Company. Some, as draughtsmen and clerks, came to Simla from the earliest period. The Kali Bari records recount that when a survey of the Simla hill tracts was made in 1823, 'The survey operations were conducted by a staff of Bengalee draughtsmen and clerks. . . . It is said that the survey party established its base in the vicinity of the place where the Kali Bari now stands.'[6]

When Government departments were transported annually during the summer months from Calcutta to Simla, Bengali clerks predominated, although it had not been easy to persuade the Bengalis to spend seven or eight months in Simla. Most low-paid clerks in Calcutta supplemented their income by undertaking private work out of office hours, such as private tuition, and writing up account books in Indian shops.[7] Since there was very limited commercial activity in Simla, this extra source of income was not available there. The Bengalis disliked the cold and discomfort of Simla; as *The Tribune* wrote sympathetically: 'Indeed the hardships the poor clerks are made to undergo in coming up here is quite immense. The ill-paid and ill-fed clerks are quite unable to stand the trying cold of Simla.'[8] In 1884, when two Bengali clerks died in Simla, resentment against the annual transfer reached the proportions of an agitation.[9] An additional problem was accommodation, and many clerks were compelled to share rooms and attics in the bazars.

But by far the greatest disadvantage from the clerks' point of view was that they had to leave their families behind in Calcutta. Government paid them travel allowances for three dependants, but since most Bengali families were much larger, the clerks came up alone. It was also Government policy to hold out inducements to the clerks to leave their families in Calcutta. Until 1908, their stay was looked upon as a tour and consequently, a Simla Allowance was paid to compensate for the increased cost of living in two places instead of one. As a junior clerk complained, 'It is the recognized principle of Government to discourage clerks bringing their families to Simla mainly on the ground that the heavy expenditure that is involved in the shape of travelling and double house rent allowance.'[10] The Government's policy had the dual aim of financial economy and of keeping the population of Simla within the bounds sketched out by its planners. Despite this, over the years it became the practice for clerks to maintain two establishments. The older children requiring high school and college education were left in Calcutta, while the younger ones travelled to Simla and studied at the municipal middle school or Bengali Boys School of Simla.

The impact of Bengali clerks on the social life of Simla is

evident from two of their institutions. The first was the Brahmo Samaj, to which an influential section of Bengalis belonged. The Brahmo Samaj was founded in Calcutta in 1824 by Raja Ram Mohan Roy. Its third leader, Keshab Chandra Sen, had organized the Samaj in various cities of north India. In 1868, Keshab Chandra stayed in Kasumpti when he visited Simla, where he delivered a lecture outlining the aims of the Samaj to an audience consisting of the Viceroy and Commander-in-Chief.[11] The Simla Brahmo Samaj was, however, formally established later, in 1876, and obtained premises in a building in a commanding position below Kennedy House. It remained active for several years although a schism which occurred in the Samaj in 1878 affected the Simla branch as well.[12] Its influence was confined to the upper-class Bengalis who had joined the Samaj, while, amongst the Punjabis, it has been pointed out, the Brahmo Samaj movement was overwhelmed and absorbed by the Arya Samaj.[13]

Kali worship was the more popular form of worship for most Bengalis:[14] the Kali temple and the institution of the Kali Bari formed a nucleus around which grew a social centre for the Bengali population of Simla. Unlike the Brahmo Samaj, the Kali Bari also attracted (and still does) the non-Bengali Hindu population of the town. Part of its appeal lay in its commanding location in the centre of the town, overlooking the Mall.

The initiative for expansion of the Kali Bari into a large complex came from the resident Bengalis, though the other Hindu residents of Simla were also involved. By 1903, the Kali Bari was converted into a trust, and a marble and concrete structure replaced the original wooden temple. In 1931, a massive four-storeyed complex adjacent to the temple, containing living rooms and a large hall which could accommodate 800 people, was constructed. The Kali Bari thus gave Simla its first public hall where middle-class Indians could hold public functions, dramatic performances and variety entertainments, and above all, hear nationalist leaders address them in the 1930s and 1940s. The politically-conscious Bengalis were instrumental in moulding the attitude of their colleagues.[15]

In 1890, they supported the demand for an elected Simla municipality and eagerly added their signatures to the petition drawn up by non-official whites for the continuance of an elected Municipal Committee. The clerks were invariably engaged to write petitions by all classes of non-English knowing Indians. Above all, the Bengalis with their higher education and heightened political consciousness were the acknowledged leaders of the clerks.

In the early twentieth century, the regional composition of the Simla clerks altered. The creation of a communication network linking all parts of India, and the spread of western education made it possible to induct clerks from other parts of India as well. While the struggle for jobs in the public services provoked considerable ill-will amongst their unsuccessful competitors towards the Bengalis, the British, on their part, were negative about the Bengali character. The stereotype of the Bengali '*baboo*', a weak, deceitful, and dangerously nationalist type, was wholly distasteful to British officials. Also, the Bengali complained time and again of the unpleasantness of the Simla climate.

The policy of dislodging Bengalis started in a small way. Non-Bengali clerks were initially recruited as a mere 'leavening';[16] however, within a few years, the Bengalis were outnumbered, and by 1911 their number had dwindled to 334. A visitor commented in 1924: 'What struck me forcibly on a visit to the offices was to find that the Bengali element had been to a great extent replaced by the Madrasi and Punjabi.'[17] The clerks were now a mixed community, and included Tamils, Punjabis and Kayasthas from the United Provinces.

The transfer of the winter capital from Calcutta to Delhi in 1911 effectively eliminated Bengali dominance in clerical positions. The proximity of Lahore and other Punjab towns to Delhi now made it possible for English-educated Punjabis to seek Government employment, and they were the chief beneficiaries of the transfer.

Although clerks from the Punjab were comparatively late entrants to the service of the Government of India, they began 'storming into this Bengali preserve in a flood'. The opportunity presented itself at the onset of World War I in 1914 when Army Headquarters and its related departments were expanded. A timely recommendation by an influential kinsman or caste fellow usually led to an appointment at the lower levels. A beneficiary of this system of patronage relates:

> The vast wartime expansion of the administration and the setting up of new bodies like the Munitions Board had opened up countless avenues to the job seeker. All that one required was a patron, and in the social dispensation of the time, to sponsor one's kith and kin for a vacancy, was not nepotism but a social obligation. [18]

Those from north India easily acclimatized themselves to the Simla weather and, indeed, regarded it as a status symbol to be posted at Simla. Secondly, the Punjabis brought their families to Simla, as the increase in the number of their dependants, from 4,050 in 1911 to 10,576 in 1921, amply indicates.

As a result, it became necessary to open many more schools for Indians. In 1921, a controversy raged on the issue of Indians being denied admission to the Anglo-Indian and European schools of Simla. [19] As a result, there was a proliferation of schools for Indians after 1921, founded both by the Government as well as by denominational organizations, which catered to the new demand for education. The Sir Harcourt Butler School for boys, opened in 1916, and the Lady Irwin School for girls, were popular English-medium schools where Indian clerks sent their children. Both schools moved with the Government offices every year to Delhi and Simla. The municipality, which had in 1885 opened one school, managed twelve primary and middle schools in 1935. The municipal school had branches for girls as well as boys in Phagli, Boileauganj, Chhota Simla and Kasumpti. The schools managed by private organizations did not lag behind. The Singh Sabha and the Anjuman Islamia had separate schools for Sikh and Muslim children respectively; the Brahmin Sabha had organized a school in 1930; and, by 1932, the College section of the Arya Samaj had opened the

Dayanand Anglo-Vedic High School, which was popular with Punjabi clerks. Simla, however, did not have an institution for higher learning, although the Raja of Jubbal had donated 1,00,000 rupees towards founding a college in Simla in 1921. The proposal matured only in May 1945 when the Sanatan Dharam Bhagat Chandra College was opened in Summer Hill.

The Indian clerks in Simla were a representative cross-section of English-educated men, belonging to middle-class families and castes from urban centres in the provinces of Bengal, Punjab, United Provinces and Madras. While they comprised a diversity of communities and castes, it is important to remember that they did not form exclusive caste-based groups; it was the bond of government service which brought them close to one another. Government service led to the emergence of common attitudes, modes of thought and style of living amongst otherwise diverse groups. These common charac-teristics were reinforced by the fact that the clerks lived in close proximity.

The Government had built about ninety-two quarters in Kainthu and Dhar for clerks and therefore could provide accom-modation for only 6 per cent of them.[20] About 50 per cent annually rented quarters in Lower and Middle Bazar, where houses with pucca walls had higher rents than makeshift structures. Some groups of clerks habitually rented blocks of houses together; for example, twelve houses in a three-storeyed block of houses between the bazars, owned by Lokenath, were rented annually by the Bengalis. They called it Bhubhan Bannerjee's Block. Others lived in the bazars at Boileauganj, Chhota Simla, Kasumpti and the pirate colony of Sanjauli, where the Maharaja of Nabha had houses which he let out to clerks.

There was a discernible pattern in the activities of the clerical staff, Hindu, Muslim or Sikh. The Simla police records of 1930 list 180 Government employees who were office-bearers of the socio-religious and caste associations of the day, although the chief donors to and organizers were of course wealthy pro-fessionals and traders.[21] The associations included the Sanatan

Dharam, both wings of the Arya Samaj, the Anjuman Islamia, the Insarul Muslamin, the Singh Sabha, the Hindu Pracharni Sabha, and caste sabhas such as the Brahman, Rajput and Jain.

For example, the Gurukul section of the Arya Samaj, with a membership of 300, had as office-bearers clerks from various Government departments. Its vice-president, Rai Sahib Ganga Ram of the Education Department, vigorously pursued the aims of the Samaj. He lived at Kasumpti, outside Simla's municipal limits, and played host to leading Arya Samaj workers. He took an active part in the *shuddhi* and *sangathan* movements and had a confrontation with the Muslims over an abduction. He was also vice-president of the Hindi Pracharni Sabha which sought to promote Hindi as the main language of India. If socio-religious activities turned into nationalist or anti-government voting stances, the government employee was censured: when Ganga Ram was host to Virender, son of the editor of the daily *Pratap*, he was given a warning by his officers.

Likewise, six of the eight office-bearers of the Singh Sabha, started in 1885, which had considerable local influence amongst Sikhs, were government employees. One of the most active was Gurdial Singh, a clerk in the General Post Office, who was also associated with the Sikh League of Simla. During the Akali movement of 1920 he passed a resolution against the treatment of Akalis by Government for which he was given a warning.

So long as these bodies retained a predominantly socio-religious character, Government staff continued to join them. Once they acquired political affiliations, it was Government pensioners rather than employees who became the principal office-bearers. It was the clerks in Government service who partnered the shopkeepers of Lower Bazar to shape the communal climate of the 1940s.

Government service forged common links in other ways too. The clerks tried to emulate their peers—the manner in which amateur dramatics as a social activity caught the imagination of all communities and classes of clerks is an example. Dramatics as a pastime also received official encouragement:

in 1893, the 'Babus of Government House' had formed their own association for staging plays.[22] The activity soon became popular with other communities as well whenever their numbers were large enough to form clubs. In 1897, the Bengali and Hindustani Samaj respectively were founded to produce and stage plays,[23] and each was permitted to rent the Gaiety Theatre once annually. The Club Committee thereafter, until 1928, refused to let Indian dramatic clubs use the theatre on the plea that they used too many stage props. In 1914, Tamil clerks formed the Madras Club and held dramatic performances at a small hall in Nabha Estate; another group of South Indian clerks living in Government quarters at Phagli organized a Daksh Club;[24] and theatricals became equally fashionable with the Punjabi clerks.

Finding a hall for their plays often posed a problem, and the denial of use of the Gaiety Theatre was often discussed as an example of racial discrimination. In 1928, Durga Das, then a Municipal Commissioner, recounted that he 'achieved some measure of success in the Indian community's fight against racial discrimination by getting the municipal-owned Gaiety Theatre on the Mall thrown open to Indian amateur dramatic clubs.'[25]

This interest in amateur dramatics was not shared by all. An Arya Samaj leader in 1926 lamented:

> The general tendency of the educated Hindu community serving in government offices, etc., in Simla is towards theatricals. Within a short span of three years, about ten Indian Amateur Dramatic clubs have sprung up here and, it is reported, that people vie with one another in trying to secure the enviable appointment of Secretary to any of these clubs.[26]

During the 1920s, both sections of the Arya Samaj launched movements for the eradication of social evils in the hills, and sought the active collaboration of the clerks in this. It was the constant endeavour of local organizations—social, religious and even political—to involve the large body of Indian Government servants in their activities. They undoubtedly participated in functions held in the evenings, after office.

The attitude of Indian Government servants towards the nationalist movement was ambivalent. They had grasped at every opportunity to obtain jobs in a Government designed to sustain imperial rule. Local political organizations often focused their attention on this class of Simla resident; the practice of addressing political meetings in the Gunj Maidan in the evening, when Government servants converged on Lower Bazar on their way home from office, was aimed at securing their attention. But it was only rarely that the clerks sided openly with the nationalists. When Gandhi came to Simla for the first time in 1921 it was a working day and the clerks could not join the reception. 'It is a pity that Mahatmaji did not arrive here on Sunday or any other holiday when the Government Clerks even would have had the honour of taking part in the reception,' the *Tribune* reported.[27] It was a lesson well learnt by local political organizations and subsequent meetings were planned only for the weekends. It was not an accident that Gandhi's mammoth meetings when he came for talks with Irwin, and the Dhami incident of 1939, were all planned to take place on a Sunday when Government servants could participate.

While Government servants as a group were sensitive to changes taking place in the country, it was perceived by them that membership of, or overt support to, political groups was inadvisable if not dangerous. Yet, no movement in Simla was deemed successful unless Government servants participated, although when they did, their support was sporadic, short-lived and could never be sustained. It was a flash in the pan, surprising alike organizers and the Government.

CHAPTER TWELVE

Human Underpinnings

A savage kick given by an Englishman to a coolie in 1925 resulted in the death of the coolie. The affair became notorious as the 'The Rickshaw Cooly Murder Case' of Simla. Over sixty years after the incident, many elderly residents point it out as one that stirred up public feeling, and some still recall the events with startling accuracy. There was a question in the House of Commons about the case as well.[1] This happening of the midnight of 3 September 1925 is worth recalling.[2]

Jageshar, a rickshaw coolie, muffled under a ragged sheet, dozed off on the porch of Yates Place, the home of Mansel-Pleydell, Controller of the Army Canteen Board. Along with several other coolies he was waiting to take his passengers, who were dining at Yates Place, home. Well past midnight, the dinner over, Mansel-Pleydell stamped out to wake up the coolies. Jageshar sat up and stumbled, as his feet were entangled in the covering sheet. An enraged, swearing Mansel-Pleydell kicked him out, off the porch, and kicking, pushed him about the garden until he collapsed into a flower-bed. Jageshar died of a ruptured spleen and three broken ribs in the early hours of the morning.

The assault on Jageshar had been witnessed in tongue-tied silence by the coolies, including his cousin Bakhia. Bakhia and his fellows returned to Yates Place after depositing their passengers, and wheeled Jageshar to the Chhota Simla Police Station. The constable on duty balked at recording the statement of the dying coolie. At this, Bakhia contacted his *chaudhri* at the Chalet shed, who hurried to Rai Bahadur Mohan Lal, Municipal Commissioner. After a call from him to the Superintendent of Police early in the morning, the case was registered at the Sadar Police Station in Lower Bazar.

The 'Rickshaw Cooly Murder Case' was one of the most

publicised crimes of Simla and was widely reported by the press, almost hearing by hearing. The proceedings were held in a court room that was packed, and a wave of sympathy built up for the hapless coolie. Twenty-three gave evidence in the case and withstood a long and rigorous cross-examination.[3] After a six-month trial, Mansel-Pleydell was convicted, sentenced to eighteen months' rigorous imprisonment, and fined 4,000 rupees. An appeal to the High Court was dismissed; Mansel-Pleydell committed suicide in jail.

The key figure in the case was Rai Bahadur Mohan Lal, the lawyer and Municipal Commissioner of Simla, on whose intervention the case was registered. The advocate for the prosecution was Kanwar Dalip Singh, assisted by Harish Chander of the local bar. But the defendant's lawyer questioned: 'Why should the Lala and prominent persons like members of the Legislative Assembly pay visits to Sardar Amar Singh, Sub-Inspector of Police to make enquiries after the case?'[4]

The case became important for a combination of reasons. Firstly, there was the personality of Mohan Lal who took up the case. He said he knew the coolies and *chaudhris* of the rickshaw stand at the Chalet, not because they were related to him, but because he hired a rickshaw there. His interest flowed from his position as Municipal Commissioner. When asked why the coolies 'salaamed' him, he retorted, in a way that was recalled as bold and true, "Half of Simla salaams Lala Mohan Lal.'[5] During a cross-examination lasting nine hours, he asserted that his interest in the case stemmed from his position as 'a citizen of Simla'. Old residents relate that despite the pressure exerted by British officials, the Lala would not retract and withdraw the case. He emerged as a champion against racial discrimination.

Secondly, the case was infused with a sense of confrontation that arose from nationalist aspirations. An interpellation question in the Punjab Legislative Assembly alleged that the Army Department was trying to 'hush up' the case, and feared that 'hot-headed persons may not be imported from England to make the lives of Indians unsafe.'[6] Congress workers seized the opportunity to highlight a sense of injustice and national hurt. They formed a conspicuous section of the crowds who attended the hearings.

Above all, the case eventually served to focus attention on the thirty per cent of Simla's summer population required every summer to pull rickshaws, carry loads, work in homes, sweep the town. They were a disparate, motley crowd of landless labourers and petty agriculturists, who flocked into the town from the hill states around Simla, Hoshiarpur and Jullundur. Low wages and lack of housing made it impossible for them to settle in Simla, nor did they bring their families with them—as is borne out by the census statistics which indicate a small percentage of women and dependants. The illiterate labouring migrant was seen as unkempt, dirty, little better than a beast of burden,[7] but in 1925, the change in perception caused by the assault was apparent, from the attitude of the labourers themselves, the disapproval of middle-class Indians, and the reports of it in sections of the nationalist press. It is worthwhile examining attitudes towards the coolies and their work conditions, and the nature of the efforts made to ameliorate and organize them.

The disciplining kick had been regarded as an accepted corrective for errant menials. It represented both the rulers' need to present a Gulliver-amongst-the-Lilliputians image, as well as an underlying fear of the mob of unruly servants. Assault was a frequent occurrence; the culprit would be let off lightly by a European jury. In any case, there was a tendency to hush up cases of assault, and in the army such cases were shielded by officers.

Physical violence appalled some fair-minded and well-meaning Britons who tried to curb the tendency, often, not because of a lack of contempt for the menial Indian, but because it soiled the paternal image of British justice. For example, when an English barrister in Agra, whose rough treatment of an Indian servant caused him to die of a ruptured spleen, was fined a paltry sum by a local magistrate, Lytton ordered the magistrate to be suspended and censured the Government of the North-Western Provinces in which the incident took place. When men of the Ninth Lancers regiment beat to death an Indian cook, Curzon ordered the offending regiments to be punished and publicly censured.

But attitudes die hard. Buck relates how an A.D.C. was directed by an angry Viceroy at the Simla Viceregal Lodge to quiet noisy domestics: 'Kick them on the shins'. But he added, since he had had to deal with more than one case in which an Indian had been assaulted, 'and be careful of their spleens.'[8]

The memory lingers of labourers that wore uniforms and turbans, but ran barefoot and smelled a lot: many would vouch with Val Prinsep that there was no smell worse than that of rickshaw coolies.[9] There are not many remnants of Simla's age of the rickshaw: only a few derelict sheds. The rickshaw used in Simla was first introduced by a chaplain, the Rev. J. Fordyce, in the early 1880s. It seated one person, was usually about nine feet long and weighed over three hundred pounds. It was far heavier than the rickshaw used in other Indian towns such as Calcutta, and four coolies were required to propel it in ascent and descent. As the only wheeled transport permitted on the roads and paths of Simla, the rickshaw was indispensable. Over 450 rickshaws served the transportation needs of Simla.[10]

Rickshaw pulling was a relatively unskilled occupation. The ability to run in step with other coolies, to develop 'wind' in order to pull the rickshaw up steep slopes, could be mastered in a few weeks. An economic report of 1934 described the rickshaw coolie as a man of simple habits, chatting to his friends, smoking the *huqqa*, and playing cards in his idle hours. He was hardy, and seldom too tired to pick up another fare.[11]

Our typical coolie was illiterate, between twenty and thirty years old. He came to Simla for the 'season' from March to October. He earned less than a bearer, *khidmutgar*, *ayah* or cook; on paper more than a sweeper, but in effect less. A sweeper normally worked in several homes and therefore his take-home earnings were correspondingly more. If a coolie was engaged by a private houseowner he was known as a *jampanee*. His salary varied in the 1930s from ten to twenty-six rupees, and he was lodged within calling distance, in one of the innumerable quarters for menials in the compound of the house. By convention he was not 'driven' more than twice a day, and was expected to wear the uniform supplied by his employer. Most private rickshaw owners employed two or three coolies and engaged others from the municipal stands whenever required.

If he was less fortunate, as most were, he was attached to one of the thirty-eight public rickshaw stands owned by the municipality. Then the figure of the *chaudhri* or contractor loomed large in his working life. The *chaudhris* owned the 450 licensed rickshaws and served as middlemen between the coolie and the municipality on the one hand, and the customer on the other.

The rates of hire, fixed in 1890, remained unchanged for almost forty years. There was an upward revision in 1914, but this increase merely covered the expenses incurred by the *chaudhri* in providing rickshaws with additional fittings, lamp and bell, and for the khaki uniform—coat, trousers and turban (but not shoes)—which the municipality decreed that he wear when 'standing or plying for hire'. The uniform cost Rs 3–8 annas; the coolie was normally charged anything upto five rupees for it by his *chaudhri*.[12]

A rickshaw could be hired for Rs 1–2 annas per hour. The *chaudhri* was entitled to take six annas from the coolie for every hour that his rickshaw was plied. He usually took eight annas and claimed it was a private arrangement. The remaining ten to twelve annas were divided amongst the four coolies.

The coolie's earnings varied from month to month, but the high watermark was August, during the monsoons, when the demand for rickshaws was greatest. On average he earned about eighteen rupees a month, of which about two-thirds were spent on essential requirements: a rupee could buy eight *seers* of rice, eight-and-a-half of wheat flour, six of jaggery (*gur*) and five-and-a-half of pulses. Normally he and his fellows set up a joint kitchen. A local shopkeeper would supply them with a brass *thali* (plate) and *katori* (bowl), ostensibly free, if they bought all their provisions at his shop. The shopkeeper re-compensed himself by hiking up the prices of rice, *atta*, *dal* and other provisions by ten or twenty per cent.

He worked and slept in his uniform. He never wore shoes, because leather ones were expensive and his *polas*, light hemp-fibre slip-ons, hampered easy running. So he ran barefoot. At night he either slept in the open or, if he was lucky, he was attached to a stand which had a shed upstairs where he could stay. Most, however, lived in dark airless godowns rented by the *chaudhri*. He paid 8 annas per month for the privilege of a roof over his head. He had neither the resources nor the utensils to heat water; so he hardly ever bathed. Consequently he was infested with body vermin. A medical test conducted by the municipality in the 1930s revealed that he was usually anaemic, and suffered from tachycardia or palpitations, an occupational hazard of running uphill. If he came from Kangra or Hoshiarpur, he may also have had chronic malaria with an enlarged spleen.

Rickshaw-pulling attracted the poorer peasants from the arid parts of the lower Kangra hills, Hamirpur and Bilaspur. They were usually landless peasants or had small uneconomic holdings; most were hopelessly in debt. The rickshaw coolies were mainly Hindu (87.2 per cent) and represented a cross-section of fourteen castes—including the Rajputs, Brahmans, Kanets and Julahas. The rest (12.8 per cent) were Muslim Gujars from Hoshiarpur.[13] Coolies belonging to the same caste ran joint kitchens and preferred to be employed together. The position of the rickshaw coolie in the caste hierarchy, however, was no index of his poverty.

The visible agent of exploitation in the rickshaw trade was the *chaudhri*. A Simla weekly stated that 'with his Shylockian propensities, he enriched himself at the expense of the coolies,'[14] and he was considered 'intractable and suspicious'. A Municipal Commissioner pronounced that the *chaudhris* 'are horrible leeches thriving on coolies' blood. . . .'[15]

Every October, the *chaudhris* made tenders for the thirty-eight rickshaw stands of the town. Upon being allotted a stand, they obtained licences for their rickshaws, and also

Captain Charles Pratt Kennedy, Political Agent, 1822–35,
'the most rigorous of dandies and sticklers for form.'

Simla's first house, Kennedy House, built in 1822. Kennedy
was associated with Simla's growth and popularity
as sanatorium.

The densest settlement sprawled across the sunny southern slopes. The incomplete Christ Church is visible on the horizon.

A *bhishti* fills his *mushak*, as an officer of the Gurkha Battalion looks on. Springs were Simla's only source of water until the 1880s.

Annandale—an amphitheatre about a quarter of a mile in
circumference, the site of countless fêtes, gymkhanas, dog shows, etc.

The Assembly Rooms and the Jubilee Theatre—the hub
of social Simla until the 1880s.

The Mall and Scandal Point. The Post Office is on the left. The new Town Hall dominates the Ridge.

The Ridge—city centre and Piazza. The bazar provided the flat stretch for annual parades and ceremonial functions. Christ Church was built in 1844–56.

Viceregal Lodge, in the Elizabethan style, was occupied by Dufferin in 1888. The terraced garden was planned by Lady Minto.

In the 1880s the offices moved into new buildings. The Army Headquarters is on the right; the timber-framed Tudor building on the hill on the left is the Telegraph Office.

The rickshaw was introduced in the 1890s. 'Licensed' rickshaw coolies wore a khaki uniform, turban and badge—but ran barefoot.

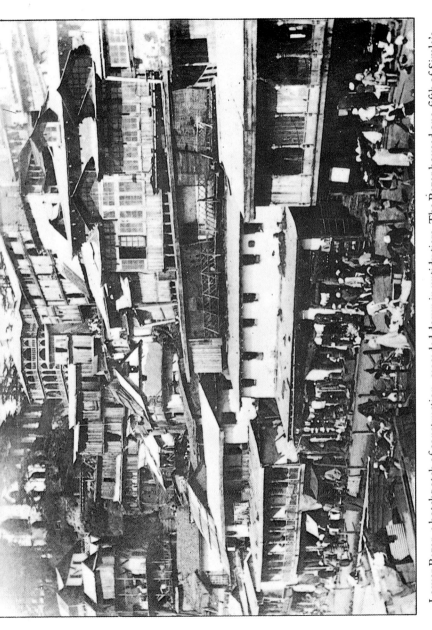

Lower Bazar, a hotchpotch of construction, cascaded down in untidy tiers. The Bazar housed one-fifth of Simla's Indian population.

Gandhiji and Mahadev Desai escorted by Lala Mela Ram Sood (right) after the Gandhi-Irwin talks in 1930. The Viceregal Lodge gate is in the background.

'Manorville', Raj Kumari Amrit Kaur's residence in Summer Hill. She is seen with Gandhi who stayed there in 1940.

The Maidan-i-Gunj in Edwards Gunj, the principal wholesale grain market. Vithalbhai Patel (below the flag) addresses a gathering in 1930. From the vantage point of the projecting balconies, many, especially women, observe the meeting.

Sunday, 27 April 1930. A procession surges across the Mall to bid farewell to Vithalbhai Patel after his resignation as President of the Legislative Assembly.

committed themselves to providing five licensed coolies for every licensed rickshaw. Although three coolies were considered necessary to propel the rickshaw, the additional ones served to meet other requirements of private rickshaw owners. They were also used as porters for carrying loads.

The *chaudhris* were responsible for the maintenance of rickshaws and rickshaw-stands according to the standards prescribed by the municipality. They paid water and electricity charges, furnished the rickshaw with rubber tyres, a glass front, a leather seat and hood, and finally ensured that their coolies were clad in khaki uniforms.

As a class the *chaudhris* were considered affluent. Their capacity to extort from the coolie more than the amount sanctioned by the municipality determined their actual profits. An instance is Chaudhri Daulat Ram of Lakkar Bazar, who was reputed to be a prosperous man. In 1929 he had been in business for ten years, and maintained fourteen to sixteen rickshaws with about eighty coolies, leasing his rickshaw stand from the municipality for 450 rupees for the season. He submitted that his gross income for the year was 3,010 rupees, with an expenditure of 2,616 rupees and a net income of about 400 rupees per season. Daulat Ram claimed he had rented five godowns and one big hall for 350 rupees as accommodation for his coolies.[16]

Technically, the *chaudhri* owned the rickshaws at his stand, but often he himself was agent for other 'financiers and secret partners' who controlled the enterprise. Sadhoo Ram, a weaver from Bilaspur, was one such. In 1894 he had set up business with five rickshaws in Kainthu. He bought another five rickshaws in the next five years. By 1929, Sadhoo Ram had 'another partner' and maintained in his own name thirty-one rickshaws. He leased out the Cecil Hotel stand of twenty rickshaws for 1,200 rupees and the municipal stand of eleven rickshaws for 980 rupees. He employed over 150 coolies and charged them one piçe per day to be accommodated in five godowns and one big hall which he rented for 350 rupees.[17]

The *chaudhris'* secret partners and financiers were often

shopkeepers or traders who owned rickshaws. Jack Blessington, the owner of a firm manufacturing and repairing rickshaws describes one such arrangement:

> I was once a lessee of the Municipal Rickshaw Shed, i.e. in front of the Station Library. I used to keep 10 Rickshaws there. The business was not run by me personally but by my agent. He used to give me Rs 2 or Rs 2/8 on account of rickshaw earnings per day. I do not say that the work was not profitable, but that it was not under my supervision, therefore, I could not make any profits.[18]

Thus, a pyramid of exploitation was constructed in the rickshaw trade. The fare which a passenger paid was shared and divided between financier, agent, *chaudhri* and coolie. The *chaudhris* in 1914 formed what was euphemistically called the Rickshaw Workers Union. The Union fought to gain from the municipality an increase in fares in 1919, which went into the *chaudhris'* pockets. The coolie remained impoverished.

Apart from the rickshaw pullers, the coolies who carried heavy loads constituted another distinct section of Simla's labouring class. They were usually Muslims from the Kashmir valley and from Ladakh,[19] who were first brought to Simla in the nineteenth century by an enterprising Kashmiri contractor. Referred to as *hathos* (a Kashmiri word meaning 'boy' or 'urchin'), they fell into two groups; one of Sunni Muslims from areas such as Shopian, Pampore, Kulgam and Anantnag in the Kashmir valley, most of whom had small holdings insufficient to sustain them and their families through the year. They stayed in Simla from March till October, and lived in the Kashmiri Mohalla in Lower Bazar. The other group, Shias, hailed from Kargil in Ladakh, and was engaged in house construction. They lived in the Ladakhi Mohalla below the Cart Road. The Imam Bara, built by Ladakhi mule-drivers and petty traders, was located in the centre of the *mohalla* and served as their social centre.[20]

Sturdy and well-built compared to the peasants from the

Simla hills, Kashmiri labourers were much in demand because of their capacity for carrying heavy loads. They therefore had the monopoly of the loading and unloading business, were engaged by wholesale merchants to carry heavy bags, and provided labour on construction sites.

Their living conditions depended on their contractor: for instance the twenty coolies retained by Nabir Mir, a Kashmiri contractor, were accommodated in a *dhara* or shed he had rented, provided with cooking utensils, and procured a licence from the municipality.[21] No commission for contractors had been fixed by the municipality, but Nabir Mir took three pies out of every eight annas (10 per cent) received by the coolies. Since the average earning of each coolie was fifteen rupees per month, the contractor gained about twenty rupees per month.

The plunge down the social scale, and to the bottommost terrace in the southern part of Simla—below the Lower Bazar, and below the Cart Road, but above the Lalpani Sewage disposal tanks—brought one to the colony of Harijans, the Balmikis of Simla. Simla's status as a sanatorium rested squarely on them. The British zeal for cleanliness, the need to clear litter from roads and hillsides, the necessity of frequently emptying commodes into receptacles placed at some distance from houses, had created a great demand for sweepers and scavengers. It opened up the possibility of a job to landless Harijans who had provided cheap labour to the large agriculturists of Jullundur and Hoshiarpur. The first to come were from the villages Badiala and Jadiala of Jullundur district. Others followed, from the nearby villages of Koravah, Jamshedpur, Podasaprai, and from the neighbouring Hoshiarpur district.

At Simla they found a way to augment the municipal salary of seven rupees per month. The municipality was short of hands; elderly Balmikis assert that there were considerably fewer than the four hundred registered in the municipal records,[22] and the more enterprising did additional work, serving as part-time hill litter cleaners. They scoured the hillside, picking up wood and pieces of coal as fuel for their cooking. It was also the accepted practice to take up part-time sweeping and scavenging jobs in private homes. During the potato season in October and November, some trudged during their off-time to Dhalli to make extra money packing potatoes for the commission agents of Simla.

Their homes near Ladakhi Mohalla were makeshift. Most returned to their village during the winter months, well dressed, strikingly different from the appearance they presented in their working life in Simla. A song sung in Badiala in Jullundur district celebrating the return of 'the boys' goes:

> *Alu-mutter pakaie hoine*
> *Bari vicho tak soniyo.*
> *Munde Shimle to aye hoine.*

> Potatoes and peas did I cook
> From Shimla have the boys come,
> O pretty one, through the window look.[23]

For peas were a delicacy, fit to be served to the young villager back from Simla. As some families then moved to Simla, references to weddings with young men settled in the summer capital began to emerge in village songs. The expectations of dowry were upgraded accordingly.

> *Ghori mere vir dhee jandhee Shimle, Shimle*
> *Bhena ne ghera pa leya, vira dheja saree vag pharien;*
> *Jo kuch mangna mangle, jyadha behna dher na layee*
> *Kurti leera reshmi bhoori bhains phariee;*
> *Ghori mere . . .*

> *Ghori mere vir dhee jaree Shimle Shimle*
> *Pharjaiyan ne ghera pa leya, dheja surma pavaiee;*
> *Jo kuch mangna mangle bhabi, bohti dher na layee*
> *Kurti leera reshmi, sone dhe nath karvaiee;*
> *Ghori mere . . .*

> To Shimla trots my brother's wedding mare.
> O brother, what'll you give us, the sisters say.
> Ask whatever you will, but hurry don't take all day.
> A silken shirt and tawny buffalo, they pray.
> To Shimla trots my brother's wedding mare.

To Shimla trots my brother's wedding mare.
And what'll you give to us, the sisters-in-law cry.
Ask whatever you will, for god's sake be spry.
A silken shirt, a gold nosering please buy.
To Shimla trots my brother's wedding mare.

These verses are sung by the women of the family when the groom departs for the bride's house. The gifts asked for such as a tawny buffalo and a gold nose-ring, were normally beyond a landless labourer's purchasing capacity.

The life history of Modhan Singh (d. 1954) is unique. His grandfather came to Simla from his village in Jullundur district in the late nineteenth century to work as a sweeper. His father, Narain Dharu, brought his family to Simla, and sent the young Modhan Singh to the municipal school at Mayfield. He was educated up to the middle school level and was, like his father and grandfather, employed by the municipality. By 1931 he was drawn into the vortex of the Congress movement for the uplift of Harijans. In Simla, Congress workers who belonged to the College section of the Arya Samaj prompted Modhan Singh to establish the Balmikiyan Temple below the Cart Road. As one of the few literate Harijans, the local Congress party made him the General Secretary of the Balmikiyan Association in 1931.

The mobilization of Simla's labour and efforts to ameliorate their work conditions after the 1930s was the result of the fusion of several strands. Gandhi's constructive work amongst the Daridnarayan merged with Nehru's efforts to give the Indian National Congress a socialist direction. In 1929 Nehru was elected President of both the Indian National Congress and the Trade Union Congress, and wrote, 'Everywhere I spoke on political independence and social freedom and made the former a step towards the attainment of the latter.'[24] Finally, religious groups such as the Arya Samaj were fired with the ideal of *shuddhi*, or re-conversion to Hinduism. The Arya Samaj joined the Congress at Simla in arousing 'national conscious-ness', although restricting it to a narrow Hindu base. At Simla it sought to prevent the Balmikis from straying into the Muslim fold by conversion.

The Balmiki Association was founded in 1931 with the active efforts of the College section of the Arya Samaj, some of whose members were also Congress activists. The Samaj provided the inspiration for the founding of the Balmiki Mandir in the Ladakhi Mohalla, a small *dhajji* structure. It also housed the new Balmiki Mandir Sabha and the Balmiki Young Men's Association, patterned on the YMCA (Young Men's Christian Association). The Balmiki Association served as a labour union, caste organization, and political organ rolled into one. Politically, it had the blessings of the local Congress.

Its meetings were held either at the Arya Samaj Hall (College section) at Lower Bazar or outside the Balmiki Mandir, between 8 p.m. and midnight when the adults of the community were free. A report of a typical meeting reads:

> A meeting was held in Arya Samaj Hall, Lower Bazar, Simla from 8.00 p.m. to 11.30 p.m., under the presidentship of Dr N. L. Varma, Municipal Commissioner, Simla, amidst a gathering of about 150 persons. Besides religious bhajans and songs that took place from 8.00 p.m. to 9.45 p.m., Dr N. L. Varma, the President, Amar Singh, Granthi Gurdwarah Nabha Estate, Master Chiranji Lal 'Prem', an Arya Samaj Preacher, L. Salig Ram, B. A., shopkeeper, Lower Bazar, Simla, Kishori Lal, President Arya Samaj, College Section, Simla, Chandan, Sweeper of Simla, and Gurdit Singh, Achhut of Faridkot (State), delivered speeches exhorting the Balmikis to organize and reform themselves and give up all habits of drinking and spending the money on evil vices.[25]

Attendance was high, with fifty to a hundred being present. The larger meetings were invariably addressed by Arya Samaj preachers and Congress members such as N. L. Varma, or Chaudhri Diwan Chand.

As a labour union, it focused on improving working conditions: shorter working hours, provision of uniforms and a salary of fifteen rupees per month were the chief of many demands. In 1931, one of the Balmiki Association's applications to the municipality was for a seat in the Municipal Committee as an 'interest' of Simla.[26] In 1935, they went on strike for higher wages. By 1939 there was an appeal for exemption from the graduate degree, prescribed as the minimum qualification required for a clerical job in the municipality.

In a chain reaction to Gandhi's fast in 1932 against giving separate political representation to the Harijans, which eventually led to the Poona Pact between the Congress and B. R. Ambedkar, the Harijan leader, the Arya Samaj Congressmen encouraged seven Balmikis (Lakhu, Gurdas, Sadhu Ram, Gulzari, Jagga, Bakha, and Santa), some of them employed in the municipality, to attend a *kirtan* in the rival Sanatan Dharam Temple; they left, when asked to by the temple priest, docilely and at once. However, the next day, a protest meeting attended by almost two hundred people took place.[27]

Dr Ambedkar, social worker and champion of the depressed classes, had drawn closer to the Muslim League after his breach with the Congress. The Muslim League opened the doors of its Islamia School to the Balmikis of Simla. Brij Lal Salhotra, former Municipal Commissioner and Up Pradhan (officebearer) of the Bharatiya Dalit Varga Sangha, remembers taking his own *bori* (gunny bag) to sit on, when he attended the Islamia School at Simla. Ambedkar's later drift away from the Muslim League as well, to found an Independent Labour Party with the major objective of propagating social equality, was reflected in the formation of a parallel association at Simla.[28] It demanded a better deal and improved working conditions for the Balmikis, exhorting them to establish themselves as a separate entity which had 'no connection with Arya Samajists and the Muslims'. The new wing, however, did not have much support,[29] the Congress–Arya Samaj combination having forged strong links, which have lasted till today.

Efforts to ameliorate the working conditions of another group of labour, the coolies, took another direction. Abdul Ghani, a labour member of the Punjab Legislative Assembly, took the initiative in welding the Kashmiri load-carrying porters and the rickshaw coolies into a labour union.

He became the first president of the Kashmiri Muslim Labour Board founded in September 1929 for improving the working and living conditions of the Kashmiri *hathos*.[30] At a mammoth meeting at the Idgah in 1929 and again in 1930, the aims of the Board were outlined: they included improvement of the working conditions and social reform of the Muslim labouring classes. By 1931, the Board had secured an increase in the coolies' rates for hire. The other major achievement was that the Kashmiri labourer was henceforth to be referred to as *khan* rather than by the derogatory term *hatho*.

Abdul Ghani's efforts to organize the rickshaw-pullers was a highly publicized event. At a meeting on 14 August 1929 convened at the Ridge, he urged them to go on strike to compel the municipality to improve their wages and conditions of work.[31] Alarmed at this prospect, the Municipal Committee conducted an inquiry into the rickshaw-pullers' grievances.

Very soon the hiring rates were revised, and the coolie's licence fee reduced from one rupee to four annas. *Chaudhris* were required to provide four instead of five coolies per rickshaw. The changes, however, merely skirted the problem, for the role of the *chaudhri* did not alter. Lala Durga Das, then a Municipal Commissioner, outlined to the committee 'a scheme . . . [to] give an incentive to the coolies themselves to become capitalists and run their own rickshaws.'[32] Durga Das proposed that the system of leasing municipal stands to the highest bidder and the institution of the *chaudhri* be abolished. In 1929 this scheme was considered a radical and impracticable one.

The initiative to implement Durga Das's scheme was taken up nine years later in 1938 by S. Partab, the Deputy Commissioner and President of the Municipal Committee. 'Moved by the pitiable condition of the coolie', Partab attempted to protect the coolie from the demands of 'that standing curse to rickshaw-coolies—the *chaudhris*'. He 'propelled' through the Municipal Committee a resolution designed to eliminate the institution of the *chaudhri*: 5,000 rupees was allocated by the municipality co enable fifty rickshaws to be owned and managed by two hundred coolies. Some rickshaw-stands were no longer given to the highest bidder, and no provision was to be made for extra coolies. After a season, the scheme was extended to cover eighteen municipal stands and 174 rickshaws. In 1941 the committee decided to eliminate the *chaudhris* altogether, but this programme was never implemented.

Dissent and opposition came from several quarters. The *chaudhris*, shopkeepers, traders, and residents, British as well as Indian, forced a reconsideration of the scheme. The political and economic ramifications of the decision also surfaced; above all, however, the proposed changes had their biggest barrier in social conservatism, the resistance to change in accepted modes.

Predictably, it was the *chaudhris* who mounted the greatest pressure. Partab was aware that their 'vested interests were so deeply rooted that they [would] not go without a stubborn fight.' What he had not anticipated was the variety of ways in which they could thwart the scheme and impel reversion to the old system. The Rickshaw Workers Union of the *chaudhris* made a plea that 'the scheme is resulting not only in ruining our ancestral profession but also telling a lot on the Municipal funds.' The *chaudhris* intensified their appeals in pamphlets and broadsheets every September before the stands were auctioned. In 1939, they engaged a local lawyer and gave notice of a civil suit, since the Act abolishing *chaudhris* was *ultra vires* of the constitution of India as it deprived a section of the public of their right to follow a particular trade. The following year, the *chaudhris* released a pamphlet which extolled the paternal relationship existing between *chaudhris* and coolies, and bore the thumb impression of 500 coolies.

The shopkeepers, traders, bankers and commission agents of the Mall, Lower Bazar, and the Lakkar Bazar, all opposed the Act. Some of them had business interests in the rickshaw trade; others were convinced the reform was not practicable. In a signature drive in 1938, they pointed out that *chaudhris* were indispensable to the trade, that the new system would be

'an army without a Commanding Officer'; also that if the coolies
had any complaint against the rickshaw *chaudhris* for not getting
their dues it was baseless: '*Chaudhris* are deprived of their
rights because coolies never let them know the actual amount
charged from the passengers.'

The *chaudhris* formed a Municipal Reforms Association,
which issued a pamphlet entitled 'The case of the Municipal
Rickshaw Chaudhris of Simla', in which the disadvantages of
the new system—the loss to the municipality, hardships to
coolies, inconvenience to the public, and deprivation of
chaudhris of their hereditary profession, were spelt out. It
added that 'in the zeal of being modern and reformists we are
diminishing all the good features of the old and incorporating
all the evils of novelty due to inexperience.'[33]

Protests poured in from several unexpected sources, the
railway authorities, the Public Works Department and the
United Service Club. Like the municipality, these organizations
also leased out sheds annually for a specified number of
rickshaws. They were quite categorical that they could not
underwrite their losses if they ceased to tender for their
rickshaw-sheds. Private complaints against the new system
from British as well as Indian residents increased.

In 1939 the Municipal Commissioners Lala Puran Chandra,
Mir Ahmed Hussain, Lala Mela Ram and P. D. Sharma, who
had enthusiastically supported the reformed system, withdrew.
A municipal election was due in 1939, though due to the outbreak of World War II, it was never held. Some Municipal
Commissioners felt compelled, for political reasons, to put up
a joint resolution for a reconsideration of the role of *chaudhris*.
The redoubtable S. Partab noted: 'Even impending election is
no justification for these gentlemen to perform such a marvellous
somersault,' and overruled their objections.

In 1940 Partab, who had initiated the reform, was transferred
from Simla. Within two years the new Committee reverted to
the old system. Soon the rickshaw-owning coolies were anxious
to obtain adequate payment for the rickshaws bought in
1939–40. The old *chaudhris*, helped by their patrons, returned

to their trade. The reform had eventually helped only the *chaudhris*, and their old financiers and secret partners.[34]

The municipality thereafter turned to less controversial methods to improve the working conditions of coolies. In 1943, labour hostels were constructed at eight different sites to accommodate 500 coolies.[35] Voluntary organizations, such as the Coolies Welfare Society, founded in 1935 under the patronage of the Vicereine, the Marchioness of Linlithgow, and headed by a few socially conscious and well-meaning individuals, attempted to improve working conditions, which amounted to conducting a few literacy classes and occasionally distributing blankets.

This detailed account of two groups of the labour force, the rickshaw coolies, and the Balmikis, illustrates two patterns of mobilization: while the Mansel-Pleydell case had generated public sympathy for rickshaw coolies, many levels of exploitation by *chaudhris*, financiers and shopkeepers, together with resistance to change, prevented the rickshaw coolies' chance of an equitable deal. Even for the few that plied until recently, the old system of ownership by the *chaudhri* continued. On the other hand, labour which was employed by the municipality was more successful in its attempts to force change. When the Balmikis, for example, struck work they were given a raise. The impulse generated by the nationalist movement against foreigners, personified by the Government or the municipality, fused with the strikers' demand. No one's interests were harmed. Everyone had something to gain.

CHAPTER THIRTEEN

1921–Simla's First Major Stir

W HEN Gandhi alighted at the Summer Hill Railway Station on 11 May 1921, there was an 'immense crowd' of Indians to receive him.[1] Preparations had been afoot since the early hours, and by the time of his arrival the town was 'garlanded and en fête,—albeit good-humouredly so—to the last degree'.[2] Scores of schoolboys had missed school and flocked to Summer Hill for a glimpse of Gandhi and to join in the festivity of the occasion.[3] During his four days' visit, crowds trailed after him whenever he set out from Shanti Kutir on Summer Hill. On 13 May, when he met Lord Reading, they followed him to the gates of Viceregal Lodge with the cry *Betaj Badshah Ki Jai* (Victory to the uncrowned king).[4] The next day, he created a sensation when he addressed the women of Simla at the Arya Samaj Hall in Lower Bazar; thereafter he was taken out in procession through 'the gaily decorated bazar' to the house of Lala Mohan Lal where an At Home took place.[5] The climax of this visit came on 15 May, a Sunday morning. Gandhi addressed an 'over-flow meeting attended by 15,000 people at the Idgah'.[6] Since it was a holiday, the large crowd included innumerable government employees. A novel feature was the presence of a multitude of hill folk who had thronged to Simla from the surrounding areas for a *darshan*. Contemporary accounts state that Gandhi's visit had aroused unprecedented enthusiasm in Simla's Indian population. In Durga Das' words, Simla experienced its 'first major stir'.[7]

Gandhi had been invited to meet Reading, the Viceroy, in order to create a favourable climate for the visit of the Prince of Wales in December 1921. The all-India response organized by Gandhi to the repressive Rowlatt Act of 1919, had been overwhelming, and apprehending another spell of protest, the Viceroy had invited Gandhi for talks.[8]

Gandhi was accompanied by Pandit Madan Mohan Malaviya and Lala Lajpat Rai, who utilized the visit to collect funds for the Tilak Swaraj Fund, and to spread the message of Swaraj in Simla. At every meeting, Gandhi spoke on non-violence, sacrifice, Hindu–Muslim unity and the use of the *charkha* as the road to freedom. Lala Lajpat Rai made impassioned addresses, stressing the need for removal of the slave mentality and making a fearless stand for the principles for which the Congress was fighting. It was the first occasion that the residents of Simla had been directly exposed to the nationalist point-of-view. Hitherto, the only public functions in Simla had been annual celebrations for the King Emperor's birthday—devices calculated to promote belief in the strength and continuity of the Empire. Gandhi's visit provided an alternative, and contrasting focus of attention. Indian public opinion in Simla now began to crystallize around the goals and ideals of Swaraj as spelt out by nationalist leaders.

The summer capital, uptil the 1920s, had been politically quiescent and public life was a 'sluggish stream . . . moving slowly, stagnating between high official banks'.[9] This tranquillity was the outcome of the design of preserving Simla as a uniquely English enclave by placing restrictions on expansion of the town and increase in its Indian population. Nevertheless, the Indian population had doubled between 1898 and 1921. Many British-owned houses and estates of Station Ward were gradually purchased and occupied by Indians. With these changes in the pattern of property ownership, and with population increase, resentment developed against features which established British racial superiority in Simla.

Several factors accelerated the pace of this resentment and also linked it with the nationalist movement. The bicameral legislature, set up under the provisions of the Government of India Act of 1919, brought politicians of an all-India reputation to Simla during the summer months.[10] Slogans and ideologies that formed a part of nationalist politics were thus introduced into Simla. Simultaneously the Congress, under Gandhi's leadership, was transformed from a party of upper-class professionals and intellectuals into a mass movement with attainment of Swaraj as its goal. The whole style of politics underwent a change and such mass involvement ushered in a new era for Simla as well. Edwards Gunj, the only unbuilt area in the crowded confines of Lower Bazar, became the venue for spontaneous political meetings, and the response of Indians in Simla to the nationalist movement changed from one of languid awareness to sporadic involvement.

Gandhi's visit affected Simla in two ways. Firstly, it activated local leaders into making elaborate arrangements for his welcome. News of his visit was widely circulated so that those living in Simla and its environs could gather to hear him. Secondly, local problems which had been the subject of petitions and memorials for several years, were now presented at public meetings before large audiences at the Gunj. Whereas leaders of an all-India stature sought to inform the Simla public about nationalist goals, local leaders cashed in on the mood to present local issues. Three personalities dominated the local political scene: Dr Kedar Nath, and Lala Harish Chandra, who were active in municipal politics, and an American missionary from Kotgarh, Samuel Evans Stokes, who aroused public opinion on the question of *begar* and encouraged the villagers of the district to converge on Simla to present their grievances.

Kedar Nath, a physician who had studied medicine at Edinburgh, made Simla his home. He is remembered as a towering figure on horseback, who lived in a house known as Ayrcliff located near the Railway Board building. Attracted both by the progressive views of the Arya Samaj and the political aims of the Congress, Kedar Nath directed his energies to mobilizing and organizing public opinion for both causes. He became president of the College section of the Arya Samaj in 1920 and spearheaded the Arya Samaj movement in the Simla hills. He was also General Secretary of the District Congress from 1914 to 1922. A moderate Congressman in 1914, he later became a convert to the mass movement policy of Gandhi. Harish

Chandra, a pleader, and Sood from Sujanpur Tira in Kangra, was president of the city Congress committee in 1914–22. Kedar Nath and Harish Chandra, both active Congressmen, tried to draw Indian attention to the unrepresentative character of the Simla municipality.

The Municipal Committee had been carefully reconstituted to function as an adjunct of the Government. The Deputy Commissioner was ex-officio President and six members were nominated, ostensibly to represent all interests. British commercial interests were safeguarded by the nomination of one member from the Punjab Trades Association, and there was one Hindu and one Muslim representative. Jai Lal continued to be a nominated member on the Municipal Committee from 1900 to 1919. Mir Mohammad Khan represented Muslim interests for over a decade.

Discontent with the functioning and constitution of Simla's 'fossil' municipality surfaced both from the non–official British residents and the Indian residents of Simla but from widely different perspectives. British traders in Simla resented a resolution passed in 1913 amending the octroi rules. This led to a debate on the wider question of the constitution and functioning of the municipality. According to British non-officials, the root cause of the ills which beset the town were 'the schemes and fads' of successive officials responsible for Simla's civic amenities. The answer lay in electing 'an able committee with business initiative and industry'.[11] Drawing parallels with the reformed municipalities in England, these British residents saw no reason why the Simla municipality should not function on the English model. To them, Simla was essentially a European town, a fact sometimes explicitly stated, often implied, but an assumption that prefaced most arguments by them. Logically, then, they argued that Simla should be administered by Europeans elected by the tax-payers.[12]

The controversy led Shadi Lal, a member of the Punjab Legislative Council, who had championed the cause of local self-government in September 1913, to raise the issue of the Simla municipality in the Punjab Legislative Council. He questioned the circumstances which deprived the tax-payers of Simla of the privilege of electing their representative to the municipality, and asked whether the Government was aware that tax-payers were dissatisfied with the municipal constitution.[13] This sparked off another lively debate in the local papers. Indians then joined in the debate—the Indian representatives were described as 'but dummies'. One anonymous letter by an Indian went on to comment, 'They can never carry their opinion nor dream of asserting themselves and always justify their existence by the graceful expression, "Yes, sir". Such is the representation the Indian rate-payers have on the Committee.'[14]

The pattern of criticism of the Simla Municipal Committee had been set by the non-official British, and was adopted by educated Indians in the middle of the twentieth century. In 1914, Kedar Nath formed the first Indian House Owners and Taxpayers' Association. Modelled on the associations formed by the British non-officials of Simla, it sought to involve a cross-section of influential middle-class Indians living in the Bazar and Station Wards. The executive committee of the Association included Puran Mal, commission agent and banker, Chaudhri Diwan Chand, Dinshaw Framji, a Parsi house-owner and merchant, and four Muslim house-owners.[15] The Association presented a representation urging restoration of the elective principle in the municipality.[16] The *Simla Times* mistakenly thought that the memorial emanated from a few 'dissatisfied babus and illiterate shopkeepers', and that house-owners had been made to sign it by misrepresentation of its contents.[17] The petition was summarily rejected.

The Government of India resolution of 16 May 1918, recommending complete popular control in local bodies, once again brought to the fore the question of the constitution of the Simla municipality.[18] The proposal to set up a self-governing local body in Simla was rejected by the president of the municipality, as a premature innovation, which raised a storm of protest from both British non-officials and traders, and from the Indian House Owners and Taxpayers' Association. The Indian protest was, however, linked to the march of

national events. The passing of the Rowlatt Act and the Jallian-
walla Bagh tragedy activated the Simla Congress; in April 1919,
Kedar Nath and Harish Chandra succeeded in persuading Simla
shopkeepers and traders to close their shops and attend a public
meeting in the Gunj. Simla, unlike Delhi, Bombay, and Lahore,
remained calm, and no violent incident occurred,[19] but, for the
first time in its history, volunteers of the Simla Rifle Corps
opened up the armoury in anticipation of violence. The *Simla
Times* reported:

> The strike of shopkeepers passed off quietly. . . . The vast
> majority of Hindus, Mohamedans and Sikhs who closed their
> shops or otherwise participated in the agitation had no evil
> intention. Unless they are acting a part they were puzzled. . . .[20]

Even if the shopkeepers appeared 'puzzled', they had nevertheless been introduced to the new weapons of the *hartal* and
the public meeting.

With a successful protest organized in 1919, Congress workers
turned their attention once again to municipal affairs. In
December 1919, they moved the Indian House Owners and
Taxpayers' Association to submit a representation for the
restoration of the elective system. They were joined by the
Punjab Trades Association and the British House Owners
Association to devise an alternative constitution for Simla.
When these efforts yielded no results, the question was taken
to the Gunj by the Indian associations. In March 1921, a resolu-
tion passed at a public meeting urged the restoration of the
elective system, and was presented by Harish Chandra to the
Municipal Committee.[21]

Throughout the summer of 1921, at largely-attended public
meetings, Harish Chandra spoke about the importance of having
a representative municipality. Meetings were held every
Sunday, leading the *Simla Times* to comment that the municipality was in for a 'hot time'.[22] As a result of this pressure, the
whole question of the municipal constitution was reopened.
In 1922, the composition of the Municipal Committee was

altered to consist of ten members, eight being nominated; two members, one each from Station and Bazar Wards being elected.[23] In 1930, the elective membership was increased to three, an additional member being elected from Bazar Ward.

Despite this concession to the elective principle, the constitution and function of the municipality continued to be tied to the concept of interests, with the Government the principal interest. It never became a self-governing institution although, under the umbrella of the Swaraj agitation, Harish Chandra and Kedar Nath had presented a local issue to the public.

The imperial summer capital was gradually undergoing a sea change. The Simla public began increasingly to witness the airing of local problems and see the rise of local leadership. One of the issues raised frequently at political meetings in the Gunj in the summer of 1921, and one that concerned the Simla Indian public only indirectly, was that of *begar*, which required peasants to serve as coolies to carry luggage virtually free. This burden fell heavily on villagers living along the more frequented routes, and provided the basis for the inexpensive hunting and sightseeing trips made by the British to the Simla hills. Such trips, especially along the Hindustan–Tibet road, were part of the attraction of Simla's summer season. It was this misuse of forced labour which was taken up by Stokes.

Samuel Evans Stokes, the son of a wealthy Philadelphian businessman, was imbued with a fervent desire for missionary service in India.[24] Not interested in following his father into business, he arrived at Sabathu at the age of 22, impatient to launch on his life as a missionary. In 1905, after a brief spell of relief work in Kangra which had been devastated by a severe earthquake, Stokes settled in Kotgarh. In 1910, together with F. J. Western, he founded a missionary society, the 'Brotherhood of the Imitation of Jesus',[25] which adopted the Indian ideal of renunciation. Stokes preached the Christian gospel in several towns in the Punjab. After a short spell he decided that Christian family life presented a higher and more relevant ideal than did renunciation, and in 1912, he married Agnes, the daughter of a local missionary and made Barubagh in Kotgarh his home.

Of a reflective and enquiring cast of mind, Stokes was unlike the stereotyped missionary—he could not shut his mind to Indian metaphysical thought. Describing himself as a 'lover of Christ' he, nevertheless, deplored the tendency of Christian missionary societies in India to establish themselves as adjuncts to Western civilization,[26] being 'anxious for the message of Christ to have the opportunity to work itself out in conjunction with Eastern thought and speculation.' He felt that evangelical Christianity need not be culturally alien to India. His philosophy of life, a subtle blending of eastern and western thought, was expounded in a book entitled *Satyakam*.[27] Stokes did not confine himself to philosophy; he was equally sensitive to the political changes sweeping the country.

On the outbreak of World War I, he volunteered his services towards the war effort, and in 1917 was appointed Recruiting Officer for the Simla Hill States.[28] Familiar with the hill people, his assignment (for which he received a letter of commendation from his Reporting Officer) brought him into even more intimate contact with the local people and their problems. The constant grievance of hill villagers living along the popular holiday routes was the exaction of forced labour. Stokes, as the 'most educated and intelligent member of the hill community', took up the question, and secured for all hill villagers who had served in World War I, a lifetime's exemption from *begar*.

Until 1918 he was convinced that if factual information about this unjust imposition was communicted to the Simla authorities, the indiscriminate issue of permits enabling visitors to requisition villagers' services to carry their luggage and serve as labourers, would cease. However, when his letters and petitions yielded no results, he looked for other ways to resolve the problem and was soon drawn into the vortex of the nationalist movement.

The Rowlatt Act and the events at Jallianwala Bagh made Stokes a critic of Government policies, and he took a strong stand against the Government's shortsighted policy of repression. He believed at that time that although loyalty to the Empire was essential, 'acquiescence in every policy of the bureaucracy' was not an inevitable corollary. The futility of the constitutional approach to the question of forced labour led him to write: 'We have to find a way to end a relation which results in a constant praying for favours on the one hand, and the condescending grant of them on the other. We have to find a way to end the situation in which foreign officials live, as inaccessible as Mahadeva on Mount Kailash, each surrounded by his vortex of parasites who fatten upon the miseries of a poor and inarticulate peasantry.'[29]

By 1920, the question of forced labour had reached crisis point. A prolonged dry spell had brought the surrounding hill areas to the brink of famine. The *rabi* wheat crop had been damaged, it was feared, beyond redemption. A summer shower could have saved the maize crop from famine 'of the worst type' but the poorer peasants would still suffer serious hardships, and the imposition of forced labour during the crucial summer season would inflict additional suffering on villagers. A tour of the towns of Punjab in November 1920 and a meeting with Gandhi and several national leaders paved the way for alternative solutions. Soon Stokes was gradually 'forced from a position of a moderate, approving British rule, to that of a thorough-going nationalist.'[30]

Stokes himself stated that politically he was not 'on all fours' with Gandhi's views, for he did not subscribe to the concept and strategy of the non-cooperation movement. He felt that there was too much theory and far too little sound constructive work, and this could lead to a general breakdown of law and order.[31] He wanted the movement to focus upon those aspects which affected relations between the people and Government, envisaging a system of vigilance committees working in close conjunction with the nationalist elements, who in turn worked in the reformed legislative councils to enforce the will of the people. The role of vigilance committees in relation to the councils was to be similar to that of the big unions in England to the Labour Party. Stokes' immediate aim was the elimination of those aspects of British rule which were based on notions of the racial superiority of the rulers; such as the system of forced labour, which he viewed as a 'key' question.

After a series of fruitless meetings with Gandhi, in December 1920 he attended the Congress session at Nagpur. His aim was to exert a modifying influence over the extremists in the party. He tried to deflect the movement from the 'perilous course of entrusting the destiny of the country to indisciplined and erratic forces as are at present to carry on most of the nationalist work.'[32] But by March 1921 Stokes, in order to present a united front, waived his reservations to accept, unstintingly, Gandhi's leadership.

Meanwhile, despite meetings with the Viceroy and the Lieutenant-Governor of the Punjab, Stokes had been unsuccessful in persuading the Government to curtail the issue of permits which forced people to work as coolies. He then decided to use the weapon of passive resistance: in a letter of March 1921, he wrote that 'he had the whole of Kotgarh organized and considerable backing in other areas similarly circumstanced.'[33]

Stokes had successfully educated and mobilized village opinion against forced labour. 'The bitterest discontent ran throughout the whole district,' his friend, C. F. Andrews, wrote in *The Tribune* after visiting Kotgarh in November 1920, 'and the people were on the edge of revolt.'[34] Andrews also raised the question with the Government, with little success.[35] In June, when the Superintendent of the Hill States visited Kotgarh, the villagers refused to render the customary services, 'so that his staff found themselves reduced to gathering their own wood and bringing their own water.'[36] Fifteen workers were arrested.

The agitation, however, culminated at Edwards Gunj in Simla. During June and July 1921, the question was given wide publicity at public meetings and a resolution presented by Stokes was passed at the Gunj.[37] He hoped that the 'Simla public would take the matter in hand and would see that justice was wrenched out of the unwilling.'[38] At a succession of meetings convened at the Gunj to spread the nationalist goal of Swaraj,

Stokes seized the opportunity to detail, in chaste Hindi, the iniquities of *begar*. For instance, at a public meeting convened on 29 June 1921 by Harish Chandra on the question of racial equality, Stokes described how sixty-eight men had been impressed at the four main stages on the Hindustan–Tibet Road for the whole season without pay, and had to subsist at their own expense.[39] At another meeting, three days later, convened to collect funds, Stokes once again spoke about the arrest of *begar* workers. The meeting passed a resolution applauding the workers in jail.

Once the anti-*begar* agitation had shifted to Simla, a series of meetings between the Government, represented by the Deputy Commissioner, and Stokes was held. In September 1921, the Government gave in and *begar* was abolished in Simla District. Buck recounts, 'The "begar" custom, or forced labour system has been abolished, and the traveller, unless he be a Government official travelling on duty, has to make his own terms with both men and mules for baggage purposes. This has added considerably to the cost of travelling in the hills.'[40]

Once the question of *begar* was solved, Stokes plunged into the larger issue of Swaraj. He made a brief tour of the towns of Punjab, spreading the message of non-cooperation and swadeshi. In December 1921, in Lahore, when accused of sedition and asked to furnish securities for good behaviour, he refused to co-operate with the authorities or to defend himself. He was consequently sentenced to six months' simple imprisonment.

After his release in June 1922, he diverged from the mainstream of the Congress movement. Although he attended the All-India Congress session in November 1922, he contributed a memorandum setting down his reasons for opposing civil disobedience as a permanent item on the Congress programme. Civil disobedience, he believed, contributed 'towards the gradual disintegration of that sense of order and discipline which is as essential to Swarajya as to any other kind of Raj.' He decided thereafter to devote himself to philosophical investigations which were published in his magnum opus,

Satyakam, in 1927, occasionally taking up social issues affecting the hill people. In 1932, under the aegis of the Arya Samaj, he became a convert to Hinduism, changing from Samuel Evans to Satyanand Stokes.

Political activity in Simla in 1921 was, quite uncharacteristically, 'no less marked than in any other busy city'.[41] Of the two recurring local questions, the plea for an elected municipality concerned Simla's literate and propertied population directly. The year 1921 marked the end of an era when Indian members were nominated as rubber stamps for decisions made by successive deputy commissioners. Indian commercial and business interests had become assertive and wanted municipal representation, as their European counterparts did. The question of *begar*, on the other hand, arose in Simla's hinterland and was effectively brought to the town. The authorities had been compelled to compromise on both issues; and by 1923 the Congress was virtually defunct.

CHAPTER FOURTEEN

Civil Disobedience and the Mall

THE right of the meanest citizen to walk on a public road is a matter of public importance,' said Gaya Prashad Singh, on the floor of the Legislative Assembly on 15 July 1930.[1] The 'public road' he referred to was the Simla Mall, and the occasion was the arrest of Congress volunteers; the legislator was voicing the general indignation that restriction of movement on the Mall evoked.

For middle-class Indians living in Simla, the Mall was more than a mere road running the length of the town. It was a symbol of humiliating subservience and of racial discrimination; a special European preserve where the Indian could not saunter along as did the European. A Simla municipal traffic by-law (No 5 Section 200) proclaimed:

> From the 15th of March till the 15th October, both days inclusive, and between the hours of 4 P.M. and 8 P.M. no job porter or coolie shall solicit employment, loiter, or carry any load in any street mentioned in the first schedule annexed to these rules [most Simla roads mentioned].

It was, however, along the Mall that the clause was insultingly enforced. The municipal rule specified coolies and job porters, but this ruling was extended to 'ill-dressed Indians' and, in 1930, to khadi-clad Congressmen as well.

Singling out instances of racial discrimination became one of the cherished objectives of the local Congress leaders. The flouting of rules and conventions regarding the Mall struck a common chord amongst Indian political workers, shopkeepers and Government employees. All were sensitive to discriminatory racial privileges, and breaches of traffic by-laws were on the margin of legality; moreover, it needed a loose interpretation of the law of sedition to be arrested. Civil disobedience in Simla was translated into defiance of the Police Act banning processions on the Mall.

The Simla Congress was revived in 1929, with a membership of sixty-seven. This reflected the impact of an energetic national membership drive spearheaded by Jawaharlal Nehru in May 1929. The Congress all-India membership figures swelled to half-a-million. The boycott of the Simon Commission stimulated the rapid growth of radical forces throughout the country, which demanded not only complete independence, but a variety of socio-economic changes of a socialist nature. These forces had been strengthened by the upsurge in the trade union movements in the major cities in 1928–9. The national movement now entered a new phase with the adoption of the aim of Purna Swaraj, complete independence, symbolized by unfurling the national tricolour at midnight on New Year's Eve 1929.

Gandhi's Dandi March (12 March to 6 April 1930), from Sabarmati to the sea through the heartland of Gujarat, with seventy-one *ashram* members drawn from all parts of India, and the large-scale illegal manufacture and sale of salt, ushered in the first civil disobedience movement. It was a sequel to Gandhi's eleven-point ultimatum to Irwin which had concretized national aspirations into a list of specific demands. These included a fifty per cent reduction of land revenue, a fifty per cent cut in expenditure on the army and civil service, reform of the Arms Act, lowering of the rupee–sterling exchange rate, protection for textiles, coastal shipping to be exclusively handled by Indians, release of political prisoners, total prohibition, and finally, abolition of the salt tax and the government monopoly of salt.

The resignation of Vithalbhai Patel as President of the Legislative Assembly on 26 April 1930 signalled the spread of civil disobedience to Simla. Vithalbhai, Sardar Vallabhai Patel's older brother, and the first Indian President of the Legislative Assembly, was a familiar figure in Simla. Vithalbhai had repeatedly asserted his prerogative as President in defiance of viceregal directives. He was reputed to have mastered the smallest detail of British parliamentry practices. His rulings were never challenged as partisan, although his sympathies lay with the nationalist opposition. His resignation from his position as a result of 'harassment, persecution, and boycott', set the Indians of Lower Bazar seething with resentment.[2] Vithalbhai was approached by local Congressmen to address a public meeting, which he suggested be followed by a procession through the Lower Bazar and across the Mall to the railway station, from where he was to leave by train.

There was a flurry of trips by Congress workers to the Simla Police Superintendent to extract permission for the procession.[3] The Punjab Government, which handled local matters, normally came to Simla in May. The Superintendent of Police apparently telephoned Vithalbhai Patel and informed him that processions were contrary to established usage, and could not be taken out without a licence, which would not be granted. However, the authorities prudently decided, because of the shortage of policemen, not to block the procession.

In a post-mortem of the incident, it was stated that the procession had been permitted as 'an act of grace'. The Home Secretary to the Government, H. W. Emerson, claimed he had given permission because he 'imagined the views of the Punjab Government would be that it was inadvisable to interfere with a procession to an ex-president of the Assembly. I did not realize that there was a local rule that processions should not be allowed on the Mall.'[4] The processionists, newspaper reports indicate, believed that they had defied the Police Act.

On 27 April 1930, a Sunday afternoon, a garlanded Vithalbhai was taken in procession, and for the first time in Simla's history, the imperial and imperious tranquillity of the Mall was shattered by a slogan-shouting anti-Government crowd of Indians. After he had addressed a large gathering at Edwards Gunj, the crowd assembled at the Telegraph Office, and then wended its way along Lower Bazar, reaching the Mall near the shop of Cotton and Morris (now Sher-i-Punjab), and then pressed

across the Mall to the railway station. Vithalbhai's flower-
decorated rickshaw was pulled by Congress volunteers, and
piloted by four traders on horseback—two Simla Ahrtis,
Nand Lal and Gokal, Rana Hoshiar Singh, proprietor of the
Simla Dairy, and Rup Lal of Bharari—and twenty schoolboys. It
was followed by ranks of schoolgirls of the Arya Girls School,
led by their headmistress, Indra Devi.[5] It was by all counts a
large procession; newspapers put the number at five thousand,
the Simla police report at eight to ten thousand, and the official
communique to the Home Member at two thousand. *The
Tribune* reported the event with obvious delight:

> Practically the whole town was out. The procession passed both
> the Lower Bazar and the Mall without a hitch. . . . Throughout
> the route typical Congress posters were hung. The volunteers
> constantly cried, 'Inqilab Zindabad', 'Up, up with the National
> Flag', 'Down, down with Union Jack'. 'Up up with Gandhi
> cap', 'Down, down with English hat'. One party asked in a chorus
> what would now happen to the Assembly, another party replied
> in a chorus that owls would cry there now.[6]

An old resident, A. S. Krishnaswami, then a boy at Harcourt
Butler School, recalls that a few days later their master tutored
them to shout, as they marched along the Mall to the railway
station to receive a visiting official dignitary, 'Up, up the Union
Jack—down down the National Flag.'[7] It was apparently a
mode of normalization after a spell of Congress activity. In the
field, the village schoolmasters would parade all the children
outside to shout suitable slogans.[8]

The emotional appeal and heroics connected with the agitation
in the summer of 1930 bore the impress of the organization
and personality of the Congress secretary, Nand Lal Varma.
Varma, a dentist by profession, had been drawn to a political
career and became, at the age of twenty-eight, general secretary
of the Simla Congress Committee. Young, ebullient and
impetuous, he was sensitive to the discriminatory treatment
meted out to Indians especially at Simla. A fiery speaker, he
was often heard at the Gunj in 1930. Despite his non-Sood
origins, he emerged as their spokesman in the newly-founded

Ahrties Association. In 1932, he was elected to the Simla Municipal Committee. An avowed nationalist, he had sharply criticised Gandhi's decision to stay at Simla in 1931 with Mohan Lal, a recipient of the title Rai Bahadur, given by a government the Congress wanted to remove. Gandhi mollified him by reminding him of the desirability of channelizing all shades of opinion towards the nationalist effort.[9] A compromise was then reached, by which Gandhi stayed at Firgrove with Mohan Lal, but was a guest of the Congress Committee.[10]

Varma had his first clash with authority in April 1930. He refused to give his particulars at the Tara Devi plague post, claiming that under the cover of a medical check-post, the police were screening and keeping a check on visitors to Simla. When he was challenged under the Epidemic Diseases Act, he deposed that he had not been medically examined.[11] The organization of Vithalbhai Patel's farewell procession and the agitation thereafter was a continuation of his stand against racial discrimination in Simla.

The Congress leadership in the 1930s was dominated by the Punjabis, while the remainder constituted a cross-section of Simla's politically conscious traders. The President of the Congress, Ganda Mal Sharma, was a watchmaker employed in Cooke and Kelvey, a jewellery shop on the Mall. Dalip Singh, a tailor by profession and member of the Sikh League, was vice-president; Bhagwan Das and Dwarka Nath, both commission agents, were joint secretary, and assistant secretary, respectively; Ghungar Mal, a cloth merchant of Lower Bazar, was treasurer of the Congress organization; Kaju Mal, of the Krishna Coal Company, was its 'financial magnate': he contributed the generous sum of 100 rupees a month to the party and 25 rupees a month to its offshoot, the Bal Bharat Sabha. Harish Chandra, the Simla pleader who had spearheaded the movement for electoral reforms in 1921, was its legal adviser; many of the secret meetings at which the policy for the future was determined were held at his house. The other activists were Bhagirath Lal, a photographer of Lower Bazar, who was assistant secretary of the Simla Congress of 1921; Kanahya Lal of the .Khaddar Bhandar; and Maulvi Ghulam Mohammad Shaidai and Maulvi Abdul Ghani who took part in the deliberations at meetings but were not visible during the agitations.[12]

Government servants formed a section of the Simla population which Congress office-bearers were anxious to involve. The success of Patel's farewell procession, although masterminded by Patel himself and by local Congress leaders, was possible because of the co-operation of several government employees. Durga Das, then a municipal commissioner and a reporter of the Associated Press, was one of the principal organizers of the farewell procession. His early career as a clerk in the Munitions Board helped him to enlist the help of other clerks, while Kirpa Ram of the Indian Stores Department, and Ganga Ram of the Education Department, clerks having contacts in the bazar, persuaded shopkeepers to decorate the bazar.

For Government, one of the most disquieting features of the procession was the presence of the 'very large number of clerks and assistants in the Legislative Department, Indian Stores Department, Army Headquarters and the Finance Department.'[13] These included a fair number of Muslims, Punjabis and Bengalis. It was one of the few occasions when a regional and religious cross-section of Government employees were mobilized. A stern Government warning followed two months later, which served as a deterrent to political participation by Government clerks.[14]

The Vithalbhai Patel procession triggered off a summer season of frenetic political activity, and civil disobedience acquired a hue that was germane to Simla. From April to September 1930, there were Congress processions, picketing of wine shops, weekly public meetings, and constant propaganda. Fifteen processions were taken out by the Congress, and fifty-three public meetings held in the Gunj under its auspices.

A symbolic salt-making ceremony by three Congress volunteers from amongst local leaders was performed and the 'manufactured' salt auctioned for the sum of eighty rupees.[15]

In response to Gandhi's anti-liquor programme, Congress volunteers picketed three liquor shops on the Mall: Bhola Ram and Sons, Framjee, and J. Morton and Co. Altogether, 106 volunteers were sent up for trial for picketing, 100 of whom were convicted. Most were convicted for three months, but leaders such as N. L. Varma were sentenced for one year.[16]

Women played a prominent part in Congress activities in 1930. In July, when the Congress office-bearers were convicted, the women continued the picketing. The wives of Ganda Mal and N. L. Varma, Lakshmi Devi and Lajja Varma, were joined by thirty-five women volunteers from Lahore, and Kamala Devi, daughter of Duni Chand, an Ambala pleader. Satyavati, from Amritsar, an eloquent speaker and poetess, was mainly responsible for organizing the women volunteers of Simla. A police report observed: 'She is a dangerous agitator who does more harm than political leaders. . . . She sings her own poems and songs in the meetings.' The women were to be seen shouting slogans below the Legislative Assembly, on the Mall and in Lower Bazar, urging legislators, including Jinnah, to resign their seats.

The volunteers of the Bal Bharat Sabha were another conspicuous group of political activists, modelled on the Naujawan Bharat Sabha. This was a secret revolutionary organization with socialist leanings, which had been founded in 1928 by Bhagat Singh and Sukhdev, as an alternative to the politically conservative Congress.[17] This small group of revolutionaries was instrumental in heightening national and anti-colonial consciousness especially in the Punjab. As according to the Congress regulations, only persons above the age of eighteen could be enlisted, the Bal Bharat Sabha was started under instructions from the Provincial Congress Committee so that younger people could also serve as volunteers.

One such young recruit to the Bal Bharat Sabha was Dina Nath 'Andhi', the son of a Sood cloth merchant from Garli. He was one of the Congress volunteers who, time and again in 1930, defied the Police Act on the Mall. He earned the nickname

'Andhi' (storm) because of the frequency with which he was produced for such offences before the magistrate. On 4 May 1930, while announcing Gandhi's arrest, he was arrested along with twelve other boys and released after a warning. In August 1930, he led Congress volunteers picketing the liquor shops on the Mall. When arrested, he gave his name as 'Andhi', son of Gandhi.[18] But in fact 'Andhi' was attracted by socialism rather than by Gandhi's political ideology, by the acts of daring involved in baiting authority rather than satyagraha. He joined the Congress Socialist Party in 1935.[19]

The Bal Bharat Sabha had a membership of forty-six and an office in a *dharamsala* at Kainthu. The office-bearers, apart from Dina Nath 'Andhi', were largely sons of local Congress workers. They were Prem Chand, son of Harish Chandra; Roshan Lal, son of Nand Lal, the commission agent from Edwards Gunj; and Jagdish Chand, son of Indra Devi, the headmistress of the Arya Girls School. The youngsters exerted some influence in the local schools which they picketed.

Varma organized and enlisted the young nationalists of the Bal Bharat Sabha to keep alive the agitation in 1930. They were a conspicuous group, dressed in red shirts, green pants and white Gandhi caps. Many of them wore three medals— the first bearing the likenesses of Bhagat Singh and Sukhdev, the second bearing a map of India with a Congress flag across it, and the third with a drawing of a Desh Sewika, a woman picketeer, holding a Congress flag aloft.[20]

Volunteers' activities were largely confined to violation of the Police Act on the Mall. *The Pioneer* of 8 May 1930 reported: 'Last evening, the local Congress Secretary sent out some boys to announce Mr Gandhi's arrest. They paraded the streets shouting revolutionary cries. A small crowd collected and joined them. After they had passed the Mall twelve of them were arrrested for obstructing traffic.'[21] On the evening of 13 May 1930, Varma and a few volunteers stood on the Mall for two hours, where a crowd gathered. Finally, the Simla Deputy Commissioner ordered the fire brigade water-hose to be turned on them, and sent them hurtling down to the Middle Bazar.[22] Varma was injured. This was the only occasion that a water hose was used to disperse a crowd in Simla.

In July, when the Legislative Assembly was in session, a special correspondent of *The Tribune* wrote: 'I should record that every afternoon, when the Assembly is in session, a batch of about a dozen volunteers . . . pass beneath the Chamber shouting, "Mahatma Gandhi *ki jai*" and "*Inquilab Zindabad*". . . . These volunteers have also scored another triumph. Their very Gandhi cap is their offence and once they come up the Mall they are arrested on the spot.'[23] Volunteers were usually arrested for obstructing traffic, and released in the evening.

In the evenings of the summer of 1930, the police was posted at the bazar on the Mall to prevent Congress volunteers climbing up to the Mall from the stairways and alleys of Middle and Lower Bazars. A typical police report reads:

> Congress Volunteers came on the Mall and announced at the top of their voices that a Congress meeting would be held that evening in the Gunj. A crowd very soon collected so a European Police Sergeant on duty stopped them and asked them to leave the Mall and go down to the Bazar. The volunteers refused . . . so they were conducted by the Sergeant to one of the alleys and made to go down.
>
> They came up again on the Mall and continued to shout and so were again removed. Eventually as they persisted in coming they were forced down to the Middle Bazar, resisting step by step, all the while. A large crowd collected in the Middle Bazar.[24]

The frequent incursions on the Mall by Congress volunteers remained a constant threat to the Simla authorities. They prepared the way for the 'monster' procession that received Gandhi the following year when he came to Simla for talks before the second Round Table Conference.

The first Round Table Conference at London was held while thousands of Indians were going to jail, or facing *lathis*, bullets and suffering damage to their property. Attempts to hammer out a constitutional compromise by a handful of largely un-representative delegates—Muslim League politicians, Hindu

Mahasabha leaders, Liberals, and a big princely contingent—
had failed. The Congress had to be involved. Talks were held
in Delhi between Gandhi and the Viceroy, Irwin, to break the
deadlock. Irwin had insisted on three conditions—federation
as the basis of the Indian constitution, reservations for the
minorities, and safeguards for defence, external affairs and the
financial credit of India. The Government offered to release
political prisoners and withdraw repressive ordinances, while
Gandhi agreed to suspend the civil disobedience movement
and to attend the Round Table Conference at London as the
sole Congress representative. The Gandhi–Irwin pact was to
be signed at Simla.

The decision that Gandhi was to come to Simla to sign the
pact sent a surge of excitement through the local Congress
leaders. They had agreed to a cessation of the agitation if 'a
friendly reception' was given to Gandhi, i.e., a conciliatory
attitude was adopted by the authorities.[25]

Gandhi had refused to travel in a rickshaw or ride on horseback from the railway station to Firgrove, in the eastern part of
Simla, where he was to stay with Rai Bahadur Mohan Lal.[26]
Gandhi's preference for walking put the authorities in a quandary
since it meant that most Indians in Simla would walk with him.
It was therefore decided to permit four cars for Gandhi and his
entourage to motor from the station. The cars were to go from
the terminal barrier via the Cart Road and along a short stretch
of the Mall, past Faridkot House (now the High Court) to
Firgrove. But even for short stretches, the only vehicles
permitted were that of the Viceroy, the Governor of the Punjab
and the Commander-in-Chief.

Municipal By-Law XXI (2) prohibited the use of wheeled
vehicles, drawn or propelled by animals (later applied to cars)
within the municipal limits. The privilege of driving a carriage
or any wheeled vehicle in Simla required viceregal assent. The
viceregal secretariat sometimes decided, after consultations
held practically in hushed whispers, to set aside the municipal
by-law to permit, on rare occasions, a visiting provincial
governor to drive down the Mall.

In 1893, the Begum of Bhopal was permitted to drive in

Simla, and to her residence at Yarrows. As the only lady who was also a ruler in her own right, it was hoped it would be an isolated case. The Military Secretary to the Viceroy had recorded: 'The Viceroy thinks it will in no way create a precedent that can be advocated by any other chief.' In 1903 and 1904, the Maharaja of Nabha was permitted 'in consideration of his age and weakness' to be driven in a carriage when he went to visit the Viceroy, the Commander-in-Chief and the Lieutenant-Governor of the Punjab.[27] Municipal records do not indicate any other Indians being accorded the privilege. The concession to Gandhi was therefore considered by local leaders to be an achievement.

On 15 May 1931, men, women, children and stragglers dressed in khadi clothes and Gandhi caps took up positions along the way that the cars were to take. A brass band, banners with 'O saint of all the world', and a flutter of the Congress national flags welcomed Gandhi.

The Simla Government authorities were well prepared for the occasion too. To offset the impact of the concession they permitted a marriage procession to precede Gandhi's motor-cade. The marriage procession of the son of the Raja of Bilaspur *en route* to Jubbal, was accompanied by Mandh infantry, Kalsia cavalary, tiny ponies, palanquins, rickshaws and even ancient pikemen and a band. The Gandhi motorcade, together with the officers, subordinates and clerks who poured out of offices to view the visit, was followed by an Indian Red Cross mule convoy. *The Pioneer* carried the heading the next day, 'Mr Gandhi's Progress up Simla Mall—Following Raja's Son's Wedding Procession.'[28]

Varma secured another triumph—permission for Gandhi to address the people on the Ridge.[29] A crowd of about ten thousand assembled, as Durga Das on behalf of the Simla Trades Association, Varma, on behalf of the Ahrties Association, and Ghulam Mohammad for the Muslims, welcomed Gandhi. Gandhi's speech was dampened by the continuous drizzle that evening.[30]

Despite the official defence, the concessions to Gandhi were viewed as having 'sullied sacred traditions'. *The Pioneer* reported that Simla was 'shocked', that the 'family pride' of Simla had received a blow. Gandhi had been permitted to drive in a car 'even though Executive Councillors and Senior Generals must walk, ride or be trundled along in a pram.'[31]

Even the Annadale Gymkhana of 1931, the British sporting event of the year, reflected the ripples caused by this event. In a written competition, during a tea interval, everybody had to use the letters of the word 'SAFE GUARDS' in a telegram to the Viceroy on the subject of Gandhi.[32] In London, a member of the House of Commons sought information on why Gandhi was granted the 'unprecedented privilege'. Wedgwood Benn, the Secretary of State for India, truthfully replied that far from being unprecedented, the facility of motoring in the summer capital was accorded to a marriage party as well.[33]

The drama of processions, and violations of traffic laws and the Police Act on the Mall were expressions of the Congress attempts to make their presence felt. Local politicians freely admitted that they could never hope to replicate the upsurge possible in the plains. This was well understood by Vithalbhai Patel. His parting words to the crowds that saw him off at the railway station were a plea that the people of Simla should at least pray for the success of the movement. The events of 1930–1 did not however result in a stronger Congress organization for recrimination between Varma and other members of the Congress led him to withdraw for a spell.[34]

The police exercised greater vigilance in screening visitors, and efforts were made to ensure that the sanctity of the European style of the Mall was preserved. An English resident in 1934 complained that the newspaper boys who shouted news headlines (presumably nationalist), were a 'source of annoyance'. A clause in the by-laws was then added, prohibiting vendors, hawkers and pedlars from shouting or calling their wares on the Mall—the prohibition was not applicable to the Lower

Bazar. A committee member did point out that newspaper vending was allowed in London, but the by-law was passed by five votes to three—the official members having succeeded in persuading Puran Chandra to vote with them.

Indians were allowed to walk on the Mall, but the myth that they were not grew, despite the happenings of 1930–1, and persists till today.

CHAPTER FIFTEEN

Communal Cleavages

A day in Lower Bazar in the 1940s often began at crack of dawn with a *prabhat pheri*, the singing of patriotic songs and nationalist slogans by Congress workers carrying lanterns and flags as they passed through the Lower Bazar, Subzi Mandi, the Cart Road and up the Gunj Road. At night, after-dinner political meetings sustained the Bazar, with the Arya Samaj Mandir and the Jami Masjid serving as the two venues. Both tended to capitalize on Hindu–Muslim differences: allegation for allegation, incident for incident, demand for demand, were traded at these well-attended nocturnal meetings. While the appeal was ostensibly to national patriotism, the sensibility was of religious appeals:[1] one of the major tasks confronting the national leadership was that of imparting a common national consciousness to the Indian people; a major hurdle was the simultaneous emergence of communalism which narrowed consciousness to religious and caste groups.

Communal consciousness, the other face of national consciousness manifest in Simla, was the result of the binding together of different sections of the Indian population. Local reactions were conditioned by local irritants, the occupational or caste patterns of society and the nature of its urbanization. Marshalling a crowd in Simla was easy. Rumours and information could in a matter of minutes be disseminated to most of its Indian population, largely confined within the Lower Bazar area. But it also made police surveillance easy, while identification and detection were not always desirable from the nationalists' point of view.

The occupational breakup of Congress membership in 1935 reveals a sharp increase of shopkeepers. Skilled artisans, tailors and carpenters, who plied their trade in the shops in the bazar, seem also to have enrolled in large numbers.[2] The new feature was the successful effort at broadening the social base of the Congress by drawing in coolies. In part, the increase in membership was due to the popularity of the movement in 1930–1, in part, the result of the leadership's ambition to secure a seat in the Provincial Congress Committee where a minimum representation of five hundred at the local level was a prerequisite.

The Congress was dominated after the 1930s by leaders from the Punjab. Chaudhri Diwan Chand and Pandit Hari Ram, both from Hoshiarpur, remained at the helm of the Simla District Congress. Chaudhri Diwan Chand, a shopkeeper of Lower Bazar, had his first taste of politics in 1921 as a signatory of the Memorandum of Association of House Owners and Taxpayers of Simla sponsored by Kedar Nath. An active Arya Samaj worker, Diwan Chand became President of the Samaj in 1935. Pandit Hari Ram came to Simla in June 1932, and worked for Surjan Mall and Co. for a year, after which, in 1933, he set up the Rama News Agency on the Mall. He became the first non-government servant president of the Brahman Sabha and activated it to establish a school for the teaching of Sanskrit. Both remained office-bearers of the Congress until 1947.

The other significant Congress functionaries and office-bearers of the City and District Congress of Simla in the 1930s and 1940s were also traders. They included Salig Ram Gupta, a bookseller in Lower Bazar; Sham Lal Khanna, a trader in the Gunj Bazar; Sultan Ahmed Butt of Middle Bazar; Janeshwari of Lower Bazar; Bhoj Raj, a rais of Lower Bazar; Baij Nath, a cloth merchant; Tufail Mohammad, a watchmaker of Lower Bazar; and Sushil Kumar, a manager of the Khaddar Bhandar. N. L. Varma remained active in the Congress and was elected to the Simla Municipal Committee in the 1936 elections, the last held before Independence.

Congress meetings were held sometimes in Dwarkagarh, the Congress office, and when that was raided in 1935, they were held in the homes of Congress workers or sympathizers such as N. L. Varma, or Kanahya Lal Butail and Rairoo Mal

Saraf, two well-known commission agents who provided the venue for a while. The Butail family, who owned the Bundla Tea Estates in Palampur, made large profits as commission agents dealing in *mishri* (crystal sugar). Their business expanded from Simla to its suburbs and they controlled the market at Kufri and Theog. Kanahya Lal Butail opened the Khaddar Bhandar at Simla and provided support to the local Congress. Rairoo Mal Saraf, who had made a fortune in the potato trade, was also a Congress sympathizer. Pandit Hari Ram, Vice-President of the Congress and Vice-President of the first elected Municipal Committee after 1947, relates that some meetings were also held at the Kareru Mandir on Prospect Hill.[3]

Local Congress leaders represented the interests of the shop-keepers and traders. Apart from championing local discontent, they picked up the message of the Indian National Congress and wove it into their political activities.

The traders of the Beopar Mandal spearheaded a protest in 1941–2 against imposition of the Punjab Sales Tax Act.[4] A week-long *hartal* compelled the municipality to open shops selling essential provisions. The sales-tax agitation mingled with oratory urging denial of all help to the war effort and championing the Quit India Movement.

Leaders of the Praja Mandals joined hands with the Congress. Padam Dev, President of the Simla Hill States Riasti Praja Mandal, addressed a meeting in the Gunj exhorting people not to contribute money towards fighting World War II as it served to tighten imperial bondage. He was arrested on 26 June 1941 and sentenced to eighteen months' rigorous imprisonment. A few days later, another worker, Salig Ram Sharma, was likewise arrested and sentenced.

In August 1942, after the Quit India call was given in Bombay, local Congressmen were activated into disseminating the message of non-violence and hoisting the national Congress flag. The Congress was banned, its office-bearers, B. D. Gupta, Tufail Mohammad and Salig Ram of Hoshiarpur, were all imprisoned for a year. The other workers, Karam Chand of Rampur, Jit Ram and Siri Ram of Arki, and Surjan Dass of

Bushahr, were arrested for shouting slogans but then released.

However, the trading community did not lend wholehearted support to the Quit India call. The commission agents, for instance, sensing troublesome days ahead, passed a resolution putting a stop to long-term credit for retail shopkeepers.[5] The reason is to be found in their links with the Arya Samaj and the Hindu Sabhas in the 1930s: the national organization of the Sabhas, the Hindu Mahasabha, had asked its members to remain at their jobs and not interfere with the war effort, and also voiced opposition to the Quit India Movement. The traders' affiliations also offer a clue to the communal disharmony of the 1940s.

The Arya Samaj was the common denominator of Congress leaders, traders and Government employees in Simla. Its donors, patrons and senior office-bearers were professional men and traders; while government clerks were also office-bearers. Both groups had spread the message of the Samaj to the hill states. Some of the leading Praja Mandal leaders were Arya Samaj workers. The link between Arya Samajis and politics had been endorsed by Lala Lajpat Rai: 'The type of man to whom the Arya Samaj appeals is the type of man to whom politics appeals, viz; the educated man who desires his country's progress.'

The Sood traders of the Bazar were linked by bonds both of commercial interest and of kinship. They looked to the more wealthy and influential Soods such as Rai Bahadur Mohan Lal, Lala Puran Mal and Jai Lal, for leadership. Mohan Lal was the moving spirit of the Gurukul section of the Arya Samaj, and the Hindu Pracharni Sabha in Simla. Although a Congress sympathizer, he did not actually join the Congress. Mohan Lal was professedly antagonistic to alleged Muslim misdemeanours; in 1922, after communal rioting in Multan, he had convened a public meeting in the Gunj to pass a resolution of sympathy for the affected Hindus.[6] In 1930, a police report noted, 'he takes a very keen part in all Hindu causes and is always ready to act as a leader of Hindu community in Simla.'[7] These attitudes were manifest in lesser Sood leaders as well.

At Simla, the Hindu Sabha had grown with the Congress

and was linked with the College section of the Arya Samaj in the persons of Dr Kedar Nath and Lala Harish Chandra. The Hindu Sabha was a forum within the Congress for the expression of Hindu views and to advance Hindu interests, of which both Lala Lajpat Rai and Pandit Madan Mohan Malaviya had been active members. Under Lala Lajpat Rai, the Sabha aimed at providing relief to Hindus who had suffered in communal riots and disturbances, the reconversion of Hindus forcibly converted to Islam, the organization of *Sewa Samitis*, the popularization of Hindi, the celebration of Hindu festivals, and improving the status of Hindu women.[8] In 1921, Harish Chandra with the blessings of Madan Mohan Malaviya convened one of the first meetings of the Hindu Sabha.[9]

Dr Kedar Nath and Harish Chandra were at the helm of the Congress in Simla. With their Congress base and Sood background it was possible for both to be elected municipal commissioners. Harish Chandra was in office during 1924–8, Kedar Nath during 1930–3. As municipal commissioners, both eschewed active Congress work, and gravitated towards the Hindu Sabha.

In the 1920s, with Kedar Nath as general secretary, the Sabha outlined its objectives as the uplift of the untouchables and low-caste *kolis* of the Simla hills.[10] It sought to involve the local Ranas of Baghat and Kothar, who attended meetings. The Hindu Orphanage, an Industrial School for Boys and an ashram for destitute women at Tutikandi were set up outside the Simla municipal limits in the hill state of Keonthal. In 1936, a sub-inspector of police observed of Kedar Nath, 'a Congressman at heart but assumes the role of a bigoted Arya Samajist whenever a communal question arises and is also very fond of giving a communal tinge to an ordinary incident when a Hindu is involved in a case.'[11] Kedar Nath was not communal in his personal life; a widower, he married a Muslim woman as his second wife, alienating orthodox Arya Samaj opinion. In the 1940s, his convictions led him to join the Praja Socialist Party.

At the national level, however, the Hindu Sabha broke from the Congress and became the Hindu Mahasabha. In 1935, after

Bhai Parmanand became president, it became an all-India Hindu organization with a strong, independent and clear cut policy which concerned itself specifically with the Hindu community, with its goal the establishment of Hindu India. It was only in December 1938 that the Congress Working Committee declared Mahasabha membership a disqualification for remaining in the Congress. At Simla, despite the directive, the breach was a superficial one for Congress both depended on, and masterminded communal opinion. For instance, Harish Chandra, although he remained associated with the Congress, was firmly entrenched in the Sabha's organization and remained its president from 1930 to 1935.

The Muslims, as already recounted, comprised a disparate group from different provinces and social classes. Kashmiri labour, skilled workers and artisans comprised the bulk of the eight thousand Muslims who lived in Simla. Of the Imams who largely provided the leadership of the Muslims in Simla, Maulvi Abdul Ghani, Imam of the Qutab Khansama Masjid, was politically the most active. He wielded great influence over a large section of the Muslim community. In 1921, he was secretary of Congress and continued to be associated with it until 1930. He was a prominent member of the Khilafat Committee of Simla in 1921, the executive committee of which comprised all the Imams of the masjids in Simla. In the 1930s he joined the Muslim League, the chief patron of which, however, was the Imam of the Jami Masjid, Maulvi Zakaullah.

A small Muslim middle-class lived in the Bazar area. In 1927, only 143 Muslims were entitled to cast their vote at municipal elections (there were 700 non-Muslim votes), but, they were, however, amply represented in the municipality to which at least three Muslims were always nominated. Their influence was, therefore, far greater than their numerical strength. Once the Hindus, and especially the Soods of Lower Bazar, turned to the communal Hindu Sabha, the Muslims gravitated towards parallel Muslim organizations. In 1921, when Gandhi came to Simla, it had been possible to secure Muslim co-operation and Gandhi addressed his largest public meeting at the Idgah. In 1931, in contrast, when he addressed the public meeting at the Ridge, the maulvis issued encyclicals asking Muslims to refrain from attending the meeting.[12]

The Ram Devi abduction case in 1934 further embittered relations between the two communities. The young daughter of a government employee, Ram Devi, was abducted by four Kashmiri Muslims on 8 June 1934. Leading Congress and Arya Samaj workers recovered the girl and the accused were arrested and convicted by August. Although it was a Muslim magistrate who sentenced her abductors to seven years rigorous imprisonment,[13] the judgment did nothing to allay communal hostility. For the Arya Samaj leaders, the case merely confirmed their mistrust.

One of the publicized and populist measures of Congressmen who were Arya Samajis was the dispatching of *jathas* or bands of satyagrahis to Hyderabad in April 1939. In the state of Hyderabad a small Muslim élite held 90 per cent of the jobs, and Urdu was maintained as the sole official language and medium of instruction in a state with a population that was 50 per cent Telugu-, 25 per cent Marathi- and 11 per cent Kannada-speaking. In 1938–9, the Arya Samaj and the Hindu Mahasabha led campaigns against the Nizam of Hyderabad and the Ittahad-ul-Musslaman. The Arya leader, Pandit Narendraji, started a satyagraha in Hyderabad city and Marathawada region demanding more jobs for the Hindus. At Simla, speeches indicated that restrictions imposed by the Nizam on the dissemination of the Arya faith and consecration of temples in Hyderabad led to the dispatching of Arya Samaj volunteers. From Simla, two *jathas*, one led by Chaudhry Diwan Chand, then vice president of the College section of the Arya Samaj, and the other by Pandit Padam Dev, secretary of the Samaj, volunteered to offer satyagraha at Hyderabad. At a large function hosted by the Dayanand Anglo-Vedic Arya Samaj School at Lakkar Bazar, and attended by an appreciative audience of over seven hundred, they were given a crusaders' farewell. There were speeches by the school staff, including the headmaster, Satya Prakash, a recitation of poems, and presentation of photographs. The function concluded with the donation of purses from individual traders and shopkeepers, school students, employees of the railway board, and even the municipal *safai* staff.[14]

They returned as victorious heroes in August. With the Nizam having acceded to their demands, they believed that they could similarly 'settle' other Muslim states. The move exacerbated Hindu–Muslim tensions, left. Muslim members of the Congress floundering, and turned the Hindu–Muslim unity meetings at the Gunj into an empty ritual.[15]

The Indians in Simla who had tumbled out in multitudes to welcome Gandhi in 1921 and 1931, greeted him in 1945 with black flags, protesting against the bartering away of Hindu rights when he came to attend the Simla Conference convened by Wavell. The conference was conceived by Wavell in the wake of the collapse of Germany and the Japanese reverses in South-east Asia and Burma. He proposed to restructure his Executive Council in order to make it more representative of organized political opinion, and giving parity to Hindus and Muslims. Churchill was strongly opposed to the Wavell Plan, indicating that the Indian problem should 'be kept on ice' for as long as possible. He then seemed to favour partition into 'Pakistan, Hindustan, Princestan,'[16] eventually accepting it under the pressure of the impending general elections.

On his return to India, Wavell ordered on 14 June the immediate release of the Congress Working Committee from jail. The Working Committee did not in principle accept the parity formula while Gandhi objected to the expression 'caste' Hindu but not to the principle of parity. The conference eventually broke down over Jinnah's insistence that the Muslim League should have the right to nominate all the Muslim members.

The conference was said, in addition, to have been sabotaged by Wavell's political masters, through the British bureaucracy at Simla. Durga Das relates that when Jinnah was asked why he had rejected the Wavell Plan, since he had won his point of parity for the League and the Congress, Jinnah replied: 'Am I a fool to accept this when I am offered Pakistan on a platter?'[17] Sir Frank Mudie, Home Member of Wavell's executive, is alleged to have first, advised Jinnah on tactics and then used his influence on the Viceroy to make sure that the tactics worked. He represented the views of British civil servants who were averse to British deals with the Congress, and resented the released Congress leaders who had become 'top dogs' at the conference.[18]

An observer, J. N. Sahni, recounts that the affair was like a political *mela*: in addition to those attending the conference, there were thousands of fun-seekers, hangers-on and observers. He captured the mood of the day when he wrote: 'Jinnah had been to Simla a hundred times. According to routine he arrived by rail motor, and then reached the Cecil by rickshaw—Nehru, however stole the show. . . . Thousands crowded the roads at Simla when he arrived. As Jinnah watched the scene from his Cecil Hotel window, he felt nauseated. He felt even worse when Nehru's car drove across the Mall.'[19]

The local authorities at Simla frowned on nationalist ideas. They professed inflexible impartiality towards religious and parochial *sabhas*, while the police records efficiently documented such affiliations which were then used as a basis for recommendations for berths on the municipality, and nominations to Government bodies. The colonial Government's distributive justice ranged itself along religious lines, thereby legitimizing such groupings. Political leaders fell an easy prey to the logic of division, and the failure of the Congress lay in the success of British efforts to promote and reinforce a divided polity.

Dual membership of the Arya Samaj and the Hindu Sabha paved the way to the popularity of the para-military Rashtriya Swayam Sevak Sangh (RSS); the cry of 'Hinduism in danger', begun by K. B. Hegdewar in Nagpur, swept across UP and Punjab in the 1930s. In the 1940s, membership of the RSS included 100,000 trained and highly disciplined militants pledged to fight for a Hindu identity. Several people at Simla recall joining the morning drills.[20]

At the close of 1946, a sub-inspector of the local *thana* wrote in his charge notes that 'the feelings amongst the two local major communities are strained and the atmosphere is surcharged with distrust and communal bickerings.'[21] Even as the Municipal Committee sanctioned ten thousand rupees for the celebration of Independence Day, Simla witnessed rioting, leading to several deaths.[22] The rioting and violence was never on the scale of the Punjab but Sylvia Corfield witnessed shops being looted and bombs hurled at rickshaw coolies' quarters in the Lower Bazar.[23] Old residents associate the period with the events of the Simla Conference of 1945. They remember it as an era of communal tension, make the sign of the scissors to signify conflict, and mutter 'Hindu–Muslim'.[24]

CHAPTER SIXTEEN

Gun Shots from Dhami

NEWS of the firing at Dhami on Sunday, 16 July 1939, hit the headlines of most nationalist newspapers. The agitation which led to it was launched from Simla. The target was Dhami, one of the small hill states nestling under the shadow of the imperial summer capital. A study of the event reveals the involvement of Simla's hill population and a large number of low-paid government servants—*daftris*, peons and gardeners employed in Simla offices and establishments.

The 'rurbanization' of Simla's hinterland, the emergence of linkages between urban centre and outlying rural regions, began with improved communications and the pull of opportunities for employment in the summer capital. Simla was a service town and jobs were available as *mundus* (low-paid domestic servants), in households, shops and eating establishments; as coolies and porters in the transport business; as *malis*, to plant, hoe, and water a patch of hillside into an English-looking garden. A modicum of literacy made possible a job in the lowest rungs of government service as 'inferior servants'—peons—carrying files and serving tea by day, and working as domestics after office hours. The Brahman village of Batal in Baghal state, with a population of about seven hundred, and small land-holdings, could boast of a high percentage of employees.[1] Others with more enterprise could think of setting up business, as the folk song describes:

> *Raja behmi ho, behmi ho meri jan*
> *Chal bhora pardeṣiya, chal Shimla kinare jaiye,*
> *Kamm tan kariye gavaliyan ra, paise*
>   *khub banaiye,*
> *Meriya jani chal. . . .*[2]

In the song a village girl urges her companion to go to Simla with her, where they will raise cows, sell their milk and make lots of money.

The story of British rule is one of disruption of the traditional isolation and self-sufficiency of the hill villages. The link between urban centre and hinterland was made more complex because of the existence of a congerie of semi-feudal hill states. Agriculture, an arduous and unprofitable proposition, was the mainstay of the people. The hill slopes were usually unirrigated and the *zamindar* (used in the Simla hills in the sense of yeoman, a small farmer who cultivates his own land), cultivated paddy and pulses during the *kharif* season and wheat or barley in the winter *rabi* season. If he was a large *zamindar*, he might own a fertile, irrigated plot of land, near a river valley. In the upper hills, a long winter set a limit to double cropping and the *zamindar* had to supplement his income by raising sheep and goats, and trading in livestock, wool, and ghee. Lastly, he depended on the forests for timber for agricultural implements and house building; grass and oak leaves for cattle bedding and fodder; and fuel for cooking. The establishment at Simla brought with it a demand for fruit and vegetables. Potatoes, easily grown and with a long storage capacity, were a crop in high demand. Some hill state capitals like Junga, in Keonthal state, emerged as a collection centre and market for potatoes from the surrounding villages.

The imperial presence also exerted an insiduous pressure. During the nineteenth century, the princely states were graded by the colonial government according to their perceived ability to handle the administration of civil and criminal justice. The Superintendent of the Simla Hill States, who was also Deputy Commissioner, soon functioned as virtual Collector for the hill states as well. The *Imperial Gazetteer* states that the hill chiefs possessed 'full powers, except that sentences of death passed by them' required the confirmation of the Superintendent. The Superintendent was expected to intervene to settle disputes between the rajas, clashes over boundaries, maladministration, or questions of regency in the case of minors. In fact, the states were gradually absorbed into the imperial system, and every state underwent a 'bureaucratizing' process, a regular revenue settlement, and a shift to cash-based revenue collection with emphasis on written rights to land. There were few areas not touched by a touring official. Between routine autumn expeditions, *shikar*, and petty ceremonial, the Superintendent oversaw the local administration. In 1908, administration of thirteen of the twenty-eight states, owing to 'minority or incapacity', was wrested from them and the Superintendent exercised control through a regency of specially-appointed officers. By the early twentieth century, most states had been pressured into making revenue settlements based on cash, through the appointment of *lumbardars*. A Superintendent thus usually added to his list of achievements a dramatic increase in revenue collection, with local Ranas usually intervening to appoint a kinsman to the post for an 'efficient' collection of revenue.

The creation of Simla town also meant a demand for fuel for cooking and wood for crackling fires in fireplaces, even in summer. The demand for charcoal made from oak wood converted forests, where villagers had traditional rights, into reserved forests, while ranas often banned local villagers from hunting and shooting in forests that were popular for *shikar*.

The state of Dhami, sixteen miles north-west of Simla, offers a typical example of the increasing pressures exerted on the hill peoples, and of their resentment gradually building into violent protest. Dhami state comprised twenty-eight square miles and had a population of 5,239. It acquired importance because part of its 2,355 acres of forest were reserved as shooting grounds for the Viceroy and his entourage.[3] Annually the Rana of Dhami played host to the Viceroy, welcoming him with a 'dolly' or presentation of trays of gold and silver, and the local produce of rice, bananas, pomegranates, dishes of honey, bundles of sugarcane and ginger, and a 'ram dragged by its horns'. Lady Dufferin recounts a trip to Dhami in 1885:

> Our destination is called Dhamin, and we are to be the guests of
> the Rana of that place, whose privilege it is to spend a certain
> sum yearly in entertaining the Viceroy at a shoot. Honour and

> glory above his fellows is all he gets by it. . . . The shooting was
> nothing to speak of—there were a thousand beaters employed, . . .
> there were about twenty-four birds killed.[4]

In an effort to conserve this *shikar*, the local *zamindars* were
prohibited from killing game such as pheasants, partridges,
ghoral and *kakkar*.[5] The game in the Dhami forests is carefully
preserved, the 1910 *Gazetteer of the Simla Hill States* stated,
'and the Rana has built a small resthouse at Ghana-ki-Hatti,
five miles from Jûtogh, for the convenience of sportsmen.'[6]

The Viceroy's annual excursion had a far-reaching impact
on the economy of the state and the lives of its people. Above
all, it reinforced the operating of a feudal structure. The Rana
could legitimately exact *begar* from his subjects. All those who
paid land revenue were required to render *begar* to the state for
seven days every month.[7] The emergence of Simla as an imperial
city multiplied the burden of *begar*, for the system soon came
to include serving parties of British officials out on *shikar*.
A purwannah or permit from the Political Agent at Simla
enabled sportsmen to avail themselves of *begarees* to serve as
porters and beaters. To mitigate this, it became the practice for
the Viceroy to make a payment to the Rana in return for such
services: 'Yet, last time Rs 800 are said to have been paid by
H.E., but not a pice was paid to those employed.'[8]

Another resented measure was the expansion of 'demarcated' forests which quadrupled over thirty years.[9] Forest
tracts apportioned to hill villages were and are governed by the
traditional right of *bartandari*, the right to use the produce of
that tract for food, fuel and fodder. Evergreen oaks, for example,
provided both fuel and fodder; their leaves are used as fodder
for cattle and goats, especially in the winter where grass is not
available. Such rights do not extend to 'demarcated' forests.
The Dhami forests were described as one of the most advanced
in forest conservation, well stocked with oak, *chir* and scrub
and well-worked for fuel and charcoal by systems of coppices
in accordance with a working plan drawn up in 1890.

This gave rise to tensions in the state: oak was a significant
source of income for the Rana; its wood could be converted to

charcoal which was always in demand at Simla. However, the villagers had been deprived of their traditional rights. In 1930 they complained that village lands had been converted into forest land.[10]

The sharp increase in land revenue after the settlement of 1916 was another burden on the local population. From Dhami's 113 villages, the land revenue collection which in 1910 was 8,000 rupees, had in 1934, almost doubled. To cope with the extra expenses of the annual *shikar*, the Rana resorted to other exactions such as fines, and confiscation of property. The failure of crops for three consecutive years before 1939 was the proverbial last straw.

Thakur Bhagmal Sautha, trained as an engineer at Baroda, but making a living by running the Imperial Hotel at Lower Bazar, was one of the four sons of Misroo Mal, a wealthy *zamindar* of Dhar village in Jubbal state. Bhagmal set up the Shri Dhami Prem Pracharni Sabha in June 1939, using his abilities and rural background to mobilize the hill villagers into the fold of the Sabha.

He made the Imperial Hotel his base for enrolling the inhabitants of Dhami who came to Simla on work. There was a regular influx of people from Dhami to sell produce in Jutogh and Simla; others came to work as porters and rickshaw-coolies. The more influential and enterprising secured employment as gardeners and peons in various government establishments. Sundays however, were spent in their homes in Dhami. This made it possible for them to maintain regular contact with the people in the state, and to retain their position as *zamindars*.

The office-bearers of the Shri Dhami Prem Pracharni Sabha were, according to the Dhami State, 'men of straw'. Narain Dass, employed in the municipality as a meter-reader, was elected president; Dhani Ram Sharma, a *daftri* in the Army Headquarters, was secretary; while the assistant secretary was a menial employed 'to clean utensils (dish washer) by a shop-keeper at Simla'. It was pointed out that: 'Narain Dass, Dhani Ram and others of their type who were holding low jobs under the Government along with other servants used to leave Simla

on the sly without taking permission of their officers every
Saturday and Sunday against the rules of the various Government Departments and used to come to Dhami and do their
propaganda work there, and as their ostensible object was the
social uplift of the zamindars these unfortunate people fell easy
prey and became members of that Pracharni Sabha.'[11] The
office-bearers of the Dhami Pracharni Sabha utilized the month
of June 1939 to spread the message of the Prajamandal and to
enlist the support of local *zamindars*.

The work at Dhami was part of a strategy planned by the
Indian National Congress which aimed at integrating the
Prajamandals, people's organizations drawn from the princely
states of India. Jawaharlal Nehru, when he was president of the
State People's Conference conceived of it as an apex body that
would become a 'clearing house' in building up Prajamandals
in the states.[12] The second rung in the hierarchy, the Himalayan
State People's Conference, was to provide the leadership for
the Prajamandals of the hill states from Kashmir to Assam,
and to consolidate the movement in Garhwal and the existing
Prajamandals of the other hill states. Their leaders, who
included Chaudhry Sher Jung of Sirmur, Pandit Padam Dev
of Bushahr, Swami Purnanand of Mandi, Thakur Hira Singh
of Baghal, and Thakur Bhagmal Sauhta of Jubbal, were co-
opted as members of the Himalayan organization.[13]

In the summer of 1939, a Pahari Sammelan was held at Simla.
Jawaharlal Nehru and M. N. Roy were its moving force. They
projected the possibilities of Simla, with its large hill population,
becoming an effective base for spearheading a movement to
the surrounding hill states. In response, on 1 June 1939, the
Simla Hill States Riasti Prajamandal was launched. Padam
Dev of Bushahr became its president; Thakur Bhagmal Sauhta
its secretary.

The first step was to enroll workers from the various hill
states who were resident in Simla: unskilled labour which
came to Simla during the summer months, and government
employees. The latter, being marginally literate and wielding
some influence in their villages, were the obvious first choice.

Accordingly, Prajamandals were formed in Kunihar, Koti, Bhajji and Dhami. That they were active is apparent from a complaint made by the Rana of Bhajji, a state adjacent to Dhami, that two *daftris* from the Army Headquarters and the Legislative Department of the Government of India were touring villages distributing literature and doing propaganda for the Praja-mandal.[14]

By July 1939, Bhagmal Sauhta calculated that the time was ripe to launch an agitation in the hill states. Since the president of the Simla Hill States Riasti Prajamandal, Pandit Padam Dev, was away at Hyderabad leading an Arya Samaj satyagraha,[15] he was free to decide on the time, and chose, as a testing ground for confrontation with the ruler, the tiny, seven-square-mile state of Kunihar. Quite astoundingly, the Rana agreed in July 1939 to the demands of the Kunihar Prajamandal. Encouraged by the initial success, Bhagmal Sauhta then turned to Dhami.

Much in the way that banquets were held for the French revolutionaries of 1848, Bhagmal issued an invitation to the people of Dhami in and outside Simla, for a *dham*, a grand feast, at the Imperial Hotel. Six hundred attended the *dham* on 13 July 1939, and passed a five-point resolution.[16] The resolution reflected a mix of well-understood realities and less-understood principles.

In the first clause, the name of the Sabha was changed from Shri Dhami Prem Pracharni Sabha to the Dhami Riasti Praja-mandal. It thus shed the guise of a social service organization and became a politically-oriented one representing the people of Dhami. It was affiliated to the Simla Hill States Riasti Praja-mandal.

The second and third resolutions sought the immediate grant of 'full responsible (representative) government' and the 'grant of civil liberties, right of free speech and platform'. As events were to show, the constitutional niceties of these demands were little understood. Resolutions four and five concerned the more tangible and easily understood demands. The abolition of *begar* was one. It had been abolished in Simla district in 1921 through Stokes' efforts: he had planned to extend the agitation to the hill states, but his retirement from active politics left the system intact. The construction of a motor road to Halog, the capital of Dhami, by forced labour in 1938 had brought *begar* into resented operation.

Another demand was for 50 per cent remission of the land revenue because of a partial but continuous failure of crops for three years. Since land revenue was collected in August, from the practical point of view this formed the core resolution, and the one which elicited the greatest support. Bhagmal Sauhta expected the Prajamandal agitation to help the *zamindars* in getting the land revenue reduced to one rupee per plough. He also hoped to get the hated forest laws, which deprived the Dhami *zamindars* of one of their props of self-sufficiency, abolished. Finally, he sought to replace the *lumbardars* holding office under the state by new ones who were democratically elected. The official Dhami view was that this was one step towards the establishment of 'a government of zamindars'.[17]

The Rana was largely supported by his kinsmen, the Rajputs, who were normally appointed to all official posts.[18] Of the ten new *lumbardars* appointed, five were Brahmans and five Kanets, the principal land-owning castes in Dhami. Three of the ten *lumbardars* proposed were Government employees at Simla—two working as peons and one as the head *mali* at Viceregal Lodge.

The resolution was sent to the Rana of Dhami for consideration and acceptance. It was decided that if the Rana failed to comply, a deputation of seven men, led by Thakur Bhagmal Sauhta, would proceed to Dhami. The Dhami Report observed: 'The 16th of July was Sunday, and that day was simply selected with the object of securing a large number of people and office employees.' The people of Dhami state had been asked to meet the deputation as it entered Dhami territory, with an understanding that they would assemble at a place called Khel Maidan, about a mile and a half from Halog, the capital.

On 15 July, the Dhami ruler issued an order under section 144 of the State Criminal Procedure Code prohibiting Bhagmal Sauhta from entering the state. The next day, at 1.30 p.m.,

Bhagmal Sauhta was stopped by the Dhami state police at Ghana-ki-Hatti, a few hundred yards from the Dhami border, and shown the order prohibiting his entry into the state. As he refused to obey the order he was arrested. The Political Agent recounted:

> The police escort with their prisoner set out for Halog, the capital of the State, some eight miles away and the crowd which accompanied him formed a procession and followed them. By the time it approached Halog the crowd is estimated by the Durbar to have numbered between 2000 and 3000.... [The police escort] reached the head of the procession shortly after [it] began to move towards the Thana, ... At this moment some of the crowd began to shout that their leader was being taken away to jail and should be prevented. ...[19]

Some aspects of the resolution had obviously not been fully comprehended by the men from Dhami. For Narain Dass, the president of the Dhami Prajamandal and meter-reader of the Simla municipality it meant, contrary to anything that the Prajamandal stood for, being appointed Rana. According to the Dhami State, the provocative appearance of Narain Dass triggered off the fire:

> Narain Dass who was coming in a rickshaw was seen coming towards the Palace. He was then seen having got a QUALGHI (a plume which is worn by the rulers on ceremonial occasions) and a man was holding an open umbrella over his head like CHHATTAR and CHANWAR behind. The people who were with him, were shouting 'Dhami *Murdabad*' and 'Rana Narain Dass *ki jai*'. ... There could not be any worse provocation that could be offered to a ruler and the loyalists within his State and in front of his palace.[20]

Then ensued a mêlée. The details vary, but it ended in two dead and forty injured.

By evening the crowd had dispersed; many to straggle back to Simla. By 10.30 p.m., the CID had begun recording at the Jutogh checkpost the names and credentials of all those who entered Simla from the direction of Dhami. The list sent to the Home Department included the names of 109 'inferior' government servants.[21] Predictably, the largest number were from offices stationed in Simla throughout the year, for example, thirty-one peons of the Army Headquarters, twenty-two from the Government of India Press, and nineteen gardeners employed at Viceregal Lodge.

News of the police firing at Dhami reached Simla and was reported in most newspapers.[22] A complete *hartal* was observed in the Simla Bazar, and at a largely-attended public meeting it was stated that the 'Paramount Power should institute an inquiry. Since many of the victims are peons of the Imperial Secretariat it is not difficult to examine them as witnesses.'[23] A Congress member of the municipality tried to get through a resolution expressing the Municipal Committee's sympathy for the rate-payers and tax-payers who suffered in the Dhami firing.

Sauhta's agitation met with disapproval from all quarters. The firing was widely publicized and an inquiry into its cause demanded. The Political Agent who visited Dhami that evening gave his verdict. The Congress made an independent inquiry in the Congress office at Lower Bazar, which was presided over by Lala Duni Chand, Advocate, Member of the Punjab Legislative Assembly, and of the All-India Congress Committee; Dev Suman, chairman of the Parvati Praja Parishad, was its secretary. The local members consisted of Lala Kishore Lal, president of the Arya Samaj, Simla and Lala Sham Lal, president of the City Congress. The Dhami durbar also held an inquiry.

The Rana of Dhami, alarmed at the censure in the press, paid a hurried visit to Gandhi to present his point of view. The 'great man', he recounted, called him a 'bad boy'.[24] Gandhi a few days later openly criticized the organizers of the event for hasty action. In an article in the *Harijan*, he pointed out that 'the Chiefs who get easily frightened and easily resort to firing ought not to possess the power they have over the life of their subjects. . . . If the people sought to overwhelm the Rana, it was undoubtedly wrong; as it was there was defiance of the order against Shri Bhagmal. It was wrong too, if outsiders joined the alleged demonstration. The lightning ultimatum, if it was that, was a preposterous thing deserving condemnation. Responsible government is made of sterner stuff.'[25] The attitude was echoed by the Congress hierarchy. Nehru, as President of the All-India States People's Conference, joined in with a note of warning to the hill states leaders.[26]

Bhagmal Sauhta was evicted from the Imperial Hotel, his belongings thrown unceremoniously into the street, and he was lodged in a jail in Ambala. Narain Dass, president of the Dhami Riasti Prajamandal, the meter-reader from the electricity department, was dismissed from municipal service despite the efforts of sympathetic Congress commissioners to delay the decision.[27]

For the organizers, it was a problem finding a new set of workers to carry on the work of the Himalaya Riasti Praja-mandal, and this resulted in a change in the base of the movement at Simla. Suman Dev, convener of the Mandal, wrote to Nehru that their activities depended upon the participation of Govern-ment servants and hence could never lead to a sustained movement; alternative support would have to be found.[28] The Simla Congress, however, capitalized on the Dhami incident by holding public meetings at the Gunj and the Arya Samaj Hall throughout July and August 1939.[29]

The Government of India was concerned at the involvement of 'inferior' government servants in the movement. Rule 23 of the Government Servants Conduct Rules forbade Government servants to take part in or assist in any way political movements in India. Until 1939 it had never been considered necessary to determine whether 'inferior' servants such as peons and *daftris* from the Government of India offices, *malis* employed in the Viceregal Lodge, etc., came within the ambit of this rule, it was also unclear whether this applied to political movements in the Indian states as well. The matter was closed with a warning and general reiteration of the application of rule 23 to all Government servants.[30]

The Dhami incident demonstrates the politicization of a section of the hill population who lived and worked in Simla. The docility of hill people had been one of the factors that made Lawrence choose Simla as summer capital. Thereafter the Government had endeavoured to insulate the summer capital from nationalist currents by cordoning off all undesirable visitors and residents. The Prajamandal movement had, however, been organized at Simla and spread out to its hinterland to involve the people of the hill states. It signalled the breakdown of the artificial isolation of the summer capital.

CHAPTER SEVENTEEN

The End of an Era

WITHDRAWAL symptoms began to show many years before 1947, for the happenings after 1921 shook the British belief in the insulated seclusion of Simla. The British reaction to inroads into its cultural enclave was to abandon long-term efforts to sustain their hold over the town. Official interest in the town sagged; the vast plans for refurbishing the town, optimistically conceived in 1914, remained incomplete and the money left unspent twenty years later. British-owned properties in Station Ward changed hands as values slumped. Indian businessmen, with a shrewd eye to bargains, bought up many highly-prized estates.

Despite nationalist criticism, officials clung 'limpet like' to the annual summer move to Simla.[1] In 1931, when Gandhi was asked where the capital of free India would be located, he had said, 'We must go down 5,000 storeys to the plains, for the Government should be among the people and for the people.'[2] The same year, Irwin curtailed the duration of the Government's Simla stay from seven to six months. Yet the logic of 'whole convoys of lorries carrying files and other documents, whole tram-loads of clerks and minor personnel, then the heads of departments, the staff officers, and finally the Viceroy himself'[3] being transported to the workshop of the Indian Empire, was still being questioned a decade later.

Simla's summer population had registered a steady rise: it was over fifty thousand in 1931, when the last summer census was taken, and the proportion of Indians had grown since then.[4] The Lee Commission recommendations of 1925 had made it possible for British officials to spend their holidays in England, and Simla lost its position as the premier holiday station.

In 1925, Edward Buck after a thirty-year stay had perceived the change: 'I should say that much of Simla's attraction from the European point of view is disappearing. . . . There is no longer one big family circle, and altogether existence is more strenuous.'[5] He attributed the change to Simla becoming more expensive, and in particular to the high wages of servants, and also to legislative reforms whereby Indians had obtained a larger share in the administration.

Some Indian families who had formed a part of the 'family circle' and could be considered social embodiments of the partnership between British and Indian ruling interests, were lured away by nationalist forces: Raj Kumari Amrit Kaur, the daughter of Raja Sir Harnam Singh, owner of Manorville, was to break out of the charmed circle of Summer Hill, and become one of the Mahatma's most ardent followers.

Harnam Singh, the second son of the Maharaja of Kapurthala, had embraced Christianity as a young man, and married the daughter of the Reverend Golaknath of Jullundur city. He managed the Kapurthala estates in Awadh from 1877 to 1895 and was secretary of the British Indian Association of the Taluqdars of Awadh for over fifty years. He received the KCIE in 1900, the title of Raja in 1907, and hereditary Raja in 1922, and was a member of the Council of State from its inception in 1921. Lady Dufferin had visited the family at Manorville and found the Kunwarani a 'very pleasing and perfect English-speaking native lady . . . remarkably nice and clever.'[6]

Rajkumari had her schooling in England, at Sherborne School in Dorsetshire, and on her return, had fitted easily into Simla society. Tennis (introduced to Simla by Dufferin), was popular with officials; since it was her forte, she occasionally won the local championships, and it kept her in close touch with officialdom.

As she matured, Rajkumari was drawn to Gandhi and nationalism. By 1930, she had turned her back on tennis and parties; she became chairperson of the All-India Women's Conference and Vice-President of the All-India Village Industries. In 1935, she placed all her personal resources at Gandhi's disposal and became a part of his inner circle. By the 1940s, the police records describe her as a 'devoted follower of Gandhi' and an 'alleged ardent supporter of non-violence'.

In autumn 1942, once the local Congress leaders were jailed, she occupied centre stage at the Gunj, distributing posters, handbills and *Harijan* bulletins, exhorting Government servants to join the civil disobedience movement. For almost two months between August and October, she urged Indian officials to quit 'sitting on the fence'; mere 'heart sympathy' was not enough.[7]

This placed the Punjab and Central Governments in a quandary, and the former shifted the responsibility of arresting her on the latter. The Chief Secretary felt that she was proving an embarrassment to the local government while her sex and 'lofty if misguided professions' were potentially dangerous. She had won a certain amount of sympathy and was capable of swinging an important section of the more impressionable towards active participation in civil disobedience.[8]

An official note recounts that she was worried by the violence generated in 1942 and 'wishes to be arrested to get out of it all.'[9] It was not thought desirable to imprison her with Gandhi and his entourage 'which is exactly what she wants.' As the Punjab Government was reluctant to treat her as a local Congress worker since she had no links with Congress in the Punjab, the Home Secretary suggested confinement at Simla. She was arrested in late October 1942 under Rule 21 of the Defence of India Rules and confined for a month at Ambala. Subsequently she was placed under house arrest and confined to the limits of the garden and house at Manorville until her release, two years later, in 1944. She played an active role at the Simla Conference a year later, in 1945.

Even in Simla's twilight years as capital, the holiday atmosphere and social life continued with the momentum given in the nineteenth century. Deborah Morris, working in the Women's Auxiliary Corps of India during World War II, reminisced about Simla: 'The hotels and restaurants which had dance floors were open two or three nights a week. Rickshaws ran gaily up and down the Mall with the crests and liveried runners of ruling princes. The Gaiety Theatre was producing one play after another. Whatever the complications of office days, the evenings grew gayer and gayer.'[10]

Implementation of the Government of India Act of 1935 and
the onset of World War II proved a turning point in deciding
the numbers who came with the Government of India. In the
early part of 1939, the Government of India reconsidered
the question of the annual move to Simla. 'They have been
influenced by the serious overcrowding in Simla and by the
prospect of this problem being made more acute when the next
and much larger Federal Legislature comes into being.'[11] The
Government therefore decided that the second annual session
of the new Legislature would be held in New Delhi between
mid-September and the beginning of November, thus further
reducing its stay in Simla. It was also considered not necessary
for the full department to be present at Simla; the upshot was
that only one-third of a staff of three thousand was privileged
to come to Simla. Heads of departments were permitted an
attached office, but the migratory ministerial staff was reduced
to 20 per cent of the total. Since heads of departments were
usually British, it enabled them to spend the summer away
from Delhi. It is curious that fear of overcrowding rather than
financial or other constraints was made the ostensible reason
for deciding Simla's fate.

At the outbreak of World War II, Army Headquarters shifted
permanently to Delhi and Simla then served as headquarters
for the émigré Burmese Government from 1942 to 1944.

The Government of India's decisions of 1939–40 sent a tremor
of 'nervousness and anxiety' through the business community
of Simla. The Municipal Committee thought that it would
prove 'disastrous to the prosperity' of the summer capital.

Once the Government of India had curtailed the numbers
travelling up to Simla, a large number of houses, especially in
the bazar area, fell vacant. Since they earned no rent, in 1940–1
the Municipal Comittee was compelled to reduce house and
water taxes to over five hundred houses.[12]

Changes in property ownership and land values are the index

of social flux. As the demand for, as well as the prestige of, larger properties in Simla diminished, property values slumped. This change in Simla can best be demonstrated by relating the history of a prestigious house known as The Crags. Situated on a huge rock jutting out on the northern face of Jakhu, with a breathtaking view of the snow ranges, it is one of the old estates, stretching over an area of 2,500 square yards. Built in 1841 by the Political Agent,'the estate had many illustrious owners, including General Sir P. S. Lumsden, in 1864–72, General E. L. Thuillier, in 1872–9, and Sir J. B. Lyall (afterwards Lieutenant-Governor of the Punjab) in 1879–83. It was then bought by Colonel A. R. D. Mackenzie for 35,000 rupees and large portions of the house were rebuilt before, in 1905, it was sold to a British houseowner, for 1,05,000 rupees. In 1915, it was bought by an Ahmedabad lawyer, Sir Chinabhoy Madaval, for the magnificent sum of 1,40,000 rupees; but by 1943 the property was sold to Pandit Thakur Datt Sharma of Lahore for a mere 80,000 rupees. [13] (Pandit Thakur Dutt Sharma had made a fortune with his patented ayurvedic medicine, amritdhara.) The main building housed the Sir Harcourt Butler School.

Indian businessmen bought up many of the commercial landmarks in the 1940s. Regent House was purchased by Mohan Singh Oberoi for his wife. George William Townley, the proprietor of Cotton and Morris, sold the Exchange Building to Khan Bahadur Sheikh Inayatullah. Northbrooke Terrace was bought by the wealthy timber contractor, Jodhamal Kuthiala, while Raja Gyan Nath, Prime Minister of Indore State, invested in the money-making venture of the new age—the New Empire Cinema (now the Ritz).

There are success stories. Mohan Singh Oberoi, at the age of twenty-five, left his plague-stricken village of Bhaun in Jhelum district to seek employment in Faletti's Hotel Cecil. 'I saw the Cecil—two beautiful buildings across the road and something told me that there was a vacancy. I took courage, walked in and met the manager. I did not even know what vermouth or sherry was, nor could I pronounce their names.' [14] He secured a job as a clerk at a salary of fifty rupees per month, and worked hard enough to be noticed by the Cecil's manager, Ernest Clarke. In 1924, when Clarke started his own Clarke's Hotel he invited Oberoi to join him as manager, storekeeper-cum-clerk at a salary of one hundred rupees; twice the amount he received at the Cecil.

The turning point came when Clarke retired and agreed to transfer the lease of the hotel to him for 30,000 rupees. Oberoi tapped all his savings and mortgaged his wife's jewellery to buy the lease. Later he bought it outright for 1,00,000 rupees, and it remains his personal property until today. It was the beginning of Oberoi's journey on the road to becoming a millionaire hotelier.

The municipal commisssioners of the 1940s were mostly Indians. This was the impact of large-scale purchases of property and trade falling from British into Indian hands—commercial interests that had to be represented. The Government further subdivided property and trade interests into Hindu and Muslim. Secondly, Indian professionals had attained the position of executive engineers and civil surgeons, and consequently were ex-officio members. The three elected members were invariably Indian.[15]

The authorities reacted to the changed complexion of the municipality by putting pressure on nominated members to vote for government-initiated resolutions. Mela Ram Sood recounted how, when N. L. Varma tabled a resolution objecting to a statement criticizing the Indian character, and Sood supported it, he was accosted by the Deputy Commissioner and reminded of his obligation as a nominated member to support the official point of view.

Mela Ram Sood was nominated to the Municipal Committee as a representative of the Simla Trades Association in 1936, a position he retained for seventeen years. He was then twenty-seven, and a timber merchant like his father and grandfather before him. He had come to Simla in 1919 as a young boy and, after his father's death, worked with his uncle, Rai Bahadur Mohan Lal. Enterprising and energetic, he had moulded himself to be the Rai Bahadur's deputy. At his uncle's request, he was made responsible for the arrangements for Gandhi's visit to Simla in 1931. Once he had learned the ropes, he expanded his business interests from timber to solidified fuel, for which he was contractor and supplier, with a shop on the Mall and a branch in New Delhi. He also became Chairman of the Hoshiarpur Electric Supply Company. He bought several properties in Lower Bazar, and then a large estate, Mythe. On his uncle's death in 1932, he championed similar causes, becoming President of the Sood Sabha and office-bearer of the Arya Samaj. In 1940, he was president of the House Owners and Merchants Association.

Despite the façade of democratization in the 1930s, the Deputy Commissioner of Simla continued to be president as well as patriarch of municipal affairs. He was vested with the authority to specially commend municipal commissioners for good work, and to report to Government on 'the general attitude of members towards their responsibilities, how far they are actuated by personal or party motives and how far they are dependent on official initiative.'[16] He thus virtually wrote annual confidential reports on them.

The Committee's control over the municipal staff and administration was curtailed. The secretary of the municipality, under the president's direction, exercised general control over the whole municipal establishment. The two officers had powers to appoint, dismiss, downgrade or fine any employee of the Committee drawing a salary of less than twenty-five rupees per month. All other cases were referred to the Committee. The incapacity of members of the Municipal Committee to take decisions was underlined in the 1940s by the Divisional Commissioner in an inspection note, who commented: 'I am also given to understand, some of the members interfere in these matters in order to get their friends appointed or retained on the staff of the Committee.'[17] On his suggestion, the Committee delegated full powers of appointment and dismissal of the whole staff to the president. Thus, despite the concession towards a constitutional framework, official control over the municipality actually increased.

The delay in implementing projects planned in 1914 by the Simla Improvement Committee provides an insight into the uncertainty of the town's future. The *Report* of 1914 had sketched out an overall plan for the projects required for the town. The three major projects were extension of the water supply, of the sewage lines, and the remodelling and reconstruction of Lower Bazar; surface drainage, improved roads, and an electric lift to Jakhu, were also envisaged. The scheme, estimated to cost 48,00,000 rupees in 1914, was sanctioned by the Secretary of State in 1916.

Improvement of the water supply to the town planned in 1914, was the largest and most successful of the projects implemented before 1947.[18] However, the implementation of plans for improving the storage system was painfully slow. In 1914, a detailed preliminary scheme and report was prepared to provide the entire town with a water-borne sanitary system. A sum of 10,00,000 rupees was allotted for laying large sewage pipes to facilitate connections to individual houses on the water carriage system, but the existing sewer pipes were not replaced by larger ones and few houses could be connected: eighteen connections were provided in 1933, but only two in 1936, five in 1938 and six in 1940–1.[19] The conversion from dry to flush water closets was likewise slow.[20]

Lower Bazar remained untouched. The 1914 Committee had found most buildings unfit for human habitation and planned major structural changes, for which 1,80,000 rupees were allocated. The report stated:

> The whole bazar should be systematically examined, each area, road and alley way should be carefully considered, and concrete schemes linking up the whole Bazar should be planned, so that ultimately the whole of the main bazar may come under systematic treatment. This will be the work of time, and can only be carried out by systematic operations carried out with some continuity of policy.[21]

The Municipal Committee felt powerless to deal with the Bazar. Under the Municipal Act, it could have prohibited the use of those houses which were unfit for habitation but it could not provide alternative accommodation because of financial constraints. The Committee had no power to remove the surplus population from this area, or to prevent the continuing influx of people. In 1922, ten of the eighteen lakh rupees sanctioned for the Bazar was spent by the Government of India for the construction of houses at Dhar and Phagli for clerks.

Hearn, who inspected the Bazar in 1936, found the majority of the houses 'ramshackle rabbit warrens', totally unfit for human habitation.[22] In addition, the entire system of drainage required remodelling but for this the whole Bazar would have had to be pulled down. The municipality did the next best by covering all the drains, utilizing only two of the eighteen lakh rupees allocated. Subsequent schemes for improvement were delayed, postponed or filed away; rebuilding the Bazar passed once again into the limbo of good intentions. Obviously, far too many interests, landlords and tenants, were involved.

By 1937, over twenty years after the sanction of the Simla Improvement Fund, only a little more than half had been spent, of which, about a quarter went to the schemes originally earmarked. The Government of India decided to suspend expenditure on it in 1937,[23] but after representations, it agreed to reframe the scheme.

In 1940–1, the Committee directed its PWD engineers to prepare a preliminary town-planning scheme for the unbuilt area and a building scheme for the built area. When contacted for assistance, the provincial town planner pointed out that the old map of Simla, made in 1923, would have to be updated because of the development which had taken place since then. As it involved technical expertise, the Committee requested the Survey of India to prepare a large-scale map. The Director, Frontier Circle, however regretted his unability to do so because of the lack of staff in view of the 'international situation'[24]. The town-planning schemes were therefore shelved for four decades, till Simla became the capital of Himachal Pradesh.

In the meanwhile, the Government of India asked the Committee to submit proposals it considered urgent:[25] these were (1) to make the Mall fit for vehicular traffic, (2) augment the water supply, (3) improve the sewage system, and (4) construct accommodation for coolies and the poorer sections of society.

The proposals were considered at a meeting in the Imperial Secretariat at Delhi, under the chairmanship of Sir Girja Shankar Bajpai. It was decided to implement schemes relating to the water supply, sewerage, and construction of houses for coolies. Only the last was implemented, resulting in the construction of the labour hostels on the Mall. The proposal of making the Mall motorable was not accepted because of the danger it would pose to pedestrians, rickshaws and ponies. Fortunately, however, to improve communications, it was decided to make a circular road that would link the Kalka road with the Hindustan–Tibet road. It was one of the last projects completed before 1947.

Simla had inexorably become an entrepôt for the hill states that lay beyond. The decision to make a circular road reflects a recognition of this fact. It provided the link to the Hindustan–Tibet road for the two new cash crops, seed potatoes and apples, which were carried on mule back. Commercial apple production was given a fillip by Satyanand Stokes who imported the Red Delicious apple along with its production technology from America. He planted the first trees on terraced fields at Barubagh in Kotgarh in 1918. When apple cultivation spread to the surrounding villages, production increased.[26] By the 1940s, 10,000–15,000 maunds of apples had to be transported from the Kotgarh area, traversed by the Hindustan–Tibet road. Stokes, in the declining years of his life, addressed himself to the problem of widening the Hindustan–Tibet road up to the apple-growing areas and linking them to the railhead at Simla.

The trace of the circular road, together with the estimates, was ready by the close of 1941.[27] Existing roads were linked up with the construction of a few stretches in between to encircle

Simla. A tunnel planned to run under Gorton Castle was shifted eastwards[28] to serve the railhead. It was named Victory Tunnel since it was commenced in 1945, at the end of World War II, to commemorate the victory of the Allied forces. The widening of the Hindustan–Tibet road had to wait till the 1950s.

CHAPTER EIGHTEEN
A Postscript

SIMLA spills over in many directions; the half-timbered Tudor mansion here and the Scottish castle there, peer from behind the thrusting new concrete structures. These spell the transformation of Simla into Shimla, from summer capital of the Raj to the all-weather provincial capital of independent India. The hill station built for the exercise of privilege, class, and eccentricity, is being turned into one of high-density colonies to meet the demands of middle-class Government employees, lawyers and bankers, contractors, shopkeepers and commission agents, and affluent fruit growers from the rural hinterland.

It is customary to highlight the meanness, squalor and vulgar health of the town, the smelly 'Shame-la', and to nurse imprisoned memories of the idyllic days of the Raj. Old residents lament the lack of 'society' and the 'graces'. There are brave, quixotic gestures, like the gentleman who walked in the centre of the road, holding up the once-restricted traffic, determined not to give way to that modern despoiler—the motor vehicle. Others would have the return of the horse, pony and rickshaw. Newspapers, sometimes reflecting élitist and exclusive views, get good copy from contrasting modern photographs of crumbling vistas with glistening images of the past.

Visually, the descent to philistine Indianness is traced to the 1950s when Simla became the capital of post-partition Punjab. In 1952, when M. S. Randhawa was posted at Simla as Development Commissioner, he noted three changes—the disappearance of the liveried rickshaw-pullers and orderlies clad in scarlet, the surplus church buildings, and the appearance of shops selling *pan* and *pakoras* on the Mall.[1] Windowpanes of the major structures ceased to be scrubbed or cleaned; the municipal *safai* staff took short cuts and now sweep garbage over the hillside—the incinerators for its disposal having fallen into disuse.

When the state of Punjab acquired the new city of Chandigarh in 1953 as its capital, Simla seemed a town without a future. Its population declined by 7.7 per cent and property values slumped. The merging of the Punjab hill areas with the new state of Himachal Pradesh in 1966 regenerated Simla once again. It was a ready-made capital, complete with houses, offices, water supply, sanitation and aura. In winter the town was covered with *him*, snow, epitomizing the new state. Its population registered a steady rise and in the 1981 census, the town showed 17,500 occupied residential houses and a population of 70,604.

We shall never know the extent of the summer population, although if the past provides any index, it would be about double the winter enumerations. The mid-summer municipal census, to assess the flood tide of summer visitors, was a useful practice. It was less detailed than the decennial census, but gave the occupational break-up of the summer population, together with dependants. The decennial census, which was taken in February or March, gave a head count of the permanent population of the town minus the migrant population that accompanied the Government of India and Punjab. There are no counts of the summer population now, although residents speak of the 'guestfall' that wipes out all 'windfalls' during the summer months.

Simla was never planned in the way New Delhi or Baguio were. However, its growth as sanatorium and holiday resort, and finally as summer capital in the last century, fixed the parameters of future growth. Its urban form was a consecration of values that implied detachment from the local people and a commitment to unequal forms of development. Station Ward and Bazar Ward: the former, the re-creation of a British town; the latter, commercial, crowded, slummy and Indian, housing about half the Indian population of Simla considered necessary to maintain the comforts of the former. The station was dominated by the élites: the bureaucracy, the judiciary, the princes, and British holiday makers. The story of Station

Ward till 1947 is that of houses and estates owned and tenanted successively by British officials, Indian aristocrats, and, in the two decades before independence, by the emerging Indian middle-classes.

Yet there is continuity in change. An Indian Rip Van Winkle awakening in Simla in the 1980s would find that Simla had reached full circle in its pattern of urbanization. The faces would be a different colour: the dominant four thousand or so European white faces would have given way to several thousand plebian brown—mostly hill folk, though better nourished and better clothed than before. But the urban problems remain striking similar.

In the 1880s, British officials lived within the encapsulated colonial world of the exile, where they were men of a superior culture, bringing enlightenment to heathens, and Simla was a little England, a haven which provided them with breathing space in the exacting task of achieving their aims.

The 'station' of the 1880s reflected their confidence and optimism in the future of empire, and also a sense of fun, of camaraderie and bonhomie. It picked from a range of Western architectural styles for its public buildings. It created large aristocratic estates that middle-class British officials eagerly bought, and made of the bazar a ghetto.

The town was the spatial embodiment of a social system; the process of urbanization expressed the colonial dynamic at the level of space. British official planners tried to preserve the urban form which had emerged in the nineteenth century well into the twentieth. Simla had been devised for an anticipated peak population of 45,000, at the most of 60,000.

There was the paranoic dread of overcrowding, of unwanted Indians, expressed in successive official reports that monitored the growth of the city, and sketched out future plans. It became a cardinal plank of official policy to 'restrict and retard' the normal growth of the town and to prevent a large-scale influx of population to the summer capital. The solution, unstated as official policy but implict in municipal decisions, was to prevent the opening up of new areas and to restrict approval for the construction of new buildings or the extension of old ones.

In the 1980s, just as it was a century ago, urban space is once again required for the proliferation of government activity, and the consequent need for offices and residential accommodation. The hill station of the 1880s was re-planned for imperial needs; it is now being re-adapted to meet the needs of the capital of Himachal Pradesh. If the combination of urban problems seems to be those of the past they are sometimes approached through the solutions of the past.

The Government's attempts to move the State Electricity Board and its offices to Sundernagar and other departments to Dharamsala are reminiscent of Curzon's efforts in 1903 to shift the Punjab Government to Dalhousie. There are contradictions: on the one hand, there are belated efforts by the state government to stay construction in the heart of the town, on the other, the local authority feels constrained to cover municipal and other deficits through the construction of commercial complexes.

The earlier structure of the hill town, the segregation of the Station and the Bazar, is being obliterated. The two begin to merge as the latter overtakes the former, and the transformation is fraught with many problems. As Dyos has said, inertia is part of the dynamic of urban change. Structures outlast the people who put them there and impose constraints on those who have to adapt them to their own use.[2]

The refurbishment of an old hill station may be a planners' nightmare. At the inception, the search for level pieces of land along the hillsides determined the location of houses, and a retaining wall would provide for a few extensions. Now it is the location of hard rock which determines the site for construction. It has become possible to build multi-storeyed structures on concrete pillars clamped to a rocky hillside. Such mushrooming blocks meet the growing demand for small apartments, though construction costs are about one and a half times that of the plains. The old single-room servant quarters have become readymade homes for the poor. When the houses were built with an acre or two of land around them, the informal layout was charming; when built close together, the corrugated iron roofing gives the scene the appearance of an outsized ironmonger's junk shop.

The initiative for building has come, as it did a century ago, from private houseowners and estate agents. There is also the familiar pattern of escalating land prices. This, together with the demand for small convenient flats, has led many an aristocratic houseowner to carve his estate into small plots, for one acre estates are expensive to maintain and lucrative to sell, having provided an excellent cushion against inflation and devaluation.

Private initiative and pressures ensure, however, that the master plan remains largely on the drawing-board, and municipal by-laws stay embalmed within the yellowing pages of the book. It is unfortunate that land readjustment projects for plots made from large, terraced estates have not been effectively implemented. In such a project, the municipality prepares a site plan, calculates the percentage of land required for services such as roads, water, sewerage and other utilities. It calculates the cost of providing services in terms of a percentage of land with sufficient improvement value to recover the cost of services.

The Government, wisely concerned about conservation of the wooded environs of Simla, continued the old prohibition on cutting trees. But even as architects worked on the aesthetic interrelationship between levels of houses *vis-à-vis* trees, it has not been possible to preserve the trees from ingenious euthanasia within private compounds. The lower half of Jakhu, for example, has become a treeless extension of Lower Bazar.

The colonial government could dictate norms and ignore Indian public opinion; popularly-elected local governments are more susceptible to pressure. New colonies have mushroomed over the years as 'planned slums'. There is the case of Sanjauli, that 'pirate' suburb which grew outside the municipal limits of Simla, both to avoid paying local taxes and octroi, and as a shelter for the middle-class unable to find a home in

Simla. Spiralling property values and soaring rents have now led to Operation Land Encroachment, and houses are spread-eagled over service lanes and roads. Perhaps in the years to come a more authoritarian municipality will carve out wider roads to let in sunlight, as well as provide ambulances and other essential services.

The local authorities at Simla have had to cope with other problems of change. For instance, as equestrian traffic gave way to vehicular, the roads had to be metalled and tarred. Before 1947, over three-quarters of the 129 kilometres of road were unmetalled. At present 112 kilometres have been provided a block top, widened where possible, to enable motor vehicles to ply.[3]

The daily water supply has been augmented from the 9,00,000 gallons per day available in 1948 to 42,00,000 gallons per day.[4] But as population outstrips supply, criticism of the lack of planning is as shrill as it was a century ago, when the water scheme of the 1880s was found inadequate within a decade and required augmentation.

The objective of connecting all residential houses to sewer lines through a waterborne system turned out to be a civic mirage. Succeeding Improvement Reports of 1907 and 1914 had detailed the sewerage scheme, but less than half the houses were connected by 1940, when the attempt was abandoned as large sewer pipes would have had to be laid. The problem is being grappled with again in the 1980s. The 1986–87 Annual Report of the Municipal Corporation has a familiar refrain: 'A request had been sent to the IPH (Irrigation and Public Health) Department to design a regular sewerage system of Shimla Town for the Municipal Corporation. Further, works of laying sewer lines shall be taken in hand only when the detailed design of sewerage system of Shimla town is received from the IPH Department.'[5] Hopefully a system will be designed and implemented by the close of the century.

Government has once again to concern itself, as it did a century ago, with housing its offices and employees. Accommodation is eagerly provided by new landlords to offices and banks, in what is calculated as a safe investment. As before, Government concern for officers rather than for lower-rung clerical staff, has led to new housing colonies being built at Kasumpti and Khalini.

The Simla municipality has traditionally functioned under the surveillance of the central Government. In the nineteenth century, municipal representation had been based on the Whig concept of 'interest', connoting that the quantum of tax paid by houseowners or tenants entitled them to a proportionate right in the running of municipal affairs. Property qualifications formed the basis on which the representative nature of the municipality rested. There was a tug-of-war between landlord and Government, as owner and tenant of property, for control of the municipality. The concept, however, nullified the need for an election, and in 1908 the municipality was a totally nominated one. With the promise of democratic rights being given in 1917, the principle of elections was reviewed again, but within the framework of representation of interests, and resulted in efforts to balance and counterpoise all interests. The meaning of the term widened to include not only property, but also traders, European and Indian, and religious groups, Hindu and Muslim. The pressure to democratize resulted in one member being elected from each of the two wards, Station and Bazar and in 1930, the Bazar Ward was given an additional seat. Despite such concessions to the elective principle, the Deputy Commissioner remained ex-officio municipal president, and functioned as a *pater familias*, specially commending members for good work.

In the post-1947 period, a representative Municipal Committee was set up. In 1953, Simla was divided into fourteen single-member wards and one double-member ward. The old property qualifications for voting were replaced by adult franchise. The last elections held according to this constitution were in November 1960.

In 1966, Simla became capital of Himachal Pradesh. Three years later, in 1969, the Municipal Committee was replaced by a corporation. The new body was headed by an administrator and consisted of ten nominated official corporators, including one woman and one scheduled-caste member. The state ruling party feared that an inconvenient political setup, singly or in combination, might embarrass the government. It may be added that such a phenomenon is not unique to India. In England, for example, the Greater London Council was abolished in 1985; it had never been controlled by the party holding national office.

In 1986, an injunction from the High Court struck down all objections to a democratic Municipal Corporation, and elections were held in May 1986. The Municipal Corporation has now lost its pivotal role in town management to a host of government departments: it surrendered transport in 1956, schools in 1957, the Bhargava College in 1961, Ripon Hospital and the dispensaries in 1968, the Fire Brigade in 1972, electricity in 1974, the food laboratory in 1976[6] and finally the bulk water supply and the pumping station. Urban expansion is overseen by the Simla Development Authority, and construction of new colonies by the Housing Board; the Town and Country Planning Department oversees its links with the region and counter-sanctions all building applicatons. The Municipal Corporation is left to look after sewerage, drainage and distribution of the water supply, and therefore, has little relevance except as a berth for small-time politicians.

The insulation of Simla town from its hinterland ended many years before 1947. The Raj created roads, within Simla and without, skirting the crest of the hills to the interior, initially for trade, and as links to the erstwhile hill states, but later also for expeditions and *shikar*. One of the more tangible developments in Simla has been its growth as an entrepôt. Efforts to monetize a traditional farm economy and raise the standard of living of farmers by the development of horticulture, seed potato and off-season vegetables, have converted Simla into a growth centre.

Development has led to a significant rise in the per capita income of Himachal Pradesh. The town now reflects its hinterland: many of the hill people have jobs at various levels in Government and quasi-Government offices, as well as links with the rural interior. As Pradesh capital, Simla has emerged once again as an administrative centre and is demographically pre-eminently a service town.

If the problems of Simla a century ago seem similar, the solutions to them have to be found in the context of the present social milieu and the technologies available today. The town is now rooted in the emerging politico-economic structure of Himachal Pradesh. As trucks trailing clouds of grey smoke roar up in low gear from July until November, transporting crates of fruit or bags of potatoes, choking traffic on Simla's circular road, they symbolise both Simla's regeneration and its struggle to cope with change.

Appendices

I. *History of Simla* Ilaqa *up to 1850*

The lands forming the pergunnah and the present station of Simla originally belonged conjointly to the Maharaja of Patiala and the Rana of Keonthal. As early as 1824, European gentlemen, chiefly invalids from the plains, had, with the permission of these chiefs, established themselves in this locality, building houses on sites granted them rent-free, and with no other stipulation than that they should refrain from the slaughter of kine and from the felling of trees, unless with previous permission of the proprietors of the land.

The station became gradually favourably known as a Sanaarium, and in 1830 the Government directed that negotiations should be entered into with the chiefs of Patiala and Keonthal, for as much land as was deemed sufficient to form a station. Accordingly Major Kennedy, the then Political Agent, negotiated an exchange with the Rana of Keonthal for his portion of the Simla hill, comprising the thirteen villages noted in the margin* and yielding an estimated annual revenue of Rs. 937, making over to the Rana the pergunnah of Rajeen, yielding an annual revenue of Rs. 1,289, which had been retained by us on the first conquest of these hills, as its position was considered to afford a good military position.

*1. Pandhore. 7. Bannowino.
2. Dumhee. 8. Pugaoo.
3. Sarran. 9. Dirwin.
4. Fagooly. 10. Khumley.
5. Dulna. 11. Khullyan.
6. Hyar. 12. Kimney.
13. Khullyar.

A portion of the retained pergunnah of Bharauli, consisting of the villages noted in the margin,* was at the same time made over to the Maharaja of Patiala in exchange for the portion of Simla which was included in his territory, and which consisted of the villages noted in the margin yielding an estimated revenue of Rs. 245 per annum.

*Dawonty, Dharaiee, Kabloun.

Kainthoo, Phungony, Chewng, Amdriee.

SOURCE: Colonel E. G. Wace, *Final Report of the First Regular Settlement of the Simla District in the Punjab 1881–1883*, pp. 20–1. Apparently the *ilaqa*, rather than any of its constituent villages, was called Simla.

II. *Simla Municipality Bye-Law for the Regulation and Prohibition of Traffic*

1.   No person shall take, keep, or use any elephant or camel in any place within Municipal limits without the previous sanction of the President or Secretary of the Municipal Committee.

Provided that nothing in this rule shall apply to camels used by any person
   (a) on the cart road as far as the Municipal Serai;
   (b) on the road leading from the Municipal Serai to the grain shops at Edwards Gunj;
   (c) on the road leading from the Municipal hydrant on the cart road below the Foreign Office to the open space below the Boileaugunj Police Station.

2.   No person shall use any wheeled vehicle in any public road or street within the limits of the Municipality except in accordance with the terms and conditions entered in a Pass to be signed by the President or Secretary of the Municipal Committee in this behalf.

Provided, first, that nothing in this rule shall apply to:-
   (a) motor-cars actually used by H.E. the Viceroy, H.E. the Governor of the Punjab, and H.E. the Commander-in-Chief in India and all other wheeled vehicles drawn by horses in their possession.
   (b) wheeled vehicles used by any person on the cart road as far as below the gate of 'Ravenswood'.
   (c) rickshaws, children's perambulators and vehicles of like nature other than wheeled barrows and hand-carts.

Provided, secondly, that nothing in this rule shall apply to bicycles the use of which is regulated by Bye-law No. XL, sanctioned in the Punjab Government Notification No. 20843, dated 31st October 1920.

Explanation:- The term 'wheeled vehicle' shall mean and include all wheeled conveyances of every description driven, drawn, or carried by animals or men or propelled by mechanical power.

Illustration:- Motor-cars, motor scooters, bicycles, hand-carts and wheeled barrows are 'wheeled vehicles' within the meaning of this rule.

3.   No cattle, sheep, goats or pigs and no mules or other animals used for draught or burden shall be permitted in the roads or streets

specified as prohibited in the second schedule annexed to these rules.

Provided that where there are very short distances to be traversed in crossing the road, mule traffic may be allowed to proceed under a General Pass issued by the Secretary of the Municipal Committee, subject to such conditions and restrictions as he may deem fit to impose.

4.   From the 15th March to 15th October, both days inclusive, and between the hours of 3 P.M. and 8 P.M. no person shall lead or drive any animal used for draught or burden, or horned cattle, and no horse dealer, syce, grass cutter, native trainer, jockey or other native servant shall lead, drive or ride any horse, pony, or mule or other animal used for riding in any street mentioned in the first schedule annexed to these rules.

Provided that nothing in this clause shall apply to
(a) saddled horse or pony which is being ridden or taken from place to place for the bona fide use of its owner, or which is being led or ridden after an owner; and
(b) any act done with the previous written sanction of the Municipal Committee.

Explanation:- The term 'owner' in this sub-clause shall be deemed to include any person to whom the said horse or pony has been or is lent or hired by the owner.

5.   From the 15th March to the 15th October, both days inclusive, and between the hours of 4 P.M. and 8 P.M. no job porter or coolie shall solicit employment, loiter, or carry any load in any street mentioned in the first schedule annexed to these rules:

Provided that nothing herein contained shall apply to:-
(a) porters or coolies carrying the personal luggage of travellers;
(b) porters or coolies carrying letters or conveying purchases from any shop or other such establishment in Simla to the residences of purchasers, such purchases not being of a size or nature calculated to cause danger, obstruction or inconvenience to passers-by;
(c) porters or coolies conveying or carrying any person in any manner;
(d) funerals; or
(e) any act done with the written sanction of the Municipal Committee.

6.   No person shall solicit alms, or expose or exhibit any sore, wound, bodily ailment or deformity in any street with the object of exciting charity or obtaining alms.

7.   No person shall carry or expose boards in any street for the purpose of advertisement except by a permit given by the Secretary of the Municipal Committee.

8.   No person shall lead or drive or ride any animal or propel or cause to be drawn or propelled any vehicle in any public road or street so rashly or negligently as to cause injury, obstruction, inconvenience or annoyance, or risk of injury, obstruction, inconvenience, or annoyance to the public or to any person.

9.   No person shall cause any animal or vehicle to stand in any public road or street longer than is necessary nor in such a position as to cause obstruction or inconvenience to the public or to the passers-by.

10.   No person shall draw or propel or cause to be drawn or propelled any rickshaw or other vehicle at a speed of more than 6 miles an hour.

11.   Persons leading horses on the public roads shall hold them close to the head with the left hand and keep to the left of the road.

12.   No person shall ride one horse, pony or mule and lead another.

13.   No person shall lead or drive or cause to be led or driven in any public road or street any cattle or other animals used for riding, driving, draught or burden, unless such animals are properly tethered and led by an attendant and not more than two animals shall be led or driven by one man.

14.   No person shall drive in any of the streets, mentioned in the first schedule, annexed to these rules, any sheep, goats or pigs, unless such animals are properly tethered and led by an attendant and not more than two such animals shall be permitted to be led or driven by one man.

15.   The recognised rules of the road in Simla shall apply to all manner of traffic in any public road or street within the limits of the Municipality.

16.   Any breach of rules 1 to 7 and 9 to 15 of the foregoing bye-laws shall be punishable with fine not exceeding Rs. 20, and any breach of rule 8 shall be punishable with fine not exceeding Rs. 50.

FIRST SCHEDULE
(Vide rules 4, 5 and 14)

1. Circular Road round Prospect Hill.
2. Circular Road round Observatory Hill.
3. Circular Road round Peterhoff Hill.
4. Circular Road from the Post Office round Jakko.
5. Circular Road round Elysium Hill.
6. Circular Road round the Convent.
7. Circular Road round Summer Hill.
8. Road from Peterhoff Hill to the Post Office.
9. Road from the Lakkar Bazar to the Elysium Hotel.
10. Road leading from the Ridge to the Main Bazar.
11. Road through the Chota Simla Bazar.
12. Road leading from Oakover to Barnes Court.
13. High level road from Barnes Court to the Convent.

SECOND SCHEDULE
(Vide rule 3)

PROHIBITED ROAD OR STREET

1. Main road from Sanjauli to the Ridge and the Lower Bazar.
2. Main road from the Telegraph Office to Boileaugunj Bazar.
3. Main road from the Exchange (Cotton and Morris) to Chota Simla Bazar.
4. Main road from the Telegraph Office to Summer Hill.

ALTERNATIVE ROUTE

1. Mule road from Sanjauli to the Lower Bazar passing below Snowdon.
2. From the Telegraph Office to Edwards Gunj and Cart Road, and via Cart Road to Boileaugunj Bazar.
3. From the Exchange to Municipal Serai and to Chota Simla via the Cart Road and the tunnel below Ravenswood and via the road above Khalini to Chota Simla rickshaw shed.
4. From Telegraph Office to Edward's Gunj, and via Cart Road to Boileau Gunj Bazar, and thence to Summer Hill via the old road leading to the temple.

Source: Act III of 1911.

III. *Membership of Simla District Congress by Occupation*

	1929	1935
Shopkeepers	21	239
Tailors	29	92
Arya Samaj Updeshiks	4	–
Government servants	2	–
Miscellaneous merchants	11	–
Carpenters	–	17
Coolies	–	63
Total	67	411

IV. Office Bearers and Members of the Congress Committee in 1932

Sr. No.	Name	Age	Occupation	Caste	Place of origin	Simla residence	Office
1.	Dr. N. L. Varma	30	Dentist	Khatri	Gujrat (Punjab)	Lower Bazar	President C.C. Simla
2.	Maulvi Gulam Mohammad	40	Private Tutor	Pirzada	Kashmir	Kashmiri Mohalla, Middle Bazar	–do–
3.	Thakur Bhagirath	40	Photographer	Rajput	Hoshiarpur	Lower Bazar	Vice President
4.	Salig Ram, BA	35	Bookseller	Sood	Hoshiarpur	Lower Bazar	Vice President
5.	Banarsi Das	45	Proprietor of Dairy Farm	Jain	Not known	Lower Bazar	Vice President
6.	Ch. Dewan Chand	42	Shopkeeper	Brahman	Hoshiarpur	Shop at Chor Bazar	Vice President
7.	Badri Das	32	Bookseller	Brahman	Hamirpur in Kangra district	Lower Bazar	Joint Secretary
8.	Bhag Mall	45	Shopkeeper	Sood	Pragpur (Kangra)	Lower Bazar	Assistant Secretary
9.	Janeshary Lalson	28	Shopkeeper	Jain	Saharanpur	Shop at Lower Bazar	Auditor

IV. *continued*

Sr. No.	Name	Age	Occupation	Caste	Place of origin	Simla residence	Office
10.	Dina Nath	35	Shopkeeper	Sood	Pragpur (Kangra)	Sabzi Mandi	Cashier
11.	Munshi Ram	35	Shopkeeper	Brahman	–	Gunj Bazar	Member
12.	Salig Ram	38	Commission Agent	Mahajan	Kalka Ambala district	Gunj Road	Member
13.	Gokul Chand	39	Commission Agent	Khatri	Hoshiarpur	Gunj Bazar	Member
14.	Ghungar Mall	50	Shopkeeper	Sood	Hoshiarpur	Lower Bazar	Member
15.	Bawa Faqir Chand	32	Cloth Merchant		Middle Bazar	Member	
16.	Hari Chand	42	Commission Agent	Kalal	Hoshiarpur	Gunj Road	Member
17.	Rana Hoshiar	42	Proprietor Simla Dairy Farm	Rajput	Kangra	Dairy Farm Market, Simla	Member
18.	Hari Lal	42		Khatri		Khalini Junga State	Member
19.	Maulvi Abdul Ghani	42	Imam, Qutub Masjid	Kashmiri	Kashmir	Lower Bazar	Member
20.	Mohd. Umar Nomani	45	Householder	Kashmiri	Lower Bazar	Lower Bazar	Member

No.	Name	Age	Occupation	Caste	District	Address	Position
21.	Nand Lal	48	Commission Agent	Kalal	Hoshiarpur	Gunj Road	Member
22.	Thakar Dass	60	Shopkeeper	Sood	Kangra	Kaithu Bazar	Member
23.	Mansa Ram	35	Shopkeeper	Sood	Kangra	Ram Bazar	Member
24.	Harish Chand	46	Vakil	Sood	Kangra	Near Jain Temple	Member
25.	Butail	45	Cloth Merchant	Sood	Kangra	Lower Bazar	Member
26.	Pt. Devi Dutt	35	Pandit	Brahman	Ambala	Kaithu Bazar	Member

Kaithu Bazar

No.	Name	Age	Occupation	Caste	District	Address	Position
1.	Mansa Ram	28	Shopkeeper	Sood	Kangra	Kaithu Bazar	President C. C. Kaithu Bazar
2.	Charanju Lal	50	Shopkeeper	Mahajan	Kangra	Kaithu Bazar	Vice President
3.	L. Ratan Chand						Secretary
4.	L. Roshan Lal		Shopkeeper				Jt. Secretary
5.	Duni Chand	50	Shopkeeper	Sood	Kangra		Cashier
6.	L. Saran Das	38	Shopkeeper	Brahman	Kangra	Kaithu Bazar	Member
7.	Ram Ditta	22	Shopkeeper	Brahman	Hoshiarpur	Kaithu Bazar	Member
8.	Bishan Das	50	Rickshaw Chaudhri	Khatri	Hoshiarpur	Kaithu Bazar	Member
9.	Faqiria	–	–	–	Hoshiarpur	–	Member

IV / *continued*

Sr. No.	Name	Age	Occupation	Caste	Place of origin	Simla residence	Office
10.	Ram Nath	26	Shopkeeper	Khosla	–	Lower Bazar	Member
11.	Pt. Padamdev	32	Updeshak Arya Samaj	Brahman	Rampur Bushahr	Arya Samaj Simla	Member
12.	Dwarka Nath	28	Ex-Secy. C. C.	Kayasth	–	Gunj Road	Member
13.	Kanaya Lal Butail	28	Shopkeeper	Sood	Jawalamukhi	Khaddar Bhandar, Simla	Member
14.	L. Kishori Lal	42	Shopkeeper	Sood	Kangra	Middle Bazar	Member
15.	Mela Ram	38	Shopkeeper	Sood	Kangra	Lower Bazar	Member
						Boileaugunj	
1.	Khushi Ram		Shopkeeper			B. Gunj	President C.C.B. Gunj
2.	Jinoo		Shopkeeper			B. Gunj	J. Secy.
3.	Chand		Shopkeeper	Sood		B. Gunj	Secy. C.C.B. Gunj

No.	Name	Age	Occupation	Caste	Place	Residence	Designation
4.	Kishan Chand		Shopkeeper			B. Gunj	Cashier
5.	Tirlok Chand	28	Shopkeeper	Bania	Kalka	Lower Bazar	Member
6.	Tirlok Nath	36	Shopkeeper	Brahman	Amritsar	Lower Bazar	Member
7.	Nanak Chand	35	Commission Agent	Sood	Solan	Lower Bazar	Member
8.	Hari Chand	26	Servant of L. Kanaya Lal of Khaddar Bhandar, Ram Bazar, Simla	Sood	Kangra	Ram Bazar	Member

SOURCE: Simla District Congress Activities, 1929–38, SPTR.

Abbreviations

ADR	Ambala Division Records
AISPC	All India States People's Conference
DDR	Delhi Division Records
HA	Haryana Archives
NAI	National Archives of India
NMML	Nehru Memorial Museum and Library
RSAC	Report of the Simla Allowances Committee, 1905
SMR	Simla Municipal Records
SPTR	Sadar Police Thana Records
1877 Report	*Report of the Simla Extension Committee, 1877*
1898 Report	*Report of the Simla Extension Committee, 1898*
1907 Report	*Report of the Simla Improvement Committee, 1907*
1914 Report	*Report of the Simla Improvement Committee, 1914*
Summer Census Report, 1911	*Report on the Summer Census of Simla, 1911*
Summer Census Report, 1921	*Report on the Summer Census of the Punjab Hill Stations—Simla, Dalhousie, 1921*

Notes

CHAPTER ONE

1. Major William Lloyd and Captain Alexander Gerard, *Narrative of a Journey from Caunpore to the Borendo Pass in the Himalaya Mountains*, Vol. I, London, 1840, p. 141.

2. Emily Eden, *Up the Country, 1837–40*, Vol. I, London, 1866, pp. 144, 161.

3. Val C. Prinsep, *Glimpses of Imperial India*, Delhi, 1979, p. 264.

4. Malcolm Muggeridge, *Chronicles of Wasted Time: The Infernal Grove*, London, 1973, p. 37.

5. Philip Woodruff, *The Men Who Ruled India*, Vol. II, London, 1954, p. 94.

6. A comment from *Simla Times Advertiser*, 11 June 1894, illustrates this: 'The use of this *khud* in an official report strikes us as rather strange. Is there no English word for it? Why must we always be interpolating our speech not only, but our documents as well with these barbarisms? "Down the Valley" would have read just as well and would have had the further recommendation of being English.'

7. Commissioner, Delhi Division to Revenue and Finance Secretary, Government of Punjab, 6 September 1898.

8. Durga Das, *India from Curzon to Nehru and After*, London, 1969, p. 86.

9. Representation by Secretary, Punjab Trades Association, 86, G/100, 3 August 1900, P–1, SMR.

10. 'Memorial to the Viceroy, by Ten Citizens of the Patiala State', *An Indictment of Patiala*, Bombay, 1939, pp. 41–9.

11. Victor Jacquemont, *Letters from India, 1829–1832*, London, 1936, pp. 91–2.

12. Eden, *Up the Country*, Vol. II, pp. 293–4.

13. William Howard Russel, *My Diary in India*, Vol. II, London, 1860, p. 149.

14. Khemi Ram Verma and Balkrishan Thakur, *Laman, Thande Pani re Dibhanu* (Folk Songs from the Hills), Shimla, n.d., p. 87.

15. Alice Elizabeth Dracott, *Simla Village Tales*, London, 1906.

16. *The Pioneer*, 20 May 1882.

17. Dracott, *Village Tales*, p. x.

18. Edward J. Buck, *Simla Past and Present*, Bombay, 1905, pp. 193–4; and M. S. Randhawa, *Travels in the Western Himalayas*, Delhi, 1974, p. 158.

19. *The Pioneer*, 20 May 1882.

20. Henry Sharp, *Good-Bye India*, London, 1946, p. 152.

21. Dufferin and Ava, *Our Viceregal Life in India*, London, 1899; Deborah Morris, *With Scarlet Majors*, London, 1960. For a fictional account, Joan Fleming, *A Pinchbeck Goddess*, London, 1898.

22. See, for example, Rudyard Kipling's delineation of Mrs Hawksbee and Strickland in several stories in *Plain Tales from the Hills*, London, 1930; and *Wee Willie Winkee and other Stories*, London, 1929.

23. *The Statesman*, 11 July 1913.

CHAPTER TWO

1. Alexander Gerard, *Account of Koonawur in the Himalaya*, London, 1841, p. 197.

2. John Pemble, *The Invasion of Nepal*, London, 1976, pp. 54–89.

3. Report on the Hill Districts occupied by the Gurkhas, No. 198, August 1914, *Records of the Ludhiana Agency*, Lahore, 1911, p. 399.

4. For a detailed account of the war in the Simla region, see Udhab Singh, *Gurkha Conquest of Arki*, Lahore, 1902; Fraser, *Journal*.

5. Report on the Hill Districts, *Records of the Ludhiana Agency*, p. 411.

6. C. U. Aitchison, *A Collection of Treaties, Engagements and Sanads*, Vol. IX, Calcutta, 1892, pp. 111–57.

7. Ibid., p. 52.

8. Also spelt Nusseeree. Means 'friendly' Gurkhas. The Battalion was later designated the 1st Gurkha Rifles.

9. Walter Hamilton, *Description of Hindostan*, Vol. I, Delhi, 1941, p. 613.

10. Jacquemont, *Letters from India*, pp. 101–2.

11. E. G. Wace, *Final Report of the First Regular Settlement of the Simla District in the Punjab 1881–1883*, Calcutta, 1884, p. 2.

12. Foreign Political, 3 April 1830, 181, NAI; Series 1/1, Bundle 10, 1831, pp. 7–8, HA ADR.

13. W. W. Hunter (ed.), *Lord Amherst and the British Advance Eastwards to Burma*, Oxford, 1889, pp. 198–203.

14. Series 1/1, Bundle 6, 1827, pp. 257–9 and 261–4, HA ADR.

15. Captain Mundy, *Pen and Pencil Sketches, being the Journal of a Tour of India*, Vol. I, London, 1832, pp. 222, 226, 240.

16. Foreign Political, 11 November 1830, 42, NAI.

17. Ibid., 12 August 1831, 16, NAI.

18. Series 1/1, Bundle 10, 1831, pp. 7–8, HA ADR.

19. Henry Edward Fane, *Five Years in India*, Vol. I, London, 1857, p. 198; Buck, *Simla Past and Present*, p. 12.

20. Wace, *Final Report*; Series 1/1, Bundle 9, 3 April 1830, pp. 87–8, HA ADR.

21. Foreign Political, Proceedings, 23 September 1831, NAI.

22. Series 1/1, Bundle 8, 1829, pp. 19–20, HA ADR.

23. Foreign Political, Proceedings, 30 July 1831, NAI.

24. Buck, *Simla Past and Present*, pp. 144–6.

25. Mundy, *Pen and Pencil Sketches*, p. 227.

26. Foreign Political, 21 November 1834, 141–2, NAI.

27. Ibid., Proceedings, 12 August 1831, NAI.

28. Indra Krishen, *An Historical Interpretation of the Correspondence of Sir George Russel Clarke, Political Agent Ambala and Ludhiana, 1831–43*, Vol. I, Delhi, 1952, p. 366; Mian Bashir Ahmed Farooqui, *British Relations with the Cis-Sutlej States, 1809–1823*, Lahore, 1941, p. 49.

29. Foreign Political, 21 November 1834, 142, NAI.

30. Ibid., 23 January 1832, pp. 381–2.

31. Ibid., 1 October 1832, p. 148.

32. Secy, Governor-General, to Resident, Delhi, 9 November 1827, pp. 289–90, HA ADR.

33. 'Lt Kennedy's Narrative of Hill States in 1824', *Records of the Delhi Residency and Agency*, Lahore, 1911, p. 274.

34. Foreign Political, Proceedings, 23 January 1832, pp. 311–83, NAI.

35. Ibid.

36. Ibid.

37. Foreign Political, 23 January 1832, 27, NAI.

38. *Supplement to the Meerutt Observer*, 21 August 1834, in Foreign Political, etc.

39. Ibid., 21 November 1834, 142.

40. Ibid.

41. Ibid., 30 March 1835, 22.

42. Ibid.

43. The list of springs has been compiled from K-50, 1904; K-58, 1905; K-66, 1907; K-89, 1909; SMR.

44. D. J. F. Newall, *The Highlands of India Strategically considered with special reference to their Colonization as Reserve Circles*, London, 1882, p. 60.

45. *Gazetteer of the Simla District, 1889*, pp. 91–114.

46. Foreign Political, 12 April 1843, 21–3, NAI.

47. Ibid., 31 December 1847, 284–7.

48. Ibid., 7 December 1852, 209–11.

49. J. G. Baird (ed.), *Private Letters of the Marquess of Dalhousie*, Ireland, 1972, p. 101.

50. Andrew Wilson, *Abode of Snow*, London, 1873, p. 94.

51. *Report on the Hill Districts*, p. 411.

52. Series 1/1, 59, 1859, HA ADR.

53. Foreign Political, 5 December 1851, 162–3, NAI.

54. St. J. Gore, *Light and Shades of Hill Life in the Afghan and Hindu Highlands of the Punjab*, London, 1895, p. 14.

55. William Edwards, *Reminiscences of a Bengal Civilian*, London, 1866, pp. 118–35.

56. Foreign Political, 3 August 1855, 221–3, NAI.

CHAPTER THREE

1. R. Bosworth Smith, *Life of Lord Lawrence*, Vol. II, London, 1883, p. 426. See also pp. 419–26.

2. Robert R. Reed, 'Remarks on the Colonial Genesis of the Hill Station in Southeast Asia with particular Reference to the Cities of Buitenzorg (Bogor) and Baguio', *Asian Profile*, Vol. 4, No. 6, December 1976; and 'The Colonial Genesis of Hill Stations: the Genting Exception', *Geographical Review*, Vol. 69, No. 4, October 1979.

3. Foreign Political, Keep Withs, 6 August 1858, 533–8, NAI.

4. 'Panics in Simla', Foreign Political, Keep Withs, 12 November 1858, 266–70, NAI.

5. W. W. Hunter, *Imperial Gazetteer of India*, Vol. XII, Calcutta, 1887, p. 493.

6. Home Public, 6 July 1864, 17–18, NAI; Bosworth Smith, *Lord Lawrence*, p. 426. See also Curzon, *British Government in India*, Vol. II, London, 1926, p. 121.

7. Home Public, 13 December 1864, 41–47 A, NAI.

8. Wood to Lawrence, 18 December 1865, Lawrence Papers, Reel 1, Acc. No. 1616, NAI.

9. Wilson, *Abode of Snow*, p. 58.

10. After annexation in 1849, Punjab was placed under a Board of Administration for four years. Thereafter it was headed by a Chief Commissioner. In 1859, when the Delhi territory was merged in Punjab, it became a Lieutenant-Governor's Province. In 1920, Punjab was declared a Governor's Province.

11. *The Tribune*, 10 April 1883.

12. Home General, July 1889, 387, NAI.

13. See, for instance, dates of annual moves of the Government of India, Home Dept., between Calcutta and Simla, Home Public, August 1884, 118–20, NAI.

14. Captain G. P. Thomas, *Views of Simla*, London, 1846, p. 37.

15. Anthony D. King, 'Colonialism and the Development of the Modern South Asian City: Theoretical Considerations', in Kenneth Ballhatchet and John Harrison (eds.), *The City in South Asia*, London, 1980.

16. Russel, *My Diary in India*, Vol. II, pp. 144–5.

17. *The Tribune*, 9 July 1881.

18. Ibid., 3 March 1883.

19. *The Bengalee*, 27 March 1889.

20. Guy Fleetwood-Wilson, *Letters to Nobody*, London, 1921, p. 126.

21. *The Bengalee*, 7 May 1887.

22. Charles Dilke, *Greater Britain*, London, 1868, p. 443.

23. *Gazetteer of the Simla District*, 1888–9, p. 1.

24. Rudyard Kipling, 'Tale of Two Cities', *Rudyard Kipling's Verse, Definitive Edition*, London, 1982, p. 77.

25. *The Tribune*, 27 March 1889.

CHAPTER FOUR

1. Lady Betty Balfour (ed.), *Personal and Literary Letters of Robert, First Earl of Lytton*, Vol. II, London, 1906, p. 16.

2. Also spelt Peterhof. Most nineteenth-century official records and maps spell it Peterhoff, which has therefore been used in the text.

3. Home Public, April 1880, 184–6, NAI.

4. Statement C showing establishment to be accommodated in 1883–4 in Central Departments; Dufferin Papers, Microfilm Reel 535, NAI.

5. H. H. Cole, *European Architecture for India: A Note*, PWD Military Works, March 1880, 4–5, NAI.

6. Asa Briggs, *Victorian Cities*, London, 1964, pp. 41–3.

7. PWD, Civil Works, Buildings, Keep Withs, March 1885, 34–7, NAI.

8. For detailed construction costs of Viceregal Lodge and government buildings, see Dufferin Papers.

9. Despatch No. 34, Public Works, 15 March 1877, Dufferin Papers.

10. A Report on the Unsatisfactory Working of the Architectural and Buildings Division at Simla', PWD Military Works, March 1880, 4–5, NAI.

11. PWD Civil Works, Buildings, Keep Withs, March 1885, 34, NAI.

12. *The Pioneer*, 13 August 1883.

13. PWD Civil Works, Buildings, Keep Withs, March 1885, 34, NAI.

14. Dufferin and Ava, *Our Viceregal Life in India*, Vol. I, p. 131.

15. PWD Civil Works, Buildings, Keep Withs, March 1885, 34, NAI.

16. Buck, *Simla Past and Present*, p. 42.

17. PWD Civil Works, Buildings, A, July 1879, 23 NAI.

18. Ibid., January 1886, 15–18, NAI.

19. *The Pioneer*, 19 July 1884.

20. *The Gazetteer of the Simla District*, 1904, p. 123; *Thacker's Guide to Simla*, 1895, p. 65.

21. Buck, *Simla Past and Present*, p. 73.

22. RSAC, pp. 184 and 28.

23. Ibid., p. 77.

24. Prinsep, *Glimpses of Imperial India*, p. 262.

25. For description of Bazar, see Foreign Political, Keep Withs, 12 November 1858, 266–70, NAI; *1877 Report*, p. 3; *1914 Report*, p. 18.

26. 'Proposed Removal of Upper Bazar', PWD, 1864, 2, HA ADR.

27. *1877 Report*, p. 8.

28. *Annual Report, 1877–78*, p. 6, SMR.

29. *The Simla Times Advertiser*, 18 June 1894.

30. Colin C. Garbett, *Christ Church, Simla*, Lahore, 1944. See also J. E. Wilkinson, *The Parochial History of Simla*, Simla, 1901.

31. 'Construction of Town Hall', M-2, Vol. I, SMR.

32. See Chapter 7.

33. See Home Public, July 1877, 29, NAI; and Public Works, General, 1877, E-4, SMR.

34. Foreign Political, Proceedings, 23 September 1831, NAI.

35. *The Pioneer*, 27 July 1883.

36. Ibid., 18 August 1883.

37. *Gazetteer of the Simla District*, 1904, p. 132.

38. Deputy Commissioner, Simla, to Commissioner, Delhi Division, 10 January 1885, E-4-1, 1887, SMR. See also *Revised Working Plan for the Simla Municipal Forests*, Part I, Simla, 1950, pp. 61–2.

39. Pamela Kanwar, 'Sources of Water Supply at Simla in the Nineteenth Century with Particular Reference to the Combermere Tunnels', June 1983, mimeo.

40. The earliest geological mapping of Simla was in H. B. Medlicott, *Memoirs of the Geological Survey of India*, Vol. III, 1865. In 1887, Thomas Oldham wrote Preliminary Sketch of the Geology of Simla, and Jutogh, (*Records, Geological Survey of India*, Vol. XX, pp. 143–53). A geological map of Simla is in S. G. Burrard and H. H. Hayden, *A Sketch of the Geography and Geology of the Himalayan Mountains and Tibet*, Calcutta, 1907.

41. Report on the Improvement of Simla, General Political, 1861, 10; and PWD, 1870, 6, HA ADR. See also 'Report on Works in Progress in Simla: The Water Supply', 4 April 1879, E-4-1, SMR

42. E 4-1, 1879, SMR.

43. Deputy Commissioner to Home Secretary, Punjab Government, 13 April 1876, ibid.

44. *Annual Report 1879–80*, SMR; *Report of the Simla Sanitary Investigation Committee*, Simla, 1905, p. 9; *Report of the Medical Officer of Health*, Simla, 1937, p. 58.

45. Dufferin's Farewell Speech in Simla, 24 September 1888, *Speeches Delivered in India 1884–8 by the Marquis of Dufferin and Ava*, London, 1890, p. 35.

CHAPTER FIVE

1. Russel, *My Diary in India*, Vol. II, p. 151.

2. Eden, *Up The Country*, Vol. I, p. 2.

3. Bradford Spangenberg, *British Bureaucracy in India*, Delhi, 1978, p. 19.

4. *The Simla Times*, 28 May 1919.

5. Conrad Corfield, *The Princely India I Knew*, Madras, 1975, pp. 30–2.

6. Colin Garbett, *Friend of Friend*, Bombay, 1943, p. 37.

7. W. R. Lawrence, *The India We Served*, London, 1939, p. 80.

8. Evan Maconochie, *Life in the Indian Civil Service*, London, 1926, p. 86.

9. Dufferin and Ava, *Our Viceregal Life in India*, Vol. II, p. 35; Sharp, *Goodbye, India*, p. 146.

10. Michael Glover, *An Assemblage of Indian Army Soldiers and Uniforms*, London, 1973, p. 83.

11. Buck, *Simla Past and Present*, pp. 115–22; William Wedderburn, *Allan Octavian Hume*, London, 1913; S. R. Mehrotra, *Towards India's Freedom and Partition*, Delhi, 1979, pp. 44–66.

12. Fleetwood-Wilson Papers, Microfilm Reel 42, NAI.

13. Ibid., and *Letters to Nobody*, p. 126.

14. P. H. Denyer, *Amateur Dramatic Club, 1837–1937*, Simla, 1937, p. 10.

15. Amateur Dramatic Club, Simla, Minutes.

16. Corfield, *The Princely India I Knew*, p. 31.

17. Charles Allen, *Plain Tales of the Raj*, London, 1980, p. 159.

18. *The Statesman*, 13 July 1913.

19. Allen, *Plain Tales*, pp. 96–7.

20. United Service Club, Simla, Papers, F-1-7/65-R4, NAI.

21. Ibid., Rules and Regulations of the New Club, Simla, 1887.

22. *A Short History of the United Service Club, Simla*, Simla, 1905, p. 3.

23. Home Public, April 1883, 195–201; June 1883, 50–1; NAI.

24. *The Englishman*, 21 January 1921.

25. Foreign Internal, July 1891, 164–5, NAI.

26. Owen Snell, *The Anglo-Indians*, Bombay, 1944, pp. 11–14.

27. Eden, *Up the Country*, Vol. I, p. 151. Attitudes towards this class in the 1880s surface in many of Kipling's stories. See, for instance, 'Beyond the Pale', 'Kidnapped', 'His Chance in Life'.

28. Ibid., p. 151.

29. Newall, *Highlands of India*, p. 61.

30. For a detailed account, see Asa Briggs, *Victorian People*, London, 1958. pp. 148–75.

31. Buck, *Simla Past and Present*, p. 87.

32. RSAC, p. 27.

33. H. M. Stowell, Superintendent in the Office of the Adjutant General in India, RSAC, p. 127.

34. *Simla Times*, 4 May 1916; 13 April 1916.

35. Ibid., 7 September 1922.

36. Ibid., 7 December 1922. See Herbert Alick Stark, *Hostages to India or the Life Story of the Anglo-Indian Race*, Calcutta, 1926, pp. 120–36.

CHAPTER SIX

1. Charles French; cf. Buck, *Simla Past and Present*, p. 13.

2. Eden, *Up the Country*, Vol. I, p. 157.

3. Philip Davies, *Splendours of the Raj*, London, 1985, pp. 109–10.

4. Dufferin and Ava, *Our Viceregal Life in India*, Vol. I, p. 131.

5. D. S. Bastavala, *Simla*, Bombay, 1925, p. 74.

6. Buck, *Simla Past and Present*, p. 127.

7. Simla Racket Court Case, Judicial, 1857, 79, HA ADR; *Civil and Military Gazette*, 24 July 1923.

8. Foreign Judicial, July 1863, 31–3 A, NAI.

9. Buck, *Simla Past and Present*, p. 127.

10. Foreign Secret Internal, Keep Withs, September 1886, 431–3, NAI.

11. Foreign Internal, July 1891, 164 5, NAI.

12. Home Public Deposit, 1890, 329, NAI.

13. Foreign Secret Internal, 1894, 72–4, NAI.

14. Ibid., Keep Withs, September 1896, 431–3, NAI.

15. Eden, *Up the Country*, Vol. I, p. 118.

16. Foreign Internal, October 1895, 107–9; and 1909, 20–2 A, NAI.

17. Foreign Internal, Proceedings, October 1897, 315–16, NAI.

18. Foreign Proceedings, June 1890, 66–70, NAI.

19. Ibid., October 1891, 16–17, NAI.

20. Ibid.

21. See Barbara N. Ramusack, 'Incident at Nabha', in Harbans Singh and N. Gerald Barrier, *Punjab Past and Present*, Patiala, 1977, pp. 433–53.

22. Foreign Secret Proceedings, June 1890, 33–7, NAI.

23. *Simla Times*, 3 June 1916.

24. Foreign Internal, Proceedings, December 1901, 3–4, NAI.

25. Iris Butler, *The Viceroy's Wife*, London, 1969, p. 136.

26. Foreign Political, Internal, April 1918, 103, NAI; and *1907 Report*, p. 16.

27. Foreign Political, Internal, September 1905, 1024, NAI.

28. Foreign Proceedings, October 1891, 16–17, NAI.

29. Curzon's Speech at Gwalior, 29 November 1899, in Earl of Ronaldshay, *The Life of Lord Curzon*, Vol. II, London, 1929, p. 90.

30. Foreign Internal Proceedings, June 1901, 42–3, NAI.

31. Ibid., 2 April 1904.

32. Ibid., February 1921, 26–7.

33. *The Pioneer*, 30 April 1930.

34. Buck, *Simla, Past and Present*, p. 31.

CHAPTER SEVEN

1. *Liddell's Simla Weekly*, 7 June 1913; 18 April 1914.

2. R. J. Moore, *Liberalism and Indian Politics, 1872–1922*, London, 1965, p. 35.

3. Foreign Political, 17 October 1851, 98–102, NAI.

4. Ibid., 26 December 1851, 80–1; see also ibid., 6 August 1852, 156–9.

5. *The Pioneer*, 18 August 1881; *The Tribune*, 20 August 1881.

6. *The Pioneer*, 26 April 1882.

7. Ibid., 20 April 1882.

8. Proceedings of the Lieutenant-General of Punjab in the Municipal Department, 2 June 1882, P-1, SMR.

9. *The Pioneer*, 22 July 1882.

10. D. E. Wacha, *Rise and Growth of Bombay Municipal Government*, Madras, 1913, pp. 296–302.

11. 'Dissent note by A. O. Hume', P-1, SMR.

12. *The Civil and Military Gazette*, 30 June 1883.

13. *The Pioneer*, 12 July 1883.

14. P-1, SMR.

15. Ibid., Hume to Aitchison, 21 July 1883.

16. Secretary, Government of India to Secretary, Government of Punjab, 1 September 1884, M-2, Vol. I, SMR.

17. President, Municipal Committee to Government of India, 8 November 1884, M-2, Vol. II, SMR.

18. Secretary, Government of Punjab to President, Municipal Committee, 23 October 1884, M-2, Vol. I, SMR.

19. Proceedings, 8 March 1885, SMR.

20. Secretary of State to Governor-General-in-Council, 15 November 1888, M-2, Vol. III, SMR.

21. Ibid., 'Note by Vice President Town Hall Sub-Committee', 1 January 1888.

22. Ibid., 'Report on Stability and Safety of Town Hall', November 1912.

23. Local Funds, 10 August 1883, H-4, DDR.

24. Memorial to Secretary, Punjab Government, 1 August 1890, p-1, Vol. II, SMR.

25. A. O. Hume had resigned from the Committee in July 1884. James Walker, president of the Committee, retired in 1887. Edward V. Cullin, a lawyer 'possessing local knowledge and professional skill' did not seek re-election after 1894.

26. *Simla Times Advertiser*, 25 June 1894.

27. Proceedings, 16 November 1883, SMR.

28. Ibid., 24 October 1883.

CHAPTER EIGHT

1. *Gazetteer of the Simla District*, 1904 and 1936.

2. *Liddell's Simla Weekly*, 6 December 1913.

3. *The Statesman*, 14 September 1924.

4. *The Pioneer*, 15 February 1896.

5. Buck, *Simla Past and Present*, pp. 173–4.

6. *The Simla Times*, 5 March 1894.

7. Home Political, A, December 1877, 24, NAI.

8. *Annual Report*, 1880–81 and 1882–83, SMR.

9. *The Pioneer*, 19 February 1896.

10. Hugh Tinker, *The Foundations of Local Self-Government in India, Pakistan and Burma*, London, 1954, p. 331.

11. *1914 Report*, Appendix 28, p. cxxxiv.

12. P-1, SMR.

13. *1907 Report*, p. 18.

14. Ibid.

15. 'Raising Simla from Class B to Class A Municipality for the purpose of Octroi', N-7, Vol. I, SMR.

16. *Annual Report*, 1884–85.

17. *Liddell's Simla Weekly*, 2 May 1914.

18. *1898 Report*, p. xx.

19. The road was proposed in 1898 and completed in 1907; *1907 Report*, p. 7.

20. *Liddell's Simla Weekly*, 7 June 1913.

CHAPTER NINE

1. Home Medical, A, July 1875, 30–40; August 1875, 69, NAI. Series 1/1, Bundle, 1875 HA ADR.

2. F. Marion Crawford, *Mr Isaacs*, London, 1894, p. 5.

3. Foreign Political, 26 December 1851, 80, NAI.

4. Ibid., Internal Secret, December 1915, 5.

5. Commissioner, Delhi Division to Financial Secretary, Punjab Government, 6 September 1898, *1898 Report*, p. 2.

6. *Census Reports*, 1911 and 1931. The table shows population variations in Simla in winter and summer.

Year	Winter	Summer
1889	–	24,179
1891	13,034	–
1911	18,490	37,895
1931	18,144	53,949

7. *Census Report*, 1904, p. 17.

8. *1898 Report*, p. 33.

9. *Summer Census Report*, 1911, p. 6.

10. *1898 Report*, p. 1.

11. Minute of 13 September 1900 to the Secretary of State.

12. Ronaldshay, *Curzon*, Vol. II, p. 140.

13. *Census Report*, 1904.

14. *The Pioneer*, 4 September 1904.

15. 24-L, SMR.

16. Foreign Political, Keep Withs, 12 November 1858, 266–70, NAI.

17. *1907 Report*, p. 46.

18. Eden, *Up the Country*, Vol. II, p. 301.

19. *Annual Report, 1887–88*, SMR.

20. *The Tribune*, 17 May 1921.

21. Ibid., 4 July 1921.

22. Ibid., 7 August 1921; 23 June 1924.

23. *The Simla Times Advertiser*, 4 June 1894.

24. *1914 Report*, p. 16.

25. *1907 Report*, p. 20.

26. Ibid., p. 8.

27. Secretary, Simla House Proprietors Association, 31 August 1907; *1907 Report*, appendix VIII, p. xxvii.

28. *1898 Report*, p. 2; *1914 Report*, Appendix A, p. 1.

29. *Report of the Simla House Accommodation Committee*, 1917, p. 11.

30. *Summer Census Report*, 1921, p. 14.

31. Foreign Political, Internal, December 1915, 5, NAI.

32. 48-L, SMR.

33. 48-L, SMR.

34. Narayani Gupta, *Delhi Between Two Empires*, Delhi, 1981, p. 93.

35. *Report of the Simla House Accommodation Committee*, 1917, p. 4.

36. *The Simla Times*, 14 September 1922.

37. 48-L, SMR.

38. Buck, *Simla Past and Present*, p. 111.

39. *The Simla Times*, 29 May 1919.

40. *Summer Census Report*, 1921, p. 13.

CHAPTER TEN

1. Denzil Ibbetson, *A Glossary of the Tribes and Castes of the Punjab and North West Frontier*, Vol. III, Lahore, 1883, p. 430.

2. William Moorcroft and George Trebeck, *Travels in the Himalayan Provinces of Hindustan and the Punjab*, Vol. I (reprint), Karachi, 1979, p. 76.

3. Foreign Political, June 1832, 18–25, NAI.

4. *1898 Report*, p. xviii.

5. Ibid.

6. The Simla commission agents maintain the following records: *Ahrties Association Simla, Rules and Regulations*, Simla 1931; and a Minute Book of meetings. The Association provided for a managing committee, elected by the general body, which consisted of a president, vice-president, a secretary and an assistant secretary. The Association was to meet twice a month, with a quorum of 40 per cent of members. The absence of any member from six consecutive meetings would result in cancellation of his membership.

7. N. B. Sen (ed.), *Punjab's Eminent Hindus*, Lahore, 1944, pp. 166–72.

8. There are several: Salamat Rai, *Mukammal Tarikh Soodan*, Lahore, 1935; Pt. Sant Ram Sastri, *Sood Vanshavali*, Lahore, n.d.; M. M. Sood, *Origin and History of Soods*, Chandigarh, n. d. There are two recent ones: Madnesh Azad, *Sood Vansh Ka Gauravshali Itihas*, Amritsar, n.d.; and M. M. Sood, *Origin and History of Soods*, Chandigarh, n.d.

9. Dispute about land known as Dedo-ka-nal with the Arya Samaj, R-11, 1885–90, SMR.

10. Kenneth W. Jones, *Arya Dharam*, Delhi, 1976, p. 224.

11. *The Tribune*, 28 April 1926.

12. Ibid., 25 April 1926.

13. Charge Note, 2 January 1936, SPTR.

14. List of Societies, No. 6, SPTR.

15. Gurdarshan Singh, 'Amritsar and the Singh Sabha Movement', in Fauja Singh (ed.), *The City of Amritsar*, Delhi, 1978, p. 97.

CHAPTER ELEVEN

1. The Government of India, Clerks' Salaries Committee, 1908, quoted in Shriram Maheshwari, *The Evolution of Indian Administration*, Agra, 1970, p. 52.

2. *The Bengalee*, 15 March 1884.

3. See Ian J. Kerr, 'Social Change in Lahore, 1849–1875', *Journal of Indian History*, Vol. LVI, Parts II and III, 1979.

4. Morris, *With Scarlet Majors*, p. 31.

5. *Census Reports*, 1911 and 1921.

6. Sudhir Chandra Sen, *The Simla Kali Bari*, p. 2.

7. Statement of P. K. Mitra, p. 67, RSAC.

8. *The Tribune*, 10 April 1883.

9. *The Pioneer*, 29 July 1884.

10. Statement of P. K. Mitra, p. 68, RSAC.

11. G. R. Elsmie, *Thirty-Five Years in the Punjab*, Edinburgh, 1908, p. 140.

12. S. D. Collet (ed.), *The Brahmo Year Book for 1878*, pp. 73–4.

13. G. S. Chhabra, *An Advanced History of the Punjab*, Vol. II, Ludhiana, 1962, p. 348.

14. Kali Baris were established in many northern towns with an appreciable Bengali population such as Lahore, Rawalpindi, Peshawar, and Kabul. Sen, *The Simla Kali Bari*, p. 3.

15. Kenneth W. Jones, 'The Bengali Elite in Post-Annexation Punjab. An Example of Inter-Regional Influence in 19th Century India', in Harbans Singh and N. Gerald Barrier, *Punjab Past and Present*, Amritsar, 1975, pp. 234–51.

16. RSAC, p. 5.

17. *The Statesman*, 14 September 1924.

18. Durga Das, *India From Curzon to Nehru*, p. 39.

19. The Anglo-Indians argued 'that the European and Christian character of their schools would be jeopardized by unconditional admission of Indians.' *The Tribune*, 7 August 1921.

20. *1914 Report*; 'Statement showing details regarding the residence of Indian employees', appendix 25; and p. 173, RSAC.

21. 'List of Government Employees who take active part in the meetings, with names of Societies 1930', SPTR.

22. Simla Amateur Dramatic Club, Minute Book, Vol. I, 1888–93, 14 September 1894.

23. Ibid., 7 September and 11 October 1897.

24. 'Holding of Dramatic Performances at the Nabha Estate by (1) The Madras Club, (2) The Daksh Club, Phagli, 1931', T-243, SMR.

25. Durga Das, *India from Curzon to Nehru*, p. 87.

26. *The Tribune*, 26 August 1926.

27. Ibid., 17 May 1921.

CHAPTER TWELVE

1. Q. No. 7, 8 March 1926.

2. Account pieced together from *The Tribune*, 5 and 7 September 1925; *The Hindustan Times*, 28 and 30 September, 7 October, and 1 November 1925; Superintendent of Police's Report 'Simla Rickshaw Case', Home Police, 1925, XXIX.F.7, NAI.

3. *The Tribune*, 20 February 1926. See also 12 February and 16 February 1926.

4. *The Hindustan Times*, 19 November 1925.

5. Ibid.

6. *The Hindustan Times*, 6 September 1925.

7. *Liddell's Simla Weekly*, 24 February 1917.

8. Buck, *Simla Past and Present*, p. 68.

9. Prinsep, *Glimpses of Imperial India*, p. 261.

10. N. Sen, *Licensed Rickshaw Coolies of Simla*, Simla, 1931; L. R. Davar, *Economic Conditions of Simla Rickshawmen*, Lahore, 1934.

11. Davar, *Simla Rickshawmen*, p. 11.

12. Note, 'Rickshaw Coolies', 14 August 1929, 66-III-W. SMR.

13. Of these, 23.8% were Rajputs, 16.9% Brahmans, 11.7% Kanets, 22.8% Juhahas; there were also Lohars, Kumars, Chhimbas, Kolis, Chamars, Nais and Doomnas. Dawar, *Simla Rickshawmen*, p. 11.

14. *Liddell's Simla Weekly*, 24 February 1917.

15. Note by N. L. Verma, 63-III-W, SMR.

16. Proceedings of Special Sub-Committee held on 26 August 1929, 63-III-W, SMR.

17. Ibid.

18. Ibid.

19. Verbal communication, Maulvi Sanaullah, Kashmiri Masjid, 5 July 1978.

20. Memo. No. 101, 25 November 1910, T-39, SMR.

21. 'Job Porters', 1931, 63-I-W, SMR.

22. Verbal communication, B. L. Salhotra.

23. Songs retold by Prakaso Devi, Safai Staff, Simla Municipal Corporation.

24. Jawaharlal Nehru, *An Autobiography*, London, 1936, p. 182.

25. Meetings of the Balmiki Sabha, Simla, 15, 17 September 1939, SPTR.

26. 'Application of Balmikiyan Sweepers Association claiming representation on the Municipal Committee', 1931, p-17, SMR.

27. Sub-Inspector, CID Report, 23 May 1933, SPTR.

28. Ibid., 18 September 1939.

29. Reports of meetings held on 12 and 28 May 1939, 1, 7, 11, 27 June 1939, SPTR.

30. Omar Nomani, a Kashmiri Muslim from Kulnag, and secretary of the Congress Committee of Simla, became the Labour Board's general secretary. Nomani was ousted from the Kashmiri Labour Board in 1935 when Pir Zakaullah, a Muslim Leaguer, became president, but he remained in the Congress. 'Grant of Leave to Muslim Coolies to attend the anniversary of the Simla Labour Board', 1930, T-236, SMR.

31. 'Application for the grant of permission to hold meetings at the Ridge', 1931, T-224, SMR. Abdul Ghani subsequently apologised to the Municipal Committee for using the Ridge for a public meeting.

32. 'Abolition of Rickshaw Chaudhries', 63-III-W, SMR.

33. 'Purchase of Rickshaws from Chaudhries and their sale to Rickshaw coolies', 64-I-L, SMR.

34. 'Rickshaw Coolies', 62-I-L, SMR.

35. Annual Report, 1942–3, P-1, SMR.

CHAPTER THIRTEEN

1. *The Simla Times*, 19 May 1921.

2. Butler, *Viceroy's Wife*, p. 32.

3. *The Tribune*, 17 May 1921; *The Simla Times*, 19 May 1921.

4. Durga Das, *India from Curzon to Nehru*, p. 91.

5. *The Pioneer*, 16 May 1921.

6. Ibid., 18 May 1921.

7. Durga Das, *India from Curzon to Nehru*, p. 92.

8. Gandhi made a political settlement on the question of Swaraj a pre-condition for the meeting. Reading, on the other hand, raised the issue of breach of trust and drew Gandhi's attention to the violence being preached at the Khilafat Conference by the Ali brothers, which had become a rallying point for Muslims all over India. Gandhi sought to obtain large-scale support from the Muslim community by supporting the Khilafat cause. Gandhi accepted Reading's position, and the main outcome of Reading's twelve-hour dialogue with Gandhi, in six sessions, was agreement on an apology from the Ali brothers.

9. *The Simla Times*, 8 September 1921.

10. The decision gave Simla one of the last public buildings of the era; the Legislative Assembly was built in 1925.

11. *Liddell's Simla Weekly*, 7 June 1913. See also 13 June and 8 November 1913.

12. Ibid.

13. P-II, SMR.

14. *Liddell's Simla Weekly*, 7 June 1913.

15. Ibid., 7 April 1914.

16. The Humble Petition of the House Owners and other Tax Payers of Simla, 9 March 1914, P-II, SMR.

17. *The Simla Times*, 9 April 1914.

18. P-1, SMR.

19. See R. Kumar (ed.), *Essays on Gandhian Politics, The Rowlatt Satyagraha of 1919*, Oxford, 1971; *Selections from the Report of the Punjab Disturbances*, Lahore, 1920.

20. *The Simla Times*, 10 April 1919.

21. 'Resolution passed at Public Meeting held at Edwards Gunj', 8 March 1921, P-1, SMR.

22. *The Simla Times*, 12 May 1921.

23. P-1, SMR.

24. Satyanand Stokes Papers, containing letters written by Stokes to his mother, 1905–28.

25. John C. B. Webster, *The Christian Community and Change in Nineteenth Century North India*, Delhi, 1976.

26. Stokes Papers, 24 August 1920. Stokes wrote to his mother that 'every Christian is expected to swallow whole the formulas evolved by the West.'

27. Satyanand Stokes, *Satyakam*, Bombay, 1942.

28. Stokes Papers, 28 December 1917, 19 March 1919.

29. Satyanand Stokes, *National Self-Realization and Other Essays*, New Delhi, 1975, p. 53.

30. Stokes Papers, 5 June 1919.

31. Stokes, *National Self Realization*, p. 154.

32. Stokes Papers, 19 October 1921.

33. Ibid., 5 March 1921.

34. *The Tribune*, 8 February 1921.

35. Andrews to Home Secretary, 9 May 1921, Home Public, July 1921, 53, NAI.

36. Stokes Papers, 18 June 1921.

37. *The Tribune*, 20 June 1921.

38. Ibid., 20, 29 June 1921; 2, 6, 8, 16 and 23 July 1921.

39. Ibid., 16 June 1921.

40. Buck, *Simla Past and Present*, p. 252.

41. *The Tribune*, 8 July 1921.

CHAPTER FOURTEEN

1. *The Legislative Assembly Debates*, Official Report, Vol. IV, 7 July to 18 July 1930, Simla, 1930, pp. 553–60.

2. *The Tribune*, 27 April 1930; *The Pioneer*, 30 April 1930.

3. Home Political, 5 No. 147, F 449, 1930, NAI.

4. Ibid.

5. 'Simla District Congress Activities, 1929–38', SPTR.

6. *The Tribune*, 30 April and 1 May 1930.

7. A. S. Krishnaswamy, Letter of 23 July 1981, and verbal communication.

8. Allen, *Plain Tales*, p. 249.

9. Gandhi to Verma, 1 May and 5 June 1931, N. L. Verma private papers.

10. *The Tribune*, 10 May 1931.

11. Ibid., 15 May 1930.

12. 'Statement Showing Names of all Societies and Movements in Simla with names of Office Bearers and Their Activities', 1930, SPTR.

13. Home Political, F. 449/30, NAI.

14. Ibid., F. 161/30.

15. *The Tribune*, 13 and 15 May 1930.

16. 'Report about Congress Activities in Simla in 1930', SPTR.

17. See Corinne Friend, 'The Hindustan Socialist Republican Army', in Singh and Barrier (ed.), *Punjab Past and Present*.

18. First Information Report, 13 August 1930, SPTR.

19. Interview with Dina Nath 'Andhi', November 1978.

20. *The Pioneer*, 15 May 1931.

21. Ibid., 8 May 1930.

22. Ibid., 14 May 1930.

23. *The Tribune*, 15 July 1931.

24. 'Report about Congress Activities in Simla in 1930', SPTR.

25. *The Tribune*, 15 May 1931.

26. Ibid.

27. 'Allowing Regal and other Nobilities to drive on the Mall', Q–1–1893 (Traffic), SMR.

28. *The Pioneer*, 16 May 1931.

29. T-224, SMR.

30. *The Pioneer*, 17 May 1931.

31. Ibid., 14 May 1931.

32. Ibid., 3 May 1931.

33. Ibid., 25 May 1931.

34. *The Tribune*, 6 July 1934.

CHAPTER FIFTEEN

1. Kumar, *Social History of Modern India*.

2. Membership of Simla District Congress. Source: 'Simla District Congress Activities, 1929–38', SPTR.

3. Verbal communication.

4. 'First Information Reports', 9 July and 13 August 1941; 10 February 1942, SPTR.

5. Minutes, Arhties Association, January 1942.

6. *The Simla Times*, 21 September 1922.

7. 'Statement showing the Names of All Societies and Movements in Simla with names of Office Bearers and their Activities', 1930, SPTR.

8. See Craig Baxter, *The Jana Sangh*, Bombay, 1971, p. 23.

9. *The Tribune*, 21 July 1921.

10. Ibid., 22 June 1924.

11. 'Charge Note', 2 January 1936, SPTR.

12. *The Pioneer*, 15 May 1931.

13. *The Tribune*, 6 August 1934.

14. Account of public meetings held on 7 and 22 April, 14, 27 and 28 August 1939, SPTR.

15. Account of public meetings held on 17 and 25 August 1939, SPTR.

16. Penderel Moon (ed.), *Wavell: The Viceroy's Journal*, London, 1973, p. 7.

17. Durga Das, *India from Curzon to Nehru*, p. 216. The Executive consisted of five 'caste' Hindus, five Muslims and two other minorities, namely the Sikhs and scheduled castes, each with one representative. Twenty-two political leaders of the Central Assembly, and the provincial chief ministers, with Gandhi and Jinnah as the recognized leaders of the two main political parties, Master Tara Singh to represent the Sikhs, and Rao Bahadur N. Shiva Raj to represent the scheduled classes, were invited to the conference.

18. Leonard Mosley, *The Last Days of the British Raj*, London, p. 15; R. J. Moore, *Escape from Empire*, pp. 350–2.

19. J. N. Sahni, *The Lid Off*, New Delhi, 1971, p. 199.

20. Verbal communication from Pandit Hari Ram and D. K. Khanna.

21. 'Charge Note 1946', SPTR.

22. Superintendent of Police's Daily Situation Reports, August, September 1947, SMR.

23. Allen, *Plain Tales*, p. 256.

24. Verbal communication, D. K. Khanna.

CHAPTER SIXTEEN

1. R. C. Pal Singh, Batal, A Village Survey, *Census of India*, Vol. XX, Part VI, 1961.

2. 'Lok Geet', *Him Prasth*, May 1958. The verse comes from the village of Markandya, 15 miles from Bilaspur.

3. Buck, *Simla Past and Present*, p. 258.

4. Dufferin and Ava, *Our Viceregal Life in India*, Vol. I, p. 186.

5. Rana of Dhami to Major R. R. Burnett, Political Agent, D. O. No. 107/ E., 25 August 1939; H. S. Chauhan, 'Dhami in 1939 A. D.', Simla, 1973.

6. *Gazetteer of the Simla Hill States*, Vol. III, Part A, 1910, Dhami State, p. 1.

7. Ibid., Vol. III, Part A, 1934, Dhami State, p. 4.

8. 'Report of the Non-official Enquiry Committee into the Tragic Happenings in Dhami State (Simla Hills) on 16th July 1939', hereafter Enquiry Committee Report, p. 4. AISPC Group I, File 22, 1937–40, NMML.

9. Figures compiled from *Gazetteer* 1910, p. 3; and *Gazetteer* 1934, p. 4.

10. 'Enquiry Committee Report', p. 4.

11. 'Brief Statement of facts leading to the most unfortunate Event that took place in the Annals of Dhami on 16 July 1939' (hereafter Dhami State Enquiry), p. 2. Home Political, 6(54) P (Secret) 1939, NAI.

12. Jawaharlal Nehru in Presidential Address at the All India State's People's Conference, Ludhiana, 15 February 1939, quoted from *Selected Works of Jawaharlal Nehru*, Vol. X, New Delhi, 1977, p. 418.

13. Ibid.

14. Rana of Bhajji to Political Agent, Political Department, F. 85-C. 0.139, 1 August 1939, NAI.

15. Ranbir Sharma, *Party Politics in a Himalayan State*, Delhi, 1977, pp. 43 and 171.

16. 'Copy of Resolution passed by the Dhami Riasti Praja Mandal on the evening of the 13th July 1939', AISPC, NMML.

17. Dhami State Enquiry, p. 2.

18. *Gazetteer of the Simla Hill States*, 1934, p. 1.

19. 'Agitation in Indian States. Riots in Dhami'. Home Political 6(54)-P-Secret, 1939, NAI.

20. Dhami State Enquiry, p. 8.

21. Ibid. 'Report against certain Government employees (mostly inferior servants) who are suspected of having participated in the demonstration against the ruler of Dhami State'. Home Public, Keep Withs, 50/12/39, 1939, NAI.

22. *The Tribune* and *The Hindustan Times*, 18 July 1939.

23. *The Hindustan Times*, 19 July 1939.

24. Verbal communication, Rana of Dhami, on 5 September 1984.

25. *Harijan*, 28 July 1931.

26. *Selected Works of Jawaharlal Nehru*, p. 531.

27. Proceedings, 19 July 1939, SMR.

28. Letter from Suman Dev to Jawaharlal Nehru, 30 July 1939, AISPC, NMML.

29. Public meetings held on 3, 8, 16, 17, and 20 August 1939, SPTR.

30. Home Public, Keep Withs, 50/12/39, 1939, NAI.

CHAPTER SEVENTEEN

1. A. S. Iyengar, *All Through the Gandhian Era*, Bombay, 1950.

2. *The Tribune*, 17 May 1931.

3. Muggeridge, *Chronicles of Wasted Time*, p. 36.

4. There were 2,988 Europeans and 48,619 Indians in 1931. In 1911, twenty years earlier, there were 4,153 Europeans, and 31,849 Indians.

5. Buck, *Simla Past and Present*, p. 280.

6. Dufferin and Ava, *Our Viceregal Life in India*, Vol. I, p. 173.

7. See *Harijan Bulletin 4*. She addressed meetings on 16 and 30 August, 13 and 27 September and 2 October 1942. 'Files Relating to Raj Kumari Amrit Kaur', SPTR.

8. Comrade Ram Chandra, *Road to Freedom*, New Delhi, 1980, pp. 292–300.

9. 'Files Relating to Raj Kumari Amrit Kaur', SPTR.

10. Morris, *With Scarlet Majors*, p. 30.

11. Draft Report on the Administration of Simla Municipality, 1939–40, pp. 3–4, Mela Ram Sood Papers; and Home Public, 5/7/42, 1942, NAI.

12. Annual Report, 1940, p. 1, SMR.

13. 'Sale of Property Register', Simla Tehsil Office; Buck, *Simla Past and Present*, p. 161.

14. *The Illustrated Weekly of India*, 8 February 1987.

15. The pressure by local Indians to widen the municipal franchise led to a constitution which was to have five elected members, three from the Bazar and two from Station Ward. The revised constitution never came into operation. The elections, scheduled for September 1939, were first postponed because of the early departure of Government offices, and then because of World War II.

16. Mentioned first in *Annual Report*, 1938–39, p. 4, SMR.

17. Inspection Note from J. W. Hearn, Commissioner, Ambala Division, 1936, p. 9, Mela Ram Sood Papers.

18. It made available twenty-one gallons of water per head per day to a population estimated at 60,000 during the peak season in the 1930s. The water supply scheme was prepared by 1922 and completed in 1924. Water from the Nauti Khad, a tributary of the Sutlej, was pumped at the Guma Pumping Station to the Simla water mains.

19. *Annual Reports*, 1933–34, p. 25; 1936–37, p. 23; 1937–38, p. 37; 1940–41, p. 32.

20. In 1937, the number of water-borne public lavatories had risen to twenty-five (with one hundred and fourteen seats); fifty-six dry latrines (with three hundred and twenty-four seats) still existed. No sewage extensions were made at municipal expense thereafter, since the government grant was withdrawn. In 1940, the municipal authorities conceded: 'Further connections on water carriage system cannot be given except in special cases, until large pipes are provided.' *Report of the Medical Officer of Health*, Simla, 1937, p. 33.

21. *1914 Report*, p. 13.

22. 'Inspection Note', Hearn, p. 17.

23. *Annual Report*, 1937–38, SMR.

24. Ibid., 1940–41.

25. Ibid., 1939–40.

26. S. M. Kanwar, *Apples: Production Technology and Economics*, New Delhi, 1987, pp. 1, 73.

27. *Annual Report*, 1940–41, SMR.

28. Proceedings, 24 May 1944, SMR.

CHAPTER EIGHTEEN

1. Randhawa, *Travels in the Western Himalayas*, p. 155.

2. H. J. Dyos and Michael Wolff, *The Victorian City*, Vol. II, London, 1973, p. 894.

3. B. K. Chauhan, 'Urban Development in Himachal Pradesh', in *Development Profile of Himachal Pradesh*, Directorate of Economics and Statistics, Himachal Pradesh, Shimla, 1985, pp. 136–7.

4. Ibid.

5. *Annual Report, 1986–87*, SMR.

6. P. N. Gautam, 'Administrative History of Simla Municipal Corporation', Mimeo, 1981, p. 32.

Glossary

anna	one-sixteenth of a rupee
arhat	commission
arhti	commission agent
atta	wheat flour
ayah	Indian nurse or maid
bara	big
bartandari	prerogative of villagers to use produce of forest tract for food, fuel and fodder
bazar	Indian market
begar/begaree	unpaid and forced labour/labourer
bhadralok	Bengali gentleman
bhisti	water carrier
bugjal	circular metallic cymbals
bunniyah/bania	trader; money lender
challan	fine
chakla	prostitute's quarter
chanwar	fly whisk
charkha	spinning wheel
charpoi	wooden frame bed with webbing
chaudhri	contractor; overseer; prefix used before name
chattar	ceremonial umbrella
chhota	small
chowki	point at which transit duty is charged, usually at state boundary
chowkidar	nightwatchman; caretaker
chowkidari	tax for policing town
chuprassi	office attendant; peon
compound	enclosed area surrounding bungalow and servant quarters

dak	post
dak bungalow	government staging house
dal	lentils
dandi	open litter
darshan	homage
dham	feast
devata	deity
dhajji	structure made of wooden frame filled with packed earth, gravel, etc.
dhara	shed or hall used as dormitory
dhol	drum
Diwali	Hindu new year and festival of lights
diwan (Sikh)	weekly meeting at gurdwara
dolly (from *dali*)	tray of gifts
durbar	court, levée
ghoral	deer
gunj	wholesale market
gwala	milkman
gymkhana	sports ground; sports meeting
halva	sweetmeat
halvai	sweetmeat seller
hartal	ceasing work or closing shop as a sign of protest
hawan	oblations
hesi	wandering minstrel of upper Himalayas
Holi	Hindu spring festival
huqqa, hookah	hubble-bubble
Idgah	a Muslim place of assembly and prayer
imambara	Shia Muslim place of worship
jagirdar	landholder
jalebi	sweetmeat
jampan	a cushioned sedan chair slung on poles and carried by four coolies

jampani	rickshaw coolie
jatha	group, band
kachchi arhat	commission agent with a temporary shed and weighing scales who buys and repacks agricultural produce for onward sale
kakkar	deer
karnal	long trumpet
katori	bowl
kharif	crop planted in summer
Khilafat	Pan-Islamic movement after the First World War to maintain the authority of the Sultan of Turkey; also spiritual leadership of Islam
khidmutgar	butler and waiter
khud	steep hillside
kilta	conical basket
kirtan	devotional singing
kotwali	police station
kutcherry	court
laddu	sweetmeat
lakh	one hundred thousand
lala	prefix used for members of trading community
laman	couplets sung in hills
Lat Sahib/ Chhota Mulk	'Lord Sahib', used for Governor/Governor-General
lumbardar	village revenue official
maidan	public land
mali	gardener
mandi	market
masalchi	kitchen boy, who ground spices
maulvi	master of Muslim law
maund	a weight—40 seers or 36 kilograms

mela	festival, fair
mishri	crystal sugar
mizajpursi	ceremonial social call
modi	wholesale trader
mohalla	an identifiable neighbourhood or area in town
mundu	low-paid servant
nautch girl	dancing girl; prostitute
nazrana	a gift given as homage
nazul	government land
newandia	plains
pahari	person from the hills
pashm	shawl wool
peon	messenger, orderly
peshwai	ceremonial presentation
polas	light hemp-fibre slip-on shoes
purwannah	permit
qualghi	plume worn by rulers on ceremonial occasions
rabi	crop planted in winter
rais	term used to indicate respectability and wealth
sabha	association
salaam	salutation
sangathan	conversion to Hinduism associated with Arya Samaj movement
satyugraha	political movement of non-violent resistance associated with Gandhi
seer	a weight, 1 seer = 0.9 kg
serai	inn
shamiana	marquee
shikar	sport: shooting and hunting

shuddhi	reconversion to Hinduism associated with Arya Samaj movement
Swaraj	Home Rule
sweeper	untouchable caste which formerly only cleaned latrines
syce	groom
tabligh	Muslim conversion movement of nineteen-twenties
taluqdar	landowner
tehsil	administrative sub-division of a district
teh zamini	tax levied in bazar
thakuraee	feudal lordships
thali	brass plate
thana	police station
thoda	folk dance of Simla hills
uchhandia	hill; uplands
vakil	Indian attorney; court pleader
Vilayat	kingdom, UK (from Blighty—derived from Britain)
zamindar	landowner; in Simla hills used in the sense of yeoman, a small farmer who cultivates his own land

Bibliography

Unpublished Material

Ahrties Association Papers, Simla
Amateur Dramatic Club, Simla, Papers
Mela Ram Sood Papers, Simla
N. L. Varma Papers

Simla, Public Works Department
Index of Buildings Register
Miscellaneous files relating to buildings

Simla Municipal Corporation Records
Minutes pertaining to the constitution.
Annual, quarterly, monthly, fortnightly and weekly reports and statements. By-laws and rules and their amendments.
Settlement Reports of Simla, purchase of land by the municipality, lease of Government land to municipality, sale of Government lands. Applications for purchase and lease of Government land.
Lease of municipal buildings Markets, quarters, godowns, Anaj Mandi, etc.
Construction and repairs of buildings Town Hall, police stations, post-office, municipal buildings, fire station.
Records relating to finance Monthly accounts, annual budgets, investment cases, grants-in-aid and loan cases, audit and inspection notes.
Records relating to civic amenities Water supply, construction of reservoirs, purchase of catchment area, supply of electricity, sanitation and health.
Educational institutions Management of middle school, grants-in-aid, libraries, management and improvement of schools.

Simla Sadar Police Thana Records
First Information Reports.
Unclassified and unsorted bundles of files.
List of Societies, 1930.
List of Government Employees who take active part in the Meetings with names of Societies, 1930.
Labour Unions 1933 and 1937–8.
Charge Notes by Station Officer, 1929–46.

Simla District Congress Activities, 1929–38.
Confidential Weekly Diary, 1939–40.
Report of Public Meetings, 1936 and 1939.
Files regarding Raj Kumari Amrit Kaur.

Tehsil Office
Registers pertaining to the sale of property.

National Archives of India, New Delhi
Dufferin Papers.
Fleetwood–Wilson Papers.
Lawrence Papers.
United Service Club Simla Papers.
Foreign Political; Foreign; Home Political; Home Public; and Public Works
    Department.

Nehru.Memorial Museum and Library, New Delhi
All India States People's Conference Papers.
Satyanand Stokes Papers.

National Library, Calcutta
Rules and Regulations of the New Club Simla, 1890.
The Simla Union Church.

Haryana State Archives, Chandigarh
Files in the office of the Commissioner, Ambala Division, pertaining to the
    nineteenth century.
Judicial Department; Political and General Department; Public Works
    Department; Revenue Department.

INTERVIEWS

Dina Nath Andhi. President of the Bal Bharat Sabha in 1930; political
    activist, and member of the Congress Socialist Party after 1935.
Puran Chandra. Advocate, member of the Municipal Committee, Simla,
    1933–6 (d. 1983).
Pandit Hari Ram. Congress activist, member of Simla Congress Committee,
    1935–47; President of the Brahmin Sabha.
B. L. Salhotra. Up-Pradhan Dalit Varga Sangha and Municipal Commis-
    sioner.

Maulvi Sanaullah. Maulvi of the Kashmiri Masjid of Simla.
Lala Mela Ram Sood. Member, Simla Municipal Committee, 1936–53.

Published Material

NEWSPAPERS

The Civil and Military Gazette, Lahore.
The Bengalee, Calcutta.
Harijan, New Delhi.
Him Prasth.
The Hindustan Times, New Delhi.
Liddell's Simla Weekly, Simla (cuttings in Simla Municipal Office, 1913–15).
The Pioneer, Allahabad.
Pioneer Daily Bulletin.
The Simla Times, Simla.
The Simla Times Advertiser, Simla.
The Statesman, Delhi.
The Tribune, Lahore.

OFFICIAL PUBLICATIONS

Aitchison, C. U., *A Collection of Treaties, Engagements and Sanads*. Calcutta, 1892.

Anderson, J. D. *Final Settlement Report of the Simla District 1915–16*. Lahore, 1917.

Census of India, 1911, Vol. XIV, Lahore, 1912.

Census of India, 1921, Vol. XV, Lahore, 1923.

Census of India, 1931, Vol. XV, Lahore, 1934.

Davar, L. R., *Economic Conditions of Simla Rickshaw Men*, Lahore, 1934.

Development Profile of Himachal Pradesh Directorate of Economics and Statis tics, Himachal Pradesh, Shimla, 1985.

Gazetteer of the Simla District, 1888–89. Calcutta, n.d.

Ibbetson, Denzil, *A Glossary of the Tribes and Castes of the Punjab and North-West Frontier Provinces*, Vol. III, Calcutta, 1883.

Imperial Gazetteer of India, Vol. XXII, London, 1908.

Legislative Assembly Debates, Vol. IV, 1930.

Pal Singh, R. C. Batal, *A Village Survey*, Census of India, Arki Tehsil, Mahasu District, Vol. XX, Part VI, 1961.

Punjab District Gazetteers

Vol. VIII B. Simla District Statistical Tables 1904. Lahore, 1913.

Vol. VIII B. Simla District Statistical Tables 1912. Lahore, 1913.

Vol. VI B. Simla District Statistical Tables 1936. Lahore, 1936.

Vol. VIII. Simla Hill States 1910. Lahore, 1911.

Vol. VIII A. Simla Hill States 1934. Lahore, 1934.

Records of the Delhi Residency and Agency, Lahore, 1911.

Records of the Ludhiana Agency, Lahore, 1911.

Report of the Simla Extension Committee, 1877.

Report of the Simla Extension Committee, 1898.

Report of the Simla Water Works Committee, 1904.

Report of the Simla Sanitary Investigation Committee, 1905.

Report of the Simla Allowances Committee, 1905.

Report of the Simla Improvement Committee, 1907.

Report of the Simla Improvement Committee, 1914.

Report of the Simla House Accommodation Committee, 1917.

Report on the Simla Census, 1904. Lahore, 1905.

Report on the Summer Census of Simla, 1911. Lahore, 1912.

Report on the Summer Census of the Punjab Hill Stations—Simla, Dalhousie, 1921. Lahore, 1923.

Settlement Report of the Station Ward of Simla Municipality, 1907.

Wace, Lt. Col. E. G., *Final Report of the First Regular Settlement of the Simla District in the Punjab 1881–83. Calcutta, 1884.*

SECONDARY SOURCES

Anand, J. K., *Simla's First Century and Who's Who*. Simla, 1938.

Azad, M., *Sood Vansh Ka Gauravshali Itihas* (Hindi). Amritsar, n.d.

Baird, J. G. (ed.), *Private Letters of the Marquess of Dalhousie*. Ireland, 1972.

Balfour, Lady Betty (ed.), *Personal and Literary Letters of Robert, First Earl of Lytton*, 2 vols. London, 1906.

Barr, Pat and Desmond, Ray, *Simla, A Hill Station in British India*. London, 1978.

Bastavala, D. S., *Simla*. Bombay, 1925.

Baxter, Craig, *The Jana Sangh*. Bombay, 1971.

Bayly, C. A., *The Local Roots of Indian Politics: Allahabad, 1880–1920*. Oxford, 1975.

———— 'Local Control in Indian Towns—The Case of Allahabad 1880–1920', *Modern Asian Studies*, Vol. V, Pt. 4, October 1971, pp. 298–311.

Blunt, W. S., *India Under Ripon. A Private Diary*. London, 1909.

Briggs, Asa, *Victorian People*. London, 1958.

———— *Victorian Cities*. London, 1964.

Brinkworth, Hugh A., *Boomba*. Simla, 1929.

Buck, Edward J., *Simla Past and Present*. Bombay, 1925.

Burrard, S. G. and Hayden, H. H. *A Sketch of the Geography and Geology of the Himalayan Mountains and Tibet*. Calcutta, 1907.

Butler, Iris, *The Viceroy's Wife*. London, 1969.

Chauhan, H. S., 'Dhami in 1939 AD', Simla, 1973.

Chhabra, G. S. *An Advanced History of the Punjab*, Vol. II. Ludhiana, 1962.

Collet, S. D. (ed.), *The Brahmo Year Book for 1976*.

Corfield, Conrad, *The Princely India I Knew*. Madras, 1975.

Cotton, H. E. A., *Calcutta Old and New*. Calcutta, 1907.

Crawford, Marion F., *Mr. Isaacs. A Tale of Modern India*. London, 1882.

Curzon, Lord, *British Government in India*. London, 1925.

Datta, V. N, *Amritsar Past and Present*. Amritsar, 1967.

Davis, Colonel Newnham, *Jadoo*. London, 1898.

Denyer, P. H. *Amateur Dramatic Club, 1837–1937*. Simla, 1937.

Dilke, Charles, *Greater Britain*. London, 1868.

Dobbin, C. E., *Urban Leadership in Western India, Politics and Communities in Bombay City, 1840–1885*. London, 1972.

Doz, *Simla in Ragtime*. Simla, 1913.

Dracott, Alice Elizabeth, *Simla Village Tales*. London, 1906.

Dufferin and Ava, *Our Viceregal Life in India*, 2 vols. London, 1899.

Durga Das, *India from Curzon to Nehru and After*. London, 1969.

Dyos, H. J. and Michael Wolff, *The Victorian City*. London, 1973.

Eden, Emily, *Up the Country, 1837–1840*, 2 vols. London, 1866.

———— *Letters from India*. London, 1872.

Edwardes, Michael, *Bound to Exile*. London, 1969.

Edwards, William, *Reminiscences of a Bengal Civilian*. London, 1866.

Elsmie, G. R., *Thirty-Five Years in the Punjab, 1858–1893*. Edinburgh, 1908.

Fane, Henry Edward, *Five Years in India*. London, 1857.

Farooqui, Mian Bashir Ahmed, *British Relations with the Cis-Sutlej States 1809–1825*. Lahore, 1941.

Fleetwood-Wilson, Guy, *Letters to Nobody*. 1921.

Fleming, Joan, *A Pinchbeck Goddess*. London, 1898.

Fraser, James Baillie, *The Journal of a Tour through part of the Himalaya Mountains*. London, 1820.

French, Charles J., *Journal of a Tour in Upper Hindustan*. London, 1853.

Friend, Corinne, 'The Hindustan Socialist Republican Army', in Harbans Singh and N. Gerald Barrier (ed.), *Punjab Past and Present*, Patiala, 1977.

Gandhi, M. K., *The Collected Works of Mahatma Gandhi*. Ahmedabad, 1977.

Garbett, Sir Colin, *Friend of Friend*. Bombay, 1943.

—— *Christ Church Simla, One Hundred Years 1844–1944*. Lahore, 1944.

Gautam, P. N., 'Administrative History of Simla Municipal Corporation', Mimeo, 1981.

Gerard, Alexander, *Account of Koonawur in the Himalaya*. London, 1841.

Gillion, K. L., *Ahmedabad: A Study in Indian Urban History*. California, 1968.

Gore, St J., *Light and Shades of Hill Life in the Afghan and Hindu Highlands of the Punjab*. London, 1895.

Gupta, Narayani, *Delhi Between Two Empires*. Delhi, 1981.

Gurdarshan Singh, 'Amritsar and the Singh Sabha Movement', in Fauja Singh (ed.), *The City of Amritsar*. Delhi, 1978.

Hamilton, Walter, *Description of Hindostan*, 2 vols. Delhi, 1941.

Harrop, F. B., *Thackers New Guide to Simla*. Simla, 1925.

Hugel, Baron Charles, *Kashmir and the Punjab*. London, 1845.

Hunter, W. W. (ed.), *Lord Amherst and the British Advance Eastward to Burma*. Oxford, 1889.

Hutchins, Francis G., *Illusion of Permanence: British Imperialism in India*. Princeton, 1967.

Hutchison, L. R. C. P. and Vogel, S. E. J., *History of the Punjab Hill States*. Lahore, 1933.

Iyengar, A. S., *All Through the Gandhian Era*. Bombay, 1950.

Jacquemont, Victor, *Letters from India, 1829–1832*. London, 1936.

Jones, Kenneth W., *Arya Dharam*. Delhi, 1976.

Kanwar, Pamela, 'The Changing Profile of the Summer Capital of British India: Simla 1864–1947', *Modern Asian Studies*, vol. 18, 2, 1984, pp. 215–36.

—— 'The Urban Growth of Shimla: An Historical Perspective', *The Journal of Himachal Pradesh Institute of Public Administration*, Vol. I, No. 1, January–June 1986.

—— 'Sources of Water Supply at Simla in the Nineteenth Century With Particular Reference to the Comberemere Tunnels'. Mimeo, 1983.

Kanwar, S. M., *Apples: Production Technology and Economics*. Delhi, 1987.

Kerr, Ian J., 'Social Change in Lahore, 1849–1975', *Journal of Indian History*, Vol. LVI, 1979.

King, Anthony D., *Colonial Urban Development*. London, 1976.

—— Colonialism and the Development of the Modern South Asian

City. Some Theoretical Considerations', in Kenneth Ballhatchet and John Harrison (ed.), *The City in South Asia*. London, 1980.

Kincaid, Dennis, *British Social Life in India*. London, 1936.

Kipling, Rudyard, *Plain Tales from the Hills*. London, 1930.

——— *Kim*. London, 1933.

Krishen, Indra, *An Historical Interpretation of the Correspondence of Sir George Russel Clarke, Political Agent Ambala and Ludhiana, 1931–43*, Vol. I. Delhi, 1952.'

Kumar, Ravinder, *Essays in the Social History of Modern India*. New Delhi, 1984.

——— 'The Changing Structure of Urban Society in Colonial India', in *The Indian Historical Review*, Vol. V, Nos. 1–2, July 1978–June 1979, pp. 200–13.

——— (ed.), *Essays on Gandhian Politics. The Rowlatt Satyagraha of 1919*. Oxford, 1971.

Lawrence, W. R. *The India We Served*. London, 1928.

Leonard, John G., 'Urban Government Under the Raj: A Case Study of Municipal Administration in 19th Century South India', *Modern Asian Studies*, Vol. VII, Pt. 2, April 1973, pp. 237–51.

Lloyd, William, and Alexander, Gerard, *Narrative of a Journey from Caunpore to the Borendo Pass in the Himalaya Mountains*, 2 vols. London, 1840.

Luard, Capt. J., *Views of India from Calcutta to the Himalayas*. London, 1833.

Maconochie, Evan, *Life in the Indian Civil Service*. London, 1926.

Maheshwari, Shriram, *The Evolution of Indian Administration*. Agra, 1970.

Mehrotra, S. R., *Towards India's Freedom and Partition*. Delhi, 1979.

Mitra (ed.), *The Indian Annual Register*, Calcutta.

Moon, Penderel (ed.), *Wavell: The Viceroy's Journal*. London, 1973.

Montagu, Edwin, *My Indian Diary*. London, 1930

Moore, R. G., *Whig Liberalism and Politics, 1872–1922*. London, 1965.

——— *Escape From Empire*. New York, 1983.

Morris, Deborah, *With Scarlet Majors*. London, 1960.

Morris, James, *Pax Britannica*. London, 1963.

Mosley, Leonard, *The Last Days of the British Raj*. London, 1961.

Mundy, Captain, *Pen and Pencil Sketches, being the Journal of a Tour of India*, 2 vols. London, 1832.

Nehru, Jawàharlal, *Selected Works of Jawaharlal Nehru*. New Delhi, 1977.

——— *An Autobiography*. London, 1936.

Newall, Major-General D. J. F., *The Highlands of India Strategically considered with special reference to their Colonization as Reserve Circles*. London, 1882.

Pemble, John, *The Invasion of Nepal*. London, 1976.

Pinch, Trevor, *Stark India*. London, 1930.

Raj, Salamat, *Mukammal Tarikh Soodan* (Urdu). Lahore, 1935.

Ramusack, Barbara N., 'Incident at Nabha', in *Punjab Past and Present*, Harbans Singh and Gerald N. Barrier (ed.). Patiala, 1977.

Randhawa, M. S., *Travels in the Western Himalayas*. Delhi, 1974.

Reed, R., 'The Colonial Genesis of Hill Stations: The Genting Exception', *Geographical Review*, Vol. 69, No. 4, October, 1979.

——— 'Remarks on the Colonial Genesis of the Hill Station in Southeast Asia with particular reference to the Cities of Buitenzorg (Bogor) and Baguio', *Asian Profile*, Vol. 4, No. 6, December, 1976.

Rees, J. D., *Travels of Lord Connemara, 1886–1890*. London, 1982.

Robinson, F. C., *Separatism among Indian Muslims. The Politics of the United Province Muslims, 1860–1918*. Cambridge, 1975.

Ronaldshay, Earl of, *The Life of Lord Curzon*. London, 1929.

Russel, William Howard, *My Diary in India*, 2 vols. London, 1860.

Sahni, J. N., *The Lid Off*. New Delhi, 1971.

Sastri, Pt. Sant Ram, *Sood Vanshavali* (Hindi). Lahore, n.d.

Sen, N., *Licensed Rickshaw Coolies of Simla*. Simla, 1934.

Sen, N. B., *Punjab's Eminent Hindus*. Lahore, 1944.

Sen, Sudhir Chandra, *The Simla Kalibari*. Simla, 1931.

Sharma, Ranbir, *Party Politics in a Himalayan State*. Delhi, 1977.

Sharp, Sir Henry, *Goodbye India*. Oxford, 1946.

Singh, Udhab, *Gurkha Conquest of Arki*. Lahore, 1902.

Smith, R. Bosworth, *Life of Lord Lawrence*, 2 vols. New York, 1883.

Snell, Owen, *The Anglo Indians*. New Delhi, 1944.

Sood, M. M., *Origin and History of the Soods*. Chandigarh, n.d.

Spangenberg, Bradford, *British Bureaucracy in India*. Delhi, 1978.

Speeches Delivered in India 1884–88, by the Marquis of Dufferin and Ava. London, 1890.

Stark, Herbert Alick, *Hostages to India or the Life Story of the Anglo-Indian Race*. Calcutta, 1926.

Stokes, Satyanand, *National Self-Realization and Other Essays*. New Delhi, 1975.

——— *Satyakam*. Bombay, 1927.

Taylor, W. W., *Thirty-Eight Years in India*. 2 vols, London, 1881.

Thomas, Capt. G. P., *Views of Simla*. London, 1846.

Tinker, Hugh, *The Foundations of Local Self-Government in India, Pakistan and Burma*. London, 1954.

Towelle's Handbook and Guide to Simla. Simla, 1890.

Verma, Khemi Ram and Balkrishan Thakur, *Laman, Thande Pani re Dibhanu* (Hindi). Collection of Folk Songs. Shimla, n.d.

Von Huber, Baron, *Through the British Empire*, 2 vols. London, 1886.

Wacha, D. E., *Rise and Growth of the Bombay Municipal Government*. Madras, 1913.

Wedderburn, William, *Allan Octavian Hume*. London, 1913.

Wilson, Andrew, *Abode of Snow*. London, 1873.

Wilkinson, J. F., *The Parochial History of Simla, 1836–1900*. Simla, 1903.

Webster, John, C. B., *The Christian Community and Change in Nineteenth Century North India*. London, 1976.

Woodruff, Philip, *The Men who Ruled India*, 2 vols. London, 1954.

Woodyatt, Nigel, *Under Ten Viceroys*. London, 1922.

Wyman, J. F., *Calcutta to the Snowy Range by an Old Indian*. London, 1865.

Index